# Practical Hydraulics

# Practical Hydraulics

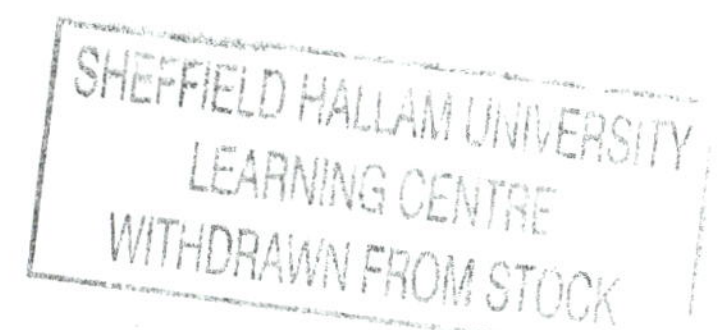


Melvyn Kay MSc DIC CEng MICE FIAgrE

*Senior Lecturer in Hydraulics and Irrigation Engineering*
*Cranfield University*
*Silsoe, UK*

E & FN SPON
An Imprint of Routledge
London and New York

First published 1998
by E & FN Spon, an imprint of Routledge
11 New Fetter Lane, London EC4P 4EE

Simultaneously published in the USA and Canada
by Routledge
29 West 35th Street, New York, NY 10001



Typeset in by Sabon by
Mathematical Composition Setters Ltd, Salisbury, Wiltshire
Printed and bound in Great Britain by
TJ International Ltd, Padstow, Cornwall



*British Library Cataloguing in Publication Data*
A catalogue record for this book is available from the British Library

*Library of Congress Cataloging in Publication data*
A catalog record for this book has been requested

ISBN 0 419 24230 9 (hbk)
ISBN 0 419 22880 2 (pbk)

# Contents

# Preface

People in many walks of life have to deal with water – from water engineers who design and operate our domestic water supply systems and hydro-electric dams to farmers who irrigate crops, environmentalists concerned about our natural rivers and wet-lands and fire crews putting out fires with high-pressure water hoses. They may be involved in storing water, pumping it, spraying it or just conveying it from one place to another in pipes or channels. All need to understand the way in which water behaves and how to deal with it. This is the study of **hydraulics**.

But hydraulics is not just about water. Many other fluids behave like water and affect a wide range of people. Doctors need to know how blood flows in arteries and veins (pipes) and how it is pumped around our bodies. Aircraft designers need to understand how air flowing around an aircraft wing can create lift. Car designers want to know how air flows around cars in order to improve road holding and reduce drag to save fuel. Sportsmen too soon learn that a ball can be made to move in a curved path by changing its velocity and the air flow around it and so confuse an opponent.

There are many misconceptions about water and those who have to deal with it often have very little knowledge of its behaviour. Many people are also afraid of hydraulics because of its reputation for being too mathematical or too complicated to understand. Hydraulics textbooks also do little to allay these fears as they are usually written by engineers for engineers and assume that the reader has a degree in mathematics.

This book tries to dispel some of these notions. It is not necessary to be an engineer and a mathematician to understand and use some of the important ideas about water. Water is all around us and is an important part of our everyday lives and we can learn a great deal about it by simply having a bath.

Have you noticed when filling your bath how the hot and cold water do not mix easily and so you stir the water to get an even temperature. This is because there is a slight density difference between hot and cold water, which makes it difficult for natural mixing to take place. Many power stations that draw cooling water from a river or the sea have similar water mixing problems. Sometimes the hot water flowing out of the station manages to find its way round to the cold water intakes and causes problems. Effective mixing to disperse the hot water with the cold avoids this problem.

When you get into your bath the water level rises. Archimedes first discovered the significance of this some 2000 years ago when he realised that the water displaced when you get into the bath has the same volume as your body. He also noticed that if you float on the water instead of sitting on the bottom then the amount of water you displace is equal to your weight. This was the beginning of our understanding of **hydrostatics** (water that is not moving) and led to formulae for the design and construction of water tanks and dams.

When sitting in your bath have you made waves by sliding up and down? If you slide back and forth a few times the water can even flow over the sides. When you stop, the waves still continue for some time. This is because there is very little friction in your bath and so there is nothing to absorb the wave energy. Water can also slosh about in harbours in the same way when wave energy from the sea enters and this can cause serious problems for ships. The wave energy is difficult to get rid of because the walls of a harbour are usually concrete and so easily reflect waves rather than absorb them. This water movement can move ships back and forth on their moorings, which can be a major problem if the ship happens to be a super-tanker and you are trying to keep it still while loading it with oil. This is why harbour entrances are narrow and specially angled to stop wave energy from entering. You may have noticed that the sea is much calmer inside a harbour than outside.

Finally when you get out of your bath and the water goes down the plug hole a whirlpool or vortex is set up which seems to be hollow down the middle. All water intakes at reservoirs and control gates along rivers suffer from vortices like this, which draw in air and reduce their efficiency. Some say that the vortex goes in a clockwise direction in the northern hemisphere and anticlockwise in the southern hemisphere. Whether this is true or not is still not clear. Experiments to test the theory are very difficult to do in a laboratory because the forces involved are very small and the flow is often influenced more by minor vibrations or temperature changes in the room.

Hydraulics can explain all these and other interesting phenomena such as: how aeroplanes fly; why the wind rushes in the gaps between buildings; why some tall chimneys and bridges collapse when the wind blows around them; why it takes two firemen to hold down a hosepipe when fighting a fire; why there is a violent banging noise in water pipes when you turn a tap off quickly; how competition swimmers can increase their speed in the water by changing their swimsuit; and why tea leaves always go to the centre of the cup when you stir your tea!

But there is a more serious side to hydraulics. It may be selecting the right size of pipes and pumps to supply domestic water to a town or choosing the right size and shape of channel to supply farms with irrigation water or solve a drainage problem.

It would have been easier to write a 'simple', descriptive book on hydraulics by omitting the more complex ideas of water flow, but this would have been simplicity at the expense of reality. It would be like writing a cookbook of recipes, rather than examining why certain things happen when ingredients are mixed together. So this book tries to cater for all levels of interest. At one level it is descriptive and provides a qualitative understanding of hydraulics. At another level it is more rigorous and quantitative. The more mathematical bits are contained in boxes for those who wish to go that extra step. It was the physicist Lord Kelvin (1824–1907) who said that it is essential to put numbers on things if we are really going to understand them. So other boxes contain worked examples that demonstrate how hydraulic problems can be solved and derivations of some of the more important formulae. The latter are for the more curious, who find it difficult to accept formulae at face value and like to see where they come from. A list of problems is provided at the ends of Chapters 2–8 for the reader to try. At this point be aware that developing a qualitative understanding of hydraulics and solving problems mathematically are two different skills. Many people achieve the first skill but then get frustrated because the second does not fall easily into place. This is a separate skill, which can only be acquired through practice – hence the reason for the worked examples. It also helps to have some basic mathematical skills – up to basic algebra should be enough.

*Melvyn Kay*
*Cranfield University*

# Acknowledgements

I would like to make special mention of two books which have greatly influenced my writing of this text. The first is *Water in the Service of Man* by H.R. Vallentine, published by Pelican Books Ltd in 1967. The second is *Fluid Mechanics for Civil Engineers* by N.B. Webber, first published in 1965 by E & FN Spon Ltd. Both are now, alas, out of print.

I would like to acknowledge my use of the method described in *Handbook of Hydraulics for the Solution of Hydrostatic and Fluid Flow Problems* by H.W. King and E.F. Brater (1963), for the design of channels using Manning's equation (section 5.5.4).

I am also grateful for ideas I have obtained from *The Economist* on the use of boundary drag on swim suits (section 3.10) and from *New Scientist* on momentum transfer (section 1.11.2) and the hydrodynamics of cricket balls (section 3.12).

I would like to thank the following people and organisations for permission to use photographs and diagrams:

Hydraulics Research Wallingford (1983) *Charts for the Hydraulic Design of Channels and Pipes*, 5th edition for Figure 4.7.

Chadwick, A. and Morfett, J. (1998) *Hydraulics in Civil and Environmental Engineering*, 3rd edition, E & FN Spon, London for Figure 5.22(b).

Fox, J. (1977) *An Introduction to Engineering Fluid Mechanics*, The Macmillan Press Ltd, London for Figure 5.26.

The Environment Agency, UK for Figure 6.3 and the front cover photograph.

Open University Oceanography COURIS Team (1995) *Waves, Tides and Shallow Water Processes*, Butterworth and Heinemann for Figures 6.2 and 6.6(b).

FC Concrete Ltd, Derby, UK for Figure 7.14.

Vallentine, H.R. (1967) *Water in the Service of Man*, Penguin Books Ltd, Harmondsworth, UK for Figure 7.2.

Fraenkel, P.L. (1986) *Water Lifting Devices*, Irrigation and Drainage Paper No. 43, Food and Agriculture Organisation, Rome for Figures 8.9 and 8.14(a) and (b).
Webber, N.B. (1971) *Fluid Mechanics for Civil Engineers*, E & FN Spon Ltd, London for Figures 8.14(c) and 8.15

Chapter 1

# Some basic mechanics

## 1.1 Introduction

This is a reference chapter rather than one for general reading, but it will be useful as a reminder about the physical properties of water and for those who want to re-visit some basic physics that is directly relevant to the behaviour of water.

## 1.2 Units

To understand hydraulics properly it is essential to be able to put numerical values on such things as pressure, velocity and discharge in order for them to have meaning. It is not enough to say the pressure is high or the discharge is large; some specific value needs to be given to quantify it. Also just providing a number on its own is quite meaningless. To say a pipeline is 6 long is not enough. It might be 6 centimetres, 6 metres or 6 kilometres. So the numbers must have units to give them some useful meaning.

Different units of measurement are used in different parts of the world. The foot, pound and second system (known as fps) is still used extensively in the USA and to some extent in the UK. The metric system, which relies on the centimetre, gram and second (known as cgs), is widely used in continental Europe. But in engineering and hydraulics the most common units are those in the SI system and it is this system which is used throughout this book.

### 1.2.1 SI base units

The Système International d'Unités (the International System of Units, usually abbreviated to SI) is not difficult to grasp and it has many advantages over the other systems. It is based on metric measurement and is slowly replacing the old fps system and the European cgs system. All length measurements are in metres, mass is in

**Table 1.1 Basic SI units of measurement**

| *Measurement* | *Unit* | *Symbol* |
|---|---|---|
| Length | metre | m |
| Mass | kilogram | kg |
| Time | second | s |

**Table 1.2 Some useful derived units**

| *Measurement* | *Unit* | *Measurement* | *Unit* |
|---|---|---|---|
| Area | $m^2$ | Force | N |
| Volume | $m^3$ | Mass density | $kg/m^3$ |
| Velocity | m/s | Specific weight | $N/m^3$ |
| Acceleration | $m/s^2$ | Pressure | $N/m^2$ |
| Viscosity | kg/ms | Momentum | kgm/s |
| Kinematic viscosity | $m^2/s$ | Energy for solids | Nm |
| | | Energy for fluids | Nm/N |

kilograms and time is in seconds (Table 1.1). SI units are simple to use and their big advantage is that they can help to avoid much of the confusion that surrounds the use of other units. For example, it is quite easy to confuse mass and weight in both fps and cgs units as they are both measured in pounds in fps and in kilograms in cgs. Any mix-up between them can have serious consequences for the design of engineering works. In the SI system the difference is clear because they have different units – mass is in kilograms whereas weight is in newtons. This is discussed later in section 1.7.

Note that there is no mention of centimetres in Table 1.1. Centimetres are part of the cgs system of units and not SI and so play no part in hydraulics or in this text. Millimetres *are* acceptable for very small measurements and kilometres for long lengths – but *not* centimetres.

### 1.2.2 Derived units

Every measurement must have a unit so that it has meaning. The units chosen for measurement do not affect the quantities measured and so, for example, 1.0 metre is exactly the same as 3.28 feet. However, when solving problems, all the measurements used must be in the same system of units. If they are mixed up (e.g. centimetres or inches instead of metres, or minutes instead of seconds) and added together, the answer will be meaningless. Some useful derived units that come from the SI system of units in Table 1.1 are included in Table 1.2.

## 1.3 Velocity and acceleration

In everyday language **velocity** is often used in place of **speed**. But they are different. Speed is the rate at which some object is travelling and is measured in metres per second (m/s) but there is no indication of the direction of travel. Velocity is speed plus direction. It defines movement in a particular direction and is also measured in metres per second (m/s). In hydraulics it is useful to know which direction water is moving and so the term 'velocity' is used instead of 'speed'. When an object travels a known distance and the time taken to do this is also known, then the velocity can be calculated as follows:

$$\text{velocity (m/s)} = \frac{\text{distance (m)}}{\text{time (s)}}$$

**Acceleration** describes change in velocity. When an object's velocity is increasing then it is **accelerating**; when it is slowing down it is **decelerating**. Acceleration is measured in metres per second per second (m/s$^2$). If the initial and final velocities are known as well as the time taken for the velocity to change, then the acceleration can be calculated as follows:

$$\text{acceleration (m/s}^2\text{)} = \frac{\text{change in velocity (m/s)}}{\text{time (s)}}$$

### Example: Calculating velocity and acceleration

An object is moving along at a steady velocity and it takes 150s to travel 100m. Calculate the velocity.

We have

$$\text{velocity} = \frac{\text{distance (m)}}{\text{time (s)}} = \frac{100}{150} = 0.67\text{m/s}$$

If the object starts from rest, calculate the acceleration if its final velocity of 1.5m/s is reached in 50s.

We have

$$\text{acceleration} = \frac{\text{change in velocity (m/s)}}{\text{time (s)}} = \frac{1.5 - 0}{50} = 0.03\text{m/s}^2$$

## 1.4 Forces

Force is not a word that can be easily described in the same way as some material object. The word 'force' is commonly used and understood to mean a pushing or a pulling action and so it is only possible to say what a force will do and not what it is. Using this idea, if a force is applied to some stationary object then, if the force is

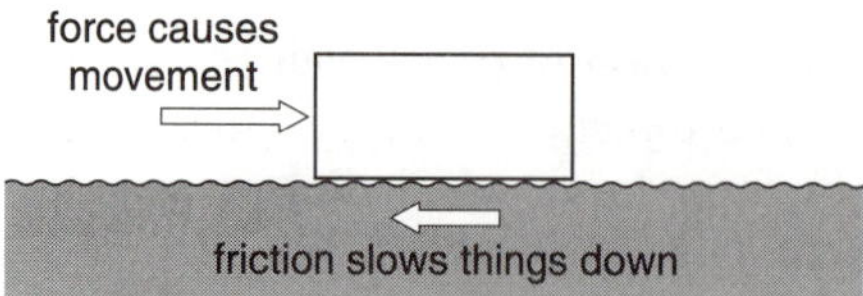


**Figure 1.1** Forces and friction

large enough, the object will begin to move (Figure 1.1). If the force is applied for long enough then the object will begin to move faster, i.e. it will accelerate. The same applies to water and to other fluids as well. It may be difficult to think of pushing water but if it is to flow along a pipeline or a channel a force will be needed to move it. So one way of describing force is to say that *a force causes movement*.

## 1.5 Friction

Friction is the name given to the force that resists movement and so causes objects to slow down (Figure 1.1). It is an important aspect of all our daily lives. Without friction between our feet and the ground surface it would be difficult to walk and we are reminded of this each time we step onto ice or some smooth oily surface. In such cases friction is essential but in others it is a great nuisance. In car engines, for example, if it were not for lubricants, which keep the moving components apart, they would quickly heat up by rubbing together and eventually would seize up. Friction also occurs in pipes and channels between flowing water and the internal surface of a pipe or the bed and sides of a channel. Indeed, much of pipe and channel hydraulics is concerned with predicting this friction force so that the right size of pipe or channel can be chosen to carry a given flow (see Chapters 4 and 5).

Friction is not only confined to boundaries, there is also friction inside fluids (internal friction), which makes some fluids flow more easily than others. The term **viscosity** is used to describe this internal friction (see section 1.12.3).

## 1.6 Newton's laws of motion

Sir Isaac Newton (1642–1728) was one of the first to begin the study of forces and how they cause movement and his work is now enshrined in three basic rules, known as **Newton's laws of motion**. They are very simple laws and at first sight they appear so obvious that they hardly seem worth writing down. But they form the basis of all our understanding of hydraulics (and movement of solid objects as well) and it took the genius of Newton to recognise their importance. They are as follows.

### Law 1: Forces cause movement

First imagine this in terms of solid objects. A block of wood placed on a table will stay there unless it is pushed (i.e. a force is applied to it). Equally, if it is moving it will continue to move unless some force (e.g. friction) causes it to slow down or to change direction. So forces are needed to make objects move or to stop them. This same law applies to water.

### Law 2: Forces cause objects to accelerate

This law builds on the first and provides the link between force, mass and acceleration (Figure 1.2a). Again think in solid material terms first. If the block of wood is to move, it will need a force to do it. The size of this force depends on the size of the block (its mass) and how fast it needs to go (its acceleration). The larger the block and the faster it must go, the larger must be the force. Water behaves in the same way. If water is to be moved along a pipeline then some force will be needed to do it. Newton linked these three together in mathematical terms to calculate the force required:

$$\text{force (N)} = \text{mass (kg)} \times \text{acceleration (m/s}^2\text{)}$$

The unit of force can be derived from multiplying mass and acceleration, i.e. kgm/s$^2$. But this is a complicated unit and so in the SI system it is simplified and called the **newton** (N) in recognition of Sir Isaac Newton's contribution to our understanding of mechanics. A force of 1 newton (1N) is defined as the force needed to cause a mass of 1kg to accelerate at 1m/s$^2$. This is not a large force. An apple held in the palm of your hand weighs approximately 1N – an interesting point since it was supposed to have been an apple falling on Newton's head that set off his thoughts on forces, gravity and motion.

Using newtons in hydraulics will produce some very large numbers and so, to overcome this, forces are measured in kilonewtons (kN):

$$1\text{kN} = 1000\text{N}$$

### Example: Calculating force using Newton's second law

A mass of 3kg is to be moved from rest to reach a speed of 6m/s and this must be done in 10s. Calculate the force needed.

First calculate the acceleration:

$$\text{acceleration (m/s}^2\text{)} = \frac{\text{change in velocity (m/s)}}{\text{time (s)}} = \frac{6}{10} = 0.6\text{m/s}^2$$

Using Newton's second law

$$\text{force} = \text{mass} \times \text{acceleration} = 3 \times 0.6 = 1.8\text{N}$$

So a force of 1.8N is needed to move a mass of 3kg to a velocity of 6m/s in 10s.

## Law 3: For every force there is always an equal and opposite force

To understand this simple but vitally important law, again think of the block of wood sitting on a table (Figure 1.2b). The block exerts a force (its weight) downwards on the table; but the table also exerts an equal but opposite upward force on the block. If it did not, the block would drop down through the table under the influence of gravity. So there are two forces, exactly equal in magnitude but in opposite directions, and so the block does not move.

The same idea can be applied to moving objects as well. In earlier times it was thought that objects were propelled forward by the air rushing in behind them. This idea was put forward by the Greeks but it failed to show how an object could be propelled in a vacuum as is the case when a rocket travels into space. What in fact happens is the downward thrust of the burning fuel creates an equal and opposite thrust which pushes the rocket upwards (Figure 1.2c). Newton helped to discredit the Greek idea by setting up an experiment which showed that, rather than encouraging an object to move faster, the air (or water) flow around it slowed it down because of the friction between the object and the air.

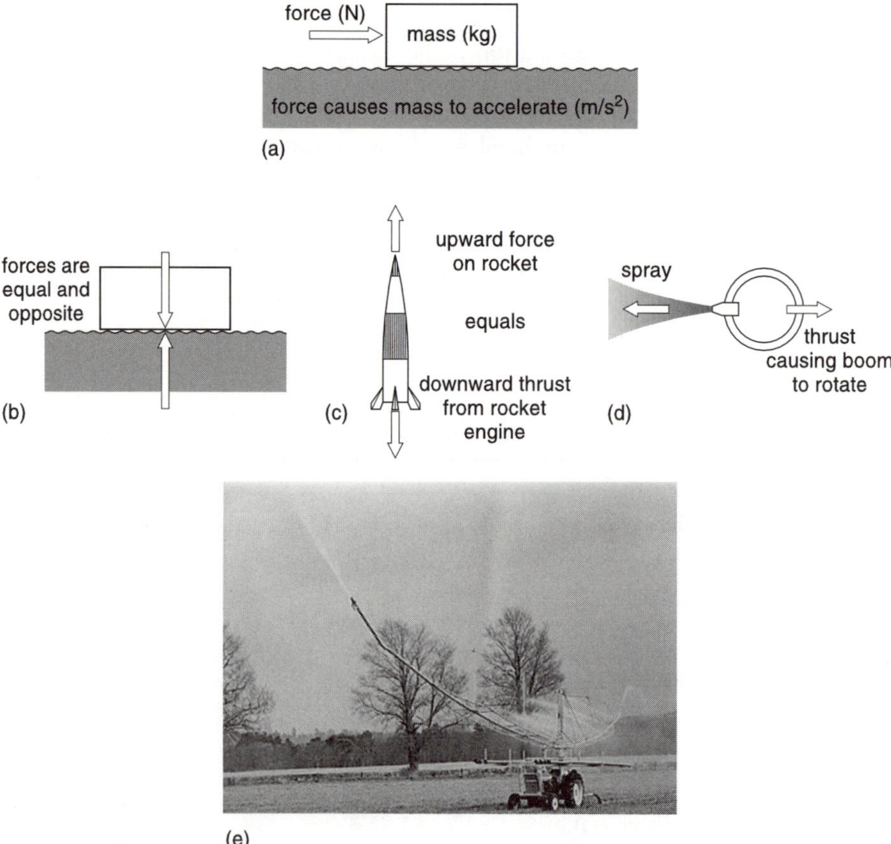


**Figure 1.2** Newton's laws of motion

Another example of Newton's third law occurs in irrigation where rotating booms spray water over crops (Figure 1.2d and e). The booms are not powered by a motor but by the reaction of the water jets. As water is forced out of the nozzles along the boom it creates an equal and opposite force on the boom itself which causes it to rotate. The same principle is used to drive the water distributors on the circular water cleaning filters at sewage works.

## 1.7 Mass and weight

There is often confusion between **mass** and **weight** and this has not been helped by the system of units used in the past. It is also not helped by our common use of the terms in everyday language. Mass and weight have very specific scientific meanings and for any study of water it is essential to have a clear understanding of the difference between them.

*Mass refers to an amount of matter or material.* It is a constant value and is measured in kilograms (kg). A specific quantity of matter is often referred to as an **object**. Hence the use of this term in the earlier description of Newton's laws.

*Weight is a force.* Weight is a measure of the force of gravity on an object and this will be different from place to place depending on the gravity. On the Earth there are only slight variations in gravity, but the gravity on the Moon is much less than it is on the Earth. So the *mass* of an object on the Moon would be the same as it is on Earth but its *weight* would be much less. As weight is a force it is measured in newtons. This clearly distinguishes it from mass, which is measured in kilograms.

Newton's second law also links mass and weight and in this case the acceleration term is the acceleration resulting from gravity. This is the acceleration that any object experiences when dropped and allowed to fall to the Earth's surface. Objects dropped in our atmosphere do, in fact, experience different rates of acceleration because of the resistance of the air – hence the reason why a feather falls more slowly than a coin. But if both were dropped at the same time in a vacuum they would accelerate at the same rate. There are also minor variations over the Earth's surface and this is the reason why athletes can sometimes run faster or throw the javelin further in some parts of the world. However, for engineering purposes, acceleration due to gravity is assumed to have a constant value of $9.81\text{m/s}^2$ – usually called the **gravity constant** and denoted by the letter $g$. The following equation based on Newton's second law provides the link between weight and mass:

$$\text{weight (N)} = \text{mass (kg)} \times \text{gravity constant (m/s}^2)$$

Confusion between mass and weight often occurs in our everyday lives. When visiting a shop and asking for 5kg of potatoes these are duly weighed out on a weigh balance. To be strictly correct we should ask for 50N of potatoes as the balance is measuring the *weight* of the potatoes (i.e. the force of gravity) and not their mass. But, because the gravity acceleration is constant all over the world the conversion factor between mass and weight is a constant value and so the shopkeeper's balance usually shows kilograms and not newtons. If shopkeepers were to change their balances to read in newtons to resolve a scientific confusion, engineers and scientists might be happy but no doubt the larger majority of shoppers would not be so happy!

### Example: Calculating the weight of an object

Calculate the weight of an object when its mass is 5kg.

Using the equation from Newton's second law

$$\text{weight} = \text{mass} \times \text{gravity constant} = 5 \times 9.81 = 49.05\text{N}$$

Sometimes engineers assume the gravity constant is $10\text{m/s}^2$ because it is easier to multiply by 10 and the error involved in this is not significant in engineering terms. In this case

$$\text{weight} = 5 \times 10 = 50\text{N}$$

## 1.8 Scalar and vector quantities

Measurements in hydraulics are either called **scalar** or **vector** quantities. Scalar measurements only indicate magnitude. Examples of this are mass, volume, area and length. So if there are 120 boxes in a room and they each have a volume of $2\text{m}^3$, both the number of boxes and the volume of each are scalar quantities.

Vectors have direction as well as magnitude. Examples of vectors include force and velocity. It is just as important to know which direction forces are pushing and water is moving as well as their magnitude.

## 1.9 Dealing with vectors

Scalar quantities can be added together by following the rules of arithmetic. Thus, 5 boxes and 4 boxes can be added to make 9 boxes, and 3m and 7m can be added to make 10m.

Vectors can also be added together providing their direction is taken into account. The addition (or subtraction) of two or more vectors results in another single vector called the **resultant** and the vectors that make up the resultant are called the **components**. If two forces, 25N and 15N, are pushing in the same direction then their resultant is found simply by adding the two together, i.e. 40N (Figure 1.3a). If they are pushing in opposite directions then their resultant is found by subtracting them, i.e. 10N. So one direction is considered positive and the opposite direction negative for the purposes of combining vectors.

But forces can also be at an angle to each other and in such cases a different way of adding or subtracting them is needed – a **vector diagram** is used for this purpose. This is a diagram drawn to a chosen scale to show both the magnitude and the direction of the vectors and hence the magnitude of the resultant vector. An example of how this is done is shown in the box.

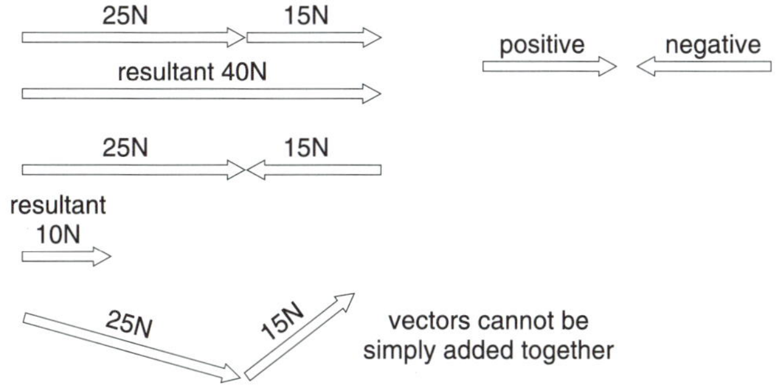


(a) Calculating the resultant

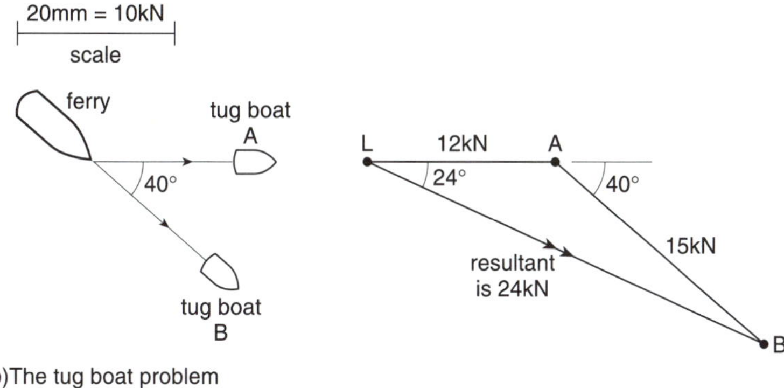


(b)The tug boat problem

**Figure 1.3 Adding and subtracting vectors**

Vectors can also be added and subtracted mathematically but a knowledge of trigonometry is needed. For those interested in this approach, it is described in most basic books on maths and mechanics.

## Example: Calculating resultant force using a vector diagram

Two tug boats A and B are pulling a large ferry boat into a harbour. Tug A is pulling with a force of 12kN, tug B with a force of 15kN and the angle between the two tow ropes is 40° (Figure 1.3b). Calculate the resultant force and show the direction in which the ferry boat will move.

First draw a diagram of the ferry and the two tugs. Then, assuming a scale of 20mm equals 10kN (this is chosen so that the diagram fits conveniently onto this book page), draw the 12kN force to scale, i.e. the line LA. Next, draw the second force, 15kN, to the same scale but starting the line at A and drawing it at an angle of 40° to the first line. This 'adds' the second force to the first one. The resultant force is found by joining the points L and B, measuring this in millimetres and converting this to a value in kilonewtons using the scale. Its value is 24kN. The line of the resultant is shown by the positioning of the line LB in the diagram.

To summarise, the ferry boat will move in a direction LB as a result of the pull exerted by the two tugs and the resultant force pulling on the ferry in that direction is 24kN.

The triangle drawn in Figure 1.3b is the **vector diagram** and shows how two forces can be added. As there are three forces in this problem it is sometimes called a **triangle of forces**. It is possible to add together many forces using the same technique. In such cases the diagram is referred to as a **polygon of forces**.

## 1.10 Work, energy and power

### 1.10.1 Work

Work refers to almost any kind of physical activity but in engineering it has a very specific meaning. Work is done when a force produces movement. A crane does work when it lifts a load against the force of gravity and a train does work when it pulls trucks. But if you hold a large weight for a long period of time you will undoubtably get very tired and feel that you have done a lot of work, but you will not have done any work in an engineering sense because nothing moved.

Work done on an object can be calculated as follows:

$$\text{work done (Nm)} = \text{force (N)} \times \text{distance moved by the object (m)}$$

As work done is the product of force (N) and distance (m) then its units are newton metres (Nm).

### 1.10.2 Energy

Energy is another word commonly used in everyday language, but in engineering and hydraulics it has a very specific meaning. Energy enables useful work to be done.

People and animals require energy to do work. This is obtained by eating food and converting it into useful energy for work through the muscles of the body. Energy is also needed to make water flow and this is why reservoirs are built in mountainous areas so that the natural energy of water can be used to make it flow downhill to a town or to a hydro-electric power station. In many cases energy must be added to water to lift it from a well or a river. This can be supplied by a pumping device driven by a motor using energy from fossil fuels such as diesel or petrol. Solar and wind energy are alternatives and so is energy provided by human hands or animals.

The amount of energy needed to do a job is determined by the amount of work to be done. So that

$$\text{energy} = \text{work done}$$

Energy, like work, is measured in Nm. But just to confuse everyone some textbooks refer to energy in **joules** (J). This is just another way of measuring energy and 1J equals 1Nm. In this text joules are not referred to in order to avoid confusion.

#### 1.10.2.1 *Changing energy*

An important aspect of energy is that it can be changed from one form of energy to another. People and animals are able to convert food into useful energy to drive their muscles. In a typical diesel engine pumping system, the energy is changed several times before it gets to the water. Chemical energy contained within the fuel (e.g. diesel oil) is burnt in a diesel engine to produce mechanical energy. This is converted to useful water energy via the drive shaft and pump (Figure 1.4). So a pump can be thought of as a device for putting additional energy into a water system.

The system of energy transfer is not perfect and energy losses occur through friction between the moving parts and is usually lost as heat energy. These losses can be significant and costly in terms of fuel use. For this reason it is important to match a pump and its power unit with the job to be done to maximise the efficiency of energy use (see Chapter 8).

### 1.10.3 Power

Power is often confused with the term 'energy'. They are related but they have different meanings. Whilst energy is the capacity to do useful work, power is the rate at which the energy is used (Figure 1.5), and so

$$\text{power (W)} = \frac{\text{energy (Nm)}}{\text{time (s)}}$$

Although logically power should be measured in newton metres per second (Nm/s) it is normally measured in **watts** (W). The relationship between the two is as follows:

$$1\text{Nm/s} = 1\text{W}$$

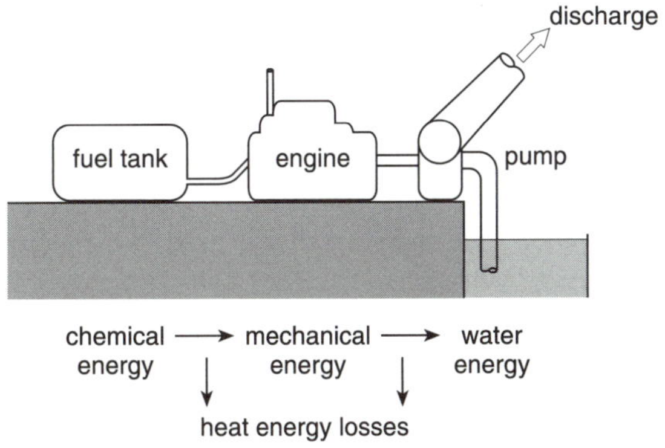


**Figure 1.4** Changing energy from one form to another

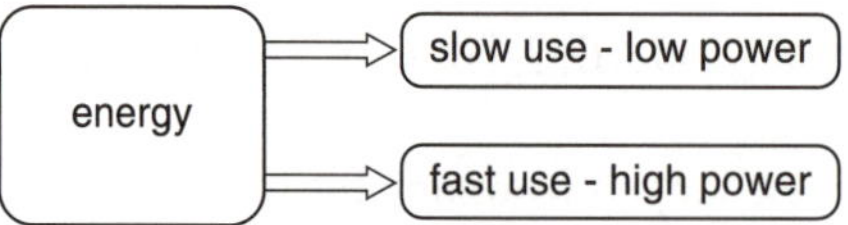


**Figure 1.5 Power is the rate of energy use**

One watt is a very small amount of power and so the **kilowatt** (kW) is more commonly used:

$$1000\text{W} = 1\text{kW}$$

To give some examples of power requirements, a typical room air conditioner has a power rating of 3kW and a small electric radiator a rating of 1 to 2kW. An average person walking up and down stairs will have a power requirement of about 0.3kW. This is the rate at which each will use energy.

Now we go back to energy for a moment. The energy used is often worked out from knowing thc power and the time the equipment will be used rather than trying to calculate it from the work done. Using the above equation for power but using the units of kW for power and hours (h) for time:

$$\text{energy (kWh)} = \text{power (kW)} \times \text{time (h)}$$

Energy is now measured in kilowatt hours (kWh). This unit for energy appears to be different to Nm referred to earlier but it is the same. In fact

$$1\text{kWh} = 3600\ 000\text{Nm} = 3 \times 10^6\ \text{Nm}$$

In many cases it is clearly easier to deal with the relatively simple numbers in kWh than it is to work in the larger numbers in Nm.

Another commonly used measure of power is **horse power** (HP). As it is not part of SI units it will not be used in this book. However, if comparison is needed:

$$1\text{kW} = 1.36\text{HP}$$

## 1.11 Momentum

The effect of applying a force to an object is to cause it to change velocity (Newton's second law). This provides another link between mass and velocity which is called **momentum**. This is another scientific term that is used in everyday language to describe something that is moving – we say that some object or a football game has momentum if it is moving along and making good progress. In engineering terms it is defined as follows:

$$\text{momentum (kgm/s)} = \text{mass (kg)} \times \text{velocity (m/s)}$$

Note that the units of momentum are a combination of those of velocity and mass.

To understand the usefulness of this idea, look first at an application to solid objects. Figure 1.6a shows two solid blocks of different masses which are to be moved by applying a force to them. The first block of mass 2kg is pushed by a force of 15N for 4s. Imagine that the surface is very smooth and there is no friction. Using Newton's second law the acceleration can be calculated together with how fast the block will be travelling after 4s:

$$\text{force} = \text{mass} \times \text{acceleration}$$

$$15 = 2 \times f$$

$$f = 7.5\text{m/s}^2$$

So for every second the force is applied the block will move faster by 7.5m/s. After 4s it will have reached a velocity of:

$$4 \times 7.5 = 30\text{m/s}$$

To calculate the momentum of the block:

$$\text{momentum} = \text{mass} \times \text{velocity}$$

$$= 2 \times 30$$

$$= 60\text{kgm/s}$$

Now holding this information for a moment, suppose a larger block of mass 10kg is pushed by the same force of 15N for the same time of 4s. Using the same calculations as before:

$$15 = 10 \times f$$

$$f = 1.5\text{m/s}^2$$

So when the same force is applied to this larger block it accelerates more slowly at 1.5m/s for every second the force is applied. After 4s it will have a velocity of:

$$4 \times 1.5 = 6\text{m/s}$$

Now calculate momentum of this block:

$$\text{momentum} = 10 \times 6$$

$$= 60\text{kgm/s}$$

The same momentum is obtained when the same force is applied for the same time although the masses are different and so are their final velocities. This means that when the same force is applied for the same time period to any mass it will produce the same momentum.

Now multiply the force by the time:

$$\text{force} \times \text{time} = 15 \times 4 = 60\text{Ns}$$

But newtons can also be written as kgm/s$^2$, and so

$$\text{force} \times \text{time} = 60\text{kgm/s}$$

This is equal to the momentum and has the same units. It is called the **impulse** and it is equal to the momentum it creates. So

$$\text{impulse} = \text{momentum}$$

$$\text{force} \times \text{time} = \text{mass} \times \text{velocity}$$

This is more commonly written as:

$$\text{impulse} = \text{change in momentum}$$

Writing 'change in momentum' is more appropriate because an object need not be starting from rest – it may already be moving. In such cases the object will have some momentum and an impulse would be increasing (changing) it. A momentum change need not be just a change in velocity but also a change in mass. If a lorry loses some of its load when travelling at speed its mass will change. In this case the lorry would gain speed as a result of being smaller in mass, the momentum before being equal to the momentum after the loss of load.

The equation for momentum change becomes:

$$\text{force} \times \text{time} = \text{mass} \times \text{change in velocity}$$

This equation works well for solid blocks that are forced to move but it is not easily applied to flowing water in its present form. For water it is better to look at the rate at which the water mass is flowing rather than thinking of the flow as a series of discrete solid blocks of water. This is done by dividing both sides of the equation by time:

$$\text{force} = \frac{\text{mass}}{\text{time}} \times \text{change in velocity}$$

Mass divided by time is the mass flow in kg/s and so the equation becomes:

$$\text{force (N)} = \text{mass flow (kg/s)} \times \text{change in velocity (m/s)}$$

So when flowing water undergoes a change of momentum by either a change in velocity or a change in mass flow (e.g. water flowing around a pipe bend or through a reducer) then a force is produced by that change (Figure 1.6b). Equally if a force is applied to water (e.g. in a pump or turbine) then the water will experience a change in momentum.

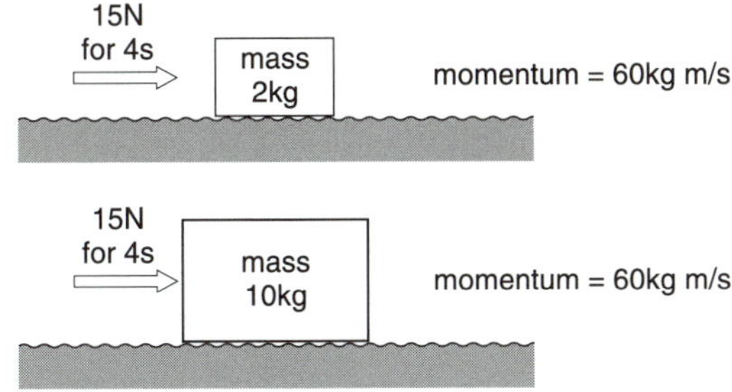


(a) Momentum for solid objects

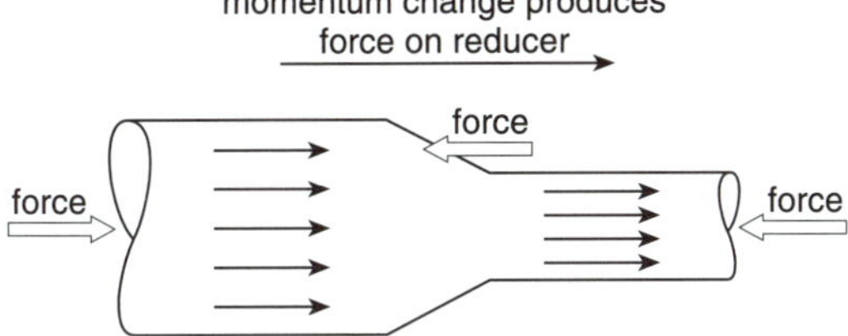


(b) Momentum change produces forces

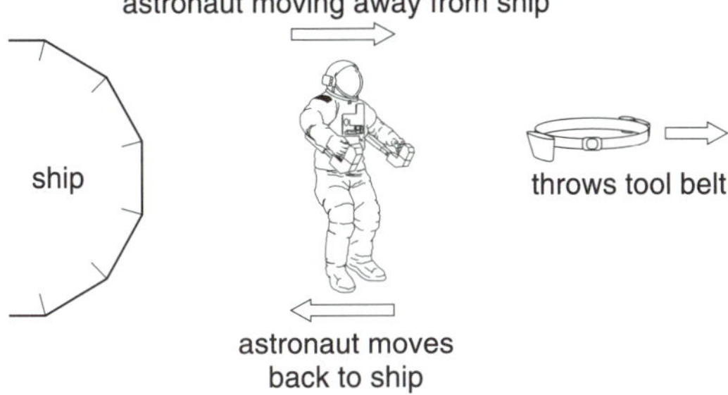


(c) The astronaut's problem

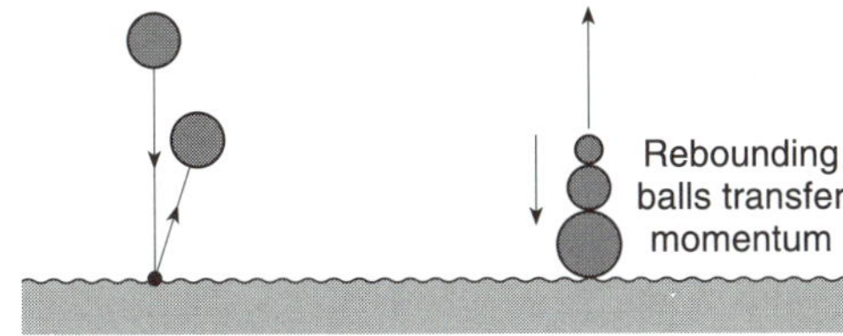


(d) Rebounding balls

**Figure 1.6 Understanding momentum**

As momentum is about forces and velocities the direction in which momentum changes is also of importance. In the simple force example, the forces are pushing from left to right and so the movement is from left to right. This is assumed to be the positive direction. Any force or movement from right to left would be considered negative. So if several forces are involved they can be added or subtracted to find a single resultant force. Another important point to note is that Newton's third law also applies to momentum. The force on the reducer (Figure 1.6b) could be drawn in either direction. It is shown in the negative direction (right to left) in the diagram and this is the force that the reducer exerts on the water. Equally it could be drawn in the opposite direction, i.e. the positive direction from left to right when it would be the force of the water on the reducer. The two forces are equal and opposite.

The application of this idea to water flow is developed further in Chapter 3.

Those not so familiar with Newton's laws might find momentum more difficult to deal with than other aspects of hydraulics. To help understand the concept here are two interesting examples of momentum change that might help.

### 1.11.1 The astronaut's problem

An astronaut has just completed a repair job on his space ship and secures his tools on his belt. He then pushes off from the ship to drift in space only to find that his life-line has come undone and he is drifting further and further away from his ship (Figure 1.6c). How can he get back? He could radio for help, but another solution would be to take off his tool belt and throw it as hard as he can in the direction he is travelling. The reaction from this will be to propel him in the reverse direction and back to his space ship. The momentum created by throwing the tool belt in one direction (i.e. mass of tool belt multiplied by velocity of tool belt) will be matched by momentum in the opposite direction (i.e. mass of astronaut multiplied by velocity of astronaut). His mass will be much larger than the tool belt and so his velocity will be smaller but at least it will be in the right direction!

### 1.11.2 Rebounding balls

Another interesting example of momentum change occurs when several balls are dropped onto the ground together (Figure 1.6d). If dropped individually they rebound to a modest height – less than the height from which they were dropped. If several balls, each one slightly smaller than the previous one, are now dropped together, one on top of the other, the top one will shoot upwards at an alarming velocity to a height far greater than any of the individual balls. The reason for this is the first ball rebounds on impact with the ground and hits the second ball and the second ball hits the third and so on. Each ball transfers its momentum to the next one. If it were possible to drop eight balls onto each other in this way the top ball would reach a velocity of 10 000m/s. This would be fast enough to put it into orbit if it did not vaporise from the heat created by friction as it went through the Earth's atmosphere! Eight balls may be difficult to manage but even with two or three the effect is quite dramatic.

## 1.12 Properties of water

The following are some of the physical properties of water. This will be a useful reference for work in later chapters.

### 1.12.1 Density

When dealing with solid objects their mass and weight are important, but when dealing with fluids it is much more useful to know about their **density**. There are two ways of expressing density: **mass density** and **weight density**.

Mass density of any material is the mass of one cubic metre of the material and is a fixed value for the material concerned. For example, the mass density of air is 1.29kg/m$^3$, steel is 7800kg/m$^3$ and gold is 19 300kg/m$^3$. Mass density can be determined by dividing the mass of some object by its volume:

$$\text{density (kg/m}^3) = \frac{\text{mass (kg)}}{\text{volume (m}^3)}$$

Mass density is usually denoted by the Greek letter $\rho$ (rho). For water the mass of one cubic metre of water is 1000kg and so:

$$\rho = 1000\text{kg/m}^3$$

Density can also be written in terms of weight as well as mass. This is referred to as weight density but engineers often use the term **specific weight** ($w$). This is the weight of one cubic metre of water. Newton's second law can be used to link mass and weight:

$$\text{weight density (kN/m}^3) = \text{mass density (kg/m}^3) \times \text{gravity constant (m/s}^2)$$

For water:

$$\begin{aligned}\text{weight density} &= 1000 \times 9.81\\ &= 9810\text{N/m}^3 \text{ (or } 9.81\text{kN/m}^3)\\ &= 10\text{kN/m}^3 \text{ (approximately)}\end{aligned}$$

Sometimes weight density for water is rounded off by engineers to 10kN/m$^3$. Usually this makes very little difference to the design of most hydraulic works. Note that the equation for weight density is applicable to all fluids and not just water. It can be used to find the weight density of any fluid provided the mass density is known.

Engineers generally use specific weight in their calculations whereas scientists tend to use $\rho g$ to describe the weight density. Either approach is acceptable but for clarity $\rho g$ is used throughout this book.

### 1.12.2 Relative density or specific gravity

Sometimes it is more convenient to use **relative density** rather than just density. It is more commonly referred to as **specific gravity** and is the ratio of the density of a material or fluid to that of some standard density – usually water. It can be written in terms of both the mass density and the weight density:

$$\text{specific gravity (SG)} = \frac{\text{density of an object (kg/m}^3)}{\text{density of water (kg/m}^3)}$$

Note that specific gravity has no units. As the volume is the same for both the object and the water, another way of writing this formula is in terms of weight:

$$\text{specific gravity} = \frac{\text{weight of an object}}{\text{weight of an equal volume of water}}$$

Some useful specific gravity values are included in Table 1.3.

The density of any other fluid (or any solid object) can be calculated by knowing the specific gravity. The mass density of mercury, for example, can be calculated from its specific gravity:

$$\text{specific gravity (SG) of mercury} = \frac{\text{mass density of mercury (kg/m}^3)}{\text{mass density of water (kg/m}^3)}$$

so

$$\begin{aligned}\text{mass density of mercury} &= \text{SG of mercury} \times \text{mass density of water}\\ &= 13.6 \times 1000\\ &= 13\,600\text{kg/m}^3\end{aligned}$$

The mass density of mercury is 13.6 times greater than that of water.

Archimedes used this concept of specific gravity in his famous principle, which is discussed in section 2.9.

**Table 1.3 Some values of specific gravity**

| *Material/fluid* | *Specific gravity* | *Comments* |
|---|---|---|
| Water | 1.0 | All other specific gravity measurements are made relative to that of water |
| Oil | 0.9 | Less than 1.0 and so it floats on water |
| Sand/silt | 2.65 | Important in sediment transport problems |
| Mercury | 13.6 | Fluid used in manometers for measuring pressure |

### 1.12.3 Viscosity

This is the friction force that exists inside a fluid as it flows. It is sometimes referred to as the **dynamic viscosity**. To understand the influence of viscosity imagine a fluid flowing along a pipe as a set of thin layers (Figure 1.7a). Although it cannot be seen and it is not very obvious, the layer nearest to the boundary actually sticks to it and does not slide along as the other layers do. The next layer away from the boundary is moving but is slowed down by friction between it and the first layer. The third layer moves faster but is slowed by the second. This effect continues until the entire flow is affected. It is similar to the sliding effect of a pack of playing cards (Figure 1.7b). This friction between the layers of fluid is known as the **viscosity**. Some fluids, such as water, have a low viscosity and this means that the friction between the layers of fluid is low and its influence is not so evident when water is flowing. In contrast engine oils have a much higher viscosity and they seem to flow more slowly. This is because the internal friction is much greater.

One way to see viscosity at work is to try to pull out a spoon from a jar of honey. Some of the honey sticks to the spoon and some sticks to the jar, demonstrating that fluid sticks to the boundaries as referred to above. There is also a resistance to pulling out the spoon and this is the influence of viscosity. This effect is the same for all fluids including water but it cannot be so clearly demonstrated as in the honey jar. In fact, viscous resistance in water is ignored in many hydraulic designs. To take account of it not only complicates the problem but also has little or no effect on the outcome because the forces of viscosity are usually very small relative to other forces involved. When forces of viscosity are ignored the fluid is described as an **ideal fluid**.

Another interesting feature of the honey jar is that the resistance changes depending on how quickly the spoon is pulled out. The faster it is pulled the more resistance there is to the pulling. Newton related this rate of movement (the velocity) to the resistance and found that they were proportional. This means the resistance increases directly as the velocity of the fluid increases. In other words the faster you try to pull the spoon out of the honey jar the greater will be the force required to do it. Most common fluids conform to this relationship and are still known today as **Newtonian fluids**.

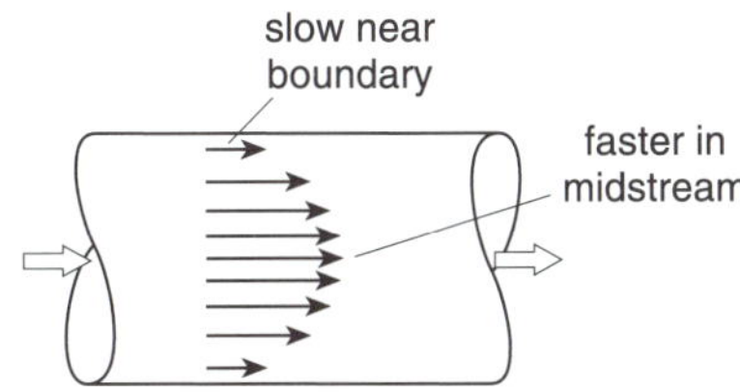


(a) Flow in a pipe as a set of thin layers

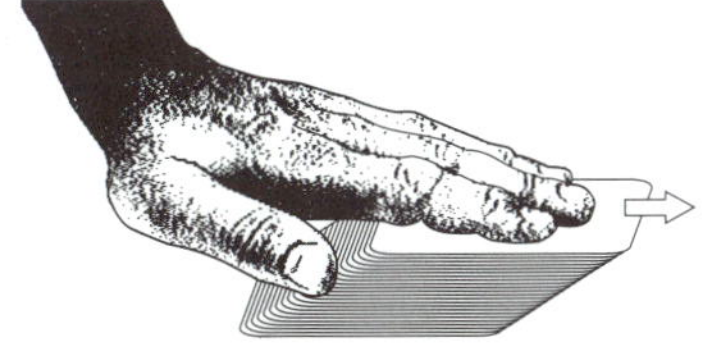

(b) Flow is similar to a pack of cards

**Figure 1.7 Understanding viscosity**

Some modern fluids, however, have different viscous properties and are called **non-Newtonian fluids**. One good example is tomato ketchup. When left on the shelf it is a highly viscous fluid which does not flow easily from the bottle. Sometimes you can turn a full bottle upside down and nothing comes out. But if you shake it vigorously (in scientific terms this means applying a shear force) its viscosity suddenly changes and the ketchup flows easily from the bottle. In other words, applying a force to a fluid can change its viscous properties, often to our advantage.

Although viscosity is often ignored, life would be difficult without it. The spoon in the honey jar would come out clean and it would be difficult to get the honey out of the jar. Rivers rely on viscosity to slow down flows otherwise they would continue to accelerate to very high speeds. The Mississippi River would reach a speed of over 300km/h as its flow gradually descends 450m towards the sea if water had no viscosity. Pumps would not work because impellers would not be able to grip the water, and swimmers would not be able to propel themselves through the water for the same reason.

Viscosity is usually denoted by the Greek letter $\mu$ (mu). For water

$$\mu = 0.001\,14 \text{kg/ms} \qquad \text{at a temperature of } 15°\text{C}$$

$$= 1.14 \times 10^{-3} \text{kg/ms}$$

The viscosity of all fluids is influenced by temperature. Viscosity decreases with increasing temperature.

### 1.12.4 Kinematic viscosity

In many hydraulic calculations viscosity and mass density go together and so they are often combined into a term known as the **kinematic viscosity**. It is denoted by the Greek letter $\nu$ (nu) and is calculated as follows:

$$\text{kinematic viscosity } (\nu) = \frac{\text{viscosity } (\mu)}{\text{density } (\rho)}$$

For water

$$\nu = 1.14 \times 10^{-6} \text{m}^2/\text{s} \qquad \text{at a temperature of } 15°\text{C}$$

Sometimes kinematic viscosity is measured in stokes (St) in recognition of the work of Sir George Stokes who helped to develop a fuller understanding of the role of viscosity in fluids:

$$10^4 \ \text{St} = 1\text{m}^2/\text{s}$$

so for water

$$\nu = 1.14 \times 10^{-2} \ \text{St}$$

### 1.12.5 Surface tension

An ordinary steel sewing needle can be made to float on water if it is placed there very carefully. A close examination of the water surface around the needle shows that the needle appears to be sitting in a slight depression and the water behaves as if it is covered with an elastic skin. This property is known as **surface tension**. The force of surface tension is very small and is normally expressed in terms of force per unit length. For water

$$\text{surface tension} = 0.51\text{N/m} \qquad \text{at a temperature of } 20^{\circ}\text{C}$$

This force is ignored in most hydraulic calculations but in hydraulic modelling, where small-scale models are constructed in a laboratory to try to work out forces and flows in large, complex problems, surface tension may influence the outcome because of the small water depths and flows involved.

### 1.12.6 Compressibility

It is easy to imagine a gas being compressible and to some extent some solid materials such as rubber. In fact all materials are compressible to some degree including water, which is 100 times more compressible than steel! Compressibility is important particularly when trying to stop water that is moving. If it were not compressible, then closing a valve on a pipeline could be a dangerous task. Imagine trying to stop suddenly a solid column of water several kilometres long. The force involved would be immense. Fortunately water is compressible and compresses like a spring to absorb the energy of the impact as the valve is closed. It behaves in a similar way to cars when they are in a pile-up. They collapse during impact and so absorb much of the energy of the collision. But the compression of water leads to another problem known as **water hammer** and this is discussed more fully in section 4.11.

Chapter 2

# Hydrostatics – water at rest

## 2.1 Introduction

**Hydrostatics** is the study of water that is not moving, i.e. it is at rest. It is important to civil engineers for the design of water storage tanks and dams. What are the forces created by water and how strong must a tank or a dam be to resist them? It is also important to naval architects who design ships and submarines. How deep can a submarine go before the pressures become too great and damage it? The answers to these questions can be found from studying hydrostatics. The theory is quite simple both in concept and in use. It is also a well established theory that was set down by Archimedes over 2000 years ago and is still used in much the same way today.

## 2.2 Pressure

The term **pressure** is used to describe the force exerted by water on each square metre of some object submerged in water, i.e. force per unit area. It may be the bottom of a tank, or the side of a dam, a ship or a submerged submarine. It is calculated as follows:

$$\text{pressure} = \frac{\text{force}}{\text{area}}$$

Introducing the units of measurement:

$$\text{pressure (kN/m}^2) = \frac{\text{force (kN)}}{\text{area (m}^2)}$$

Force is in kilonewtons (kN), area is in square metres ($m^2$) and so pressure is measured in $kN/m^2$. Sometimes pressure is measured in **pascals** (Pa) in recognition of Blaise Pascal (1620–1662) who clarified much of modern-day thinking about pressure and barometers for measuring atmospheric pressure:

$$1\text{Pa} = 1\text{N/m}^2$$

One pascal is a very small quantity and so kilopascals are often used so that:

$$1\text{kPa} = 1\text{kN/m}^2$$

Although it is in order to use pascals, kilonewtons per square metre is used throughout this text for the units of pressure.

## Example: Calculating pressure

Calculate the pressure on a plate 3m × 2m when a mass of 50kg rests upon it. Calculate the change in pressure when the plate is reduced in size to 1.5m × 2m.

First calculate the force on the plate (remember weight is a force):

$$\text{mass of water in tank} = 50\text{kg}$$

$$\text{weight of water in tank} = \text{mass} \times \text{gravity constant}$$

$$= 50 \times 9.81 = 490.5\text{N}$$

Also

$$\text{area of tank base} = 3 \times 2 = 6\text{m}^2$$

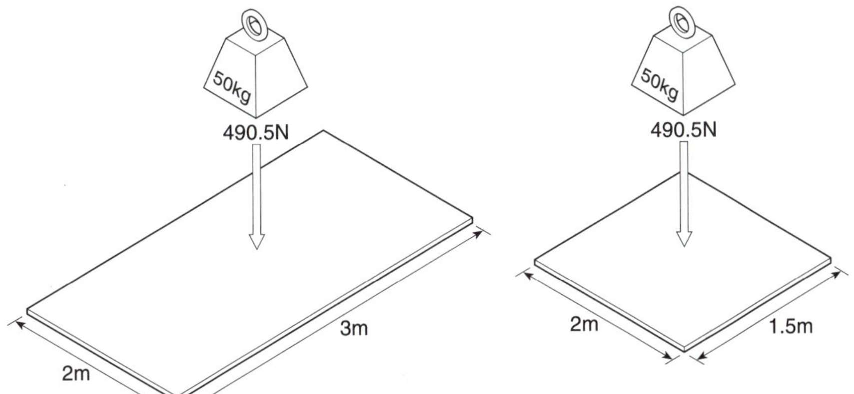


**Figure 2.1** Calculating pressure

so

$$\text{pressure} = \frac{\text{force}}{\text{area}} = \frac{490.5}{6} = 81.75\text{N/m}^2$$

When the plate is reduced to 1.5m by 2m

$$\text{area} = 1.5 \times 2 = 3\text{m}^2$$

$$\text{pressure} = \frac{490.5}{3} = 163.5\text{N/m}^2$$

so the mass and weight are the same but the areas are different and so the pressures are also different.

There is clearly a difference between force and pressure but there is often confusion between them. Take, for example, an elephant's foot and a woman's high heel shoe (Figure 2.2). Which exerts the greater pressure on the floor, the elephant or the heel of the shoe? The answer is the high heel shoe (see the example in the box). Although the weight (force) in the shoe is small in comparison to the weight of the elephant, the area of the shoe heel is very small and so the pressure is extremely high. Hence the reason why high heel shoes are sometimes banned from indoors as they can so easily damage wooden floors!

Pressure greater under the high heel shoe
than under the elephant's foot


**Figure 2.2** Difference between force and pressure

### Example: Calculating pressure under foot

Which produces the larger pressure, a 0.3m diameter foot of an elephant of mass 5000kg or 0.01m diameter heel of a woman's shoe when she has a mass of 60kg?

Consider first the pressure under the elephant's foot:

$$\text{mass of elephant} = 5000\text{kg}$$

$$\text{weight of elephant} = 49\ 050\text{N} = 49\text{kN}$$

$$\text{weight per foot} = \frac{49}{4} = 12.25\text{kN}$$

$$\text{area of foot} = \frac{\pi d^2}{4} = \frac{\pi 0.3^2}{4} = 0.07\text{m}^2$$

$$\text{pressure under foot} = \frac{\text{force}}{\text{area}} = \frac{12.25}{0.07} = 175\text{kN/m}^2$$

Now consider the pressure under the woman's shoe heel:

$$\text{mass of woman} = 60\text{kg}$$

$$\text{weight of woman} = 589\text{N} = 0.59\text{kN}$$

$$\text{weight per foot} = \frac{0.59}{2} = 0.29\text{kN}$$

$$\text{area of shoe heel} = \frac{\pi d^2}{4} = \frac{\pi 0.01^2}{4} = 0.0001\text{m}^2$$

$$\text{pressure under heel} = \frac{\text{force}}{\text{area}} = \frac{0.29}{0.0001} = 2900\text{kN/m}^2$$

The pressure under the woman's heel is 16 times greater than under the elephant's foot. So which would you rather have standing on your foot!

## 2.3 Pressure and depth

The pressure on some object under water is determined by the depth of water above it. The deeper the object is below the surface, the higher will be the pressure. This can be calculated using the pressure–head equation:

$$p = \rho g h$$

where $p$ is pressure (kN/m$^2$), $\rho$ is mass density of water (kN/m$^3$), $g$ is gravity constant (m/s$^2$) and $h$ is depth of water (m). This formula can be derived from basic principles. For those who wish to pursue this, look in the box below.

## Derivation: Pressure–head equation

A tank of water has a depth of water $h$ and a cross-sectional area $a$ (Figure 2.3a). The weight of water on the bottom of the tank (remember that weight is a force and is acting downwards) is balanced by an upward force from the bottom of the tank supporting the water (Newton's third law). So the formula is derived by calculating these two forces and putting them equal to each other.

First calculate the downward force. This is the weight of water. To do this calculate the volume and then the weight using the density:

$$\text{volume of water} = \text{cross-sectional area} \times \text{depth}$$

$$= a \times h$$

and so

$$\text{weight of water in tank} = \text{volume} \times \text{density} \times \text{gravity constant}$$

$$= a \times \rho \times h \times g$$

This is the downward force of the water. Next calculate the upward force from the base:

$$\text{supporting force} = \text{pressure} \times \text{area}$$

$$= p \times a$$

Put these two forces equal to each other

$$p \times a = a \times \rho \times h \times g$$

The area $a$ cancels out from both sides of the equation and so

$$p = \rho g h$$

$$\text{pressure} = \text{mass density} \times \text{gravity constant} \times \text{depth of water}$$

This is the pressure–head equation and this links pressure with the depth of water. It shows that pressure increases directly as the depth increases. It is independent of the shape of the tank or its base area.

### 2.3.1 The hydrostatic paradox

The area of the base of the tank has no effect on the pressure nor does the weight of the water in the tank (Figure 2.3b). It does not matter if the water is in a large reservoir or in a narrow tube. When the depth is the same then the pressure is the same.

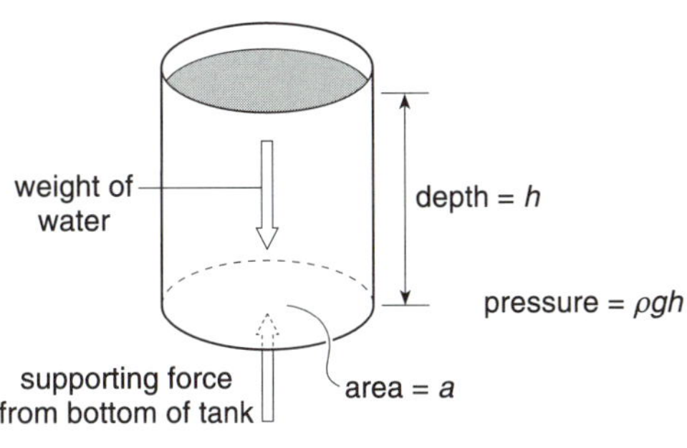


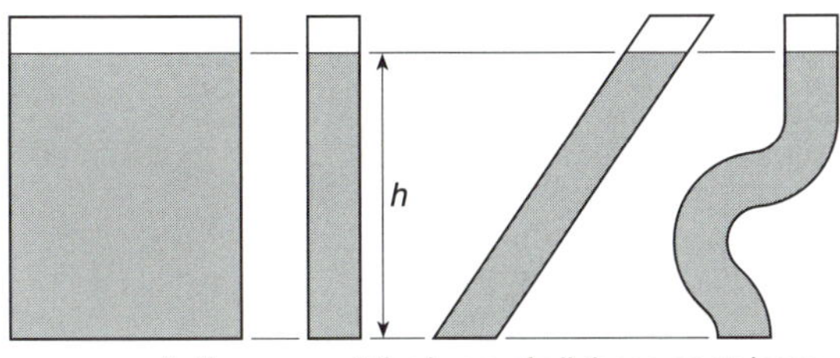


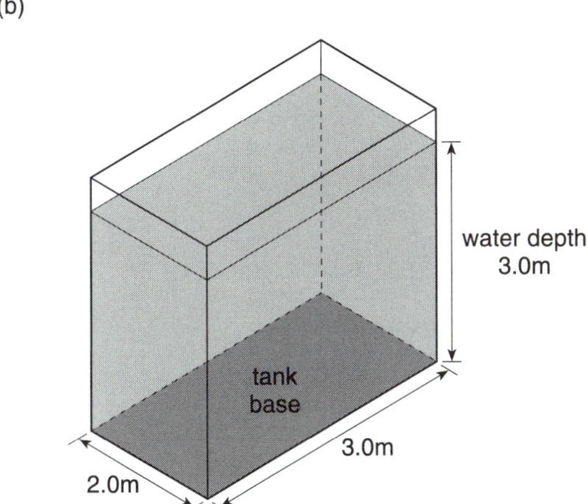


**Figure 2.3 Pressure and head**

Note that the equation $p = \rho gh$ works for all fluids and not just water, provided of course that the correct value of density is used for the fluid concerned.

Although the example in the box is concerned with pressure pushing vertically downwards, pressure does in fact push in all directions. Think of a cube immersed in water (Figure 2.4). The pressure of the water is pushing on all sides of the cube and not just on the top. If the cube was very small then the pressure on all six faces would be almost the same. If the cube gets smaller and smaller until it almost disappears, it becomes clear that *the pressure at a point in the water is the same in all directions*. So the pressure pushes in all directions and not just vertically. This idea is important in the design of dams because it is the horizontal action of pressure that pushes on a dam which must be resisted if the dam is not to fail. Note

## Example: Calculating the pressure and force on the base of a tank

A rectangular tank of water is 3m deep. If the base measures 3m by 2m, calculate the pressure and force on the base of the tank (Figure 2.3c).
Using the pressure–head equation we get

$$\begin{aligned} p &= \rho g h \\ &= 1000 \times 9.81 \times 3.0 \\ &= 29\ 430\text{N/m}^2 \\ &= 29.43\text{kN/m}^2 \end{aligned}$$

Calculate the force on the bottom of the tank:

area of the base $= 3 \times 2 = 6\text{m}^2$.

$$\begin{aligned} \text{force} &= \text{pressure} \times \text{area} \\ &= 29.43 \times 6.0 \\ &= 176.6\text{kN} \end{aligned}$$

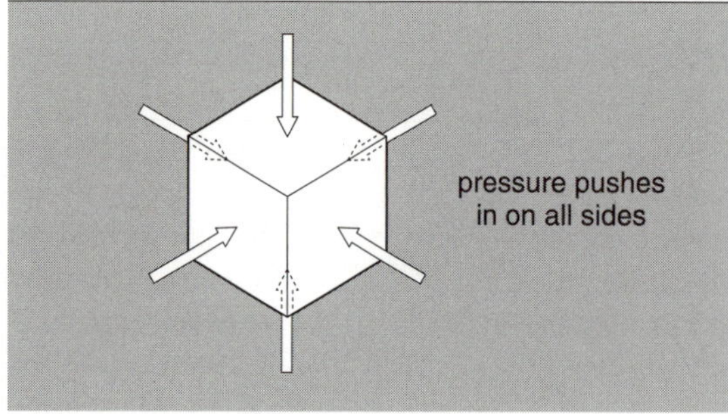
water surface
pressure pushes in on all sides
as cube gets smaller
pressure at a point is the same in all directions

**Figure 2.4 Pressure is the same in all directions**

also that the pressures in Figure 2.4 are drawn acting inwards. They could equally have been drawn pushing outwards according to Newton's third law.

## 2.4 Pressure head

Pressure is often referred to as so many metres of water rather than as a pressure in $kN/m^2$. It is called the **pressure head** or just **head** and is measured in metres. It is the same depth of water $h$ referred to in the equation $p = \rho gh$. As the density of water and gravity acceleration are constants, the pressure can be referred to either way. In the example in the box, the pressure is $29.43kN/m^2$ but this could be stated as 3m head of water. Both are correct and one can easily be converted to the other using the pressure–head equation.

Engineers prefer to use head measurements because, as will be seen later, differences in ground level can affect the pressure in a pipeline. It is then an easy matter to add (or subtract) changes in ground level to pressure values because they both have the same units.

When head is used to measure water pressure it is important to say that it is water, i.e. head of water. If another liquid is used, e.g. mercury, then the term 'head of mercury' must be used. Even though the pressure may be the same, the head will be quite different for different liquids. See the box for an example.

### Example: Calculating pressure head in mercury

Using the previous example, calculate the depth of mercury needed in the tank to produce the same pressure as 3m depth of water ($29.43kN/m^2$). Specific gravity (SG) of mercury is 13.6.

First calculate the density of mercury:

$$\rho_{mercury} = \rho_{water} \times SG_{mercury}$$
$$= 1000 \times 13.6$$
$$= 13\,600 N/m^3$$

Use the pressure–head equation to calculate the head of mercury:

$$p = \rho gh$$

where $\rho$ is now the density and $h$ is the depth of mercury, and so

$$29\,430 = 13\,600 \times 9.81 \times h$$
$$h = 0.22\text{m of mercury}$$

Note that when $\rho$ is in $N/m^3$ then pressure must be in $N/m^2$ and when $\rho$ is in $kN/m^3$ then pressure is in $kN/m^2$. So the depth of mercury required to create the same pressure as 3m of water is only 0.22m. This is because mercury is much denser than water.

## 2.5 Atmospheric pressure

The pressure of the atmosphere is all around us pressing on our bodies. Although air seems to be very light, when there is a large depth of it, as on the Earth's surface, it creates a very high pressure of approximately $100\text{kN/m}^2$. The average person has a skin area of $2\text{m}^2$ and so the force acting on each of us due to the air around us is approximately 200kN (the equivalent of 200 000 apples or approximately 20 tonnes). This is a very large force indeed! Fortunately there is an equal and opposite pressure from within our bodies that balances this pressure and so we feel no effect (Newton's third law). If for some reason one side of this pressure system was removed then the result would be catastrophic. For example, a person stepping from our normal atmosphere into a vacuum (like stepping out from a pressurised space rocket into space) would probably explode because the outside pressure is removed but the internal pressure remains.

At high altitudes, where atmospheric pressure is less than at the Earth's surface, some people suffer from nose bleeds because their blood pressure is much higher than the pressure of the surrounding atmosphere.

It was only in the seventeenth century that scientists began to understand about atmospheric pressure. They previously explained atmospheric effects by saying that *nature abhors a vacuum*. By this they meant that if the air is sucked out of a bottle it will immediately fill by sucking air back in again when it is opened to the atmosphere. Nowadays we know that this is not the way it works. When the bottle is opened to the atmosphere, it is the higher air pressure outside the bottle that pushes air into it until the pressures inside and outside are equal. The end-result is the same (i.e. the bottle is filled with air), but the mechanism is quite different. This principle is very important because it affects what we can do with pumps. Pumps do not suck up water as is commonly thought. First the air is removed from a pump by a process known as priming and it is atmospheric pressure that pushes water up into it. This means that pumps cannot 'suck' up water more than atmospheric pressure will allow (this is discussed fully in section 8.4). Siphons also rely on atmospheric pressure in a similar way (section 4.7).

Atmospheric pressure varies over the surface of the Earth and this is the reason for high winds when air flows from high-pressure areas to low-pressure areas. But for most hydraulics problems atmospheric pressure can be assumed to have a constant value.

One way of experiencing atmospheric pressure is to place a large sheet of paper on a table over a thin piece of wood (Figure 2.5a). If you hit the wood sharply it is possible to strike a considerable blow without disturbing the paper. You may even break the wood. This is because the paper is being held down by the pressure of the atmosphere. If the paper is $1.0\text{m}^2$ then the force holding down the paper can be calculated as follows:

$$\text{force} = \text{pressure} \times \text{area}$$

In this case

$$\text{pressure} = \text{atmospheric pressure} = 100\text{kN/m}^2$$

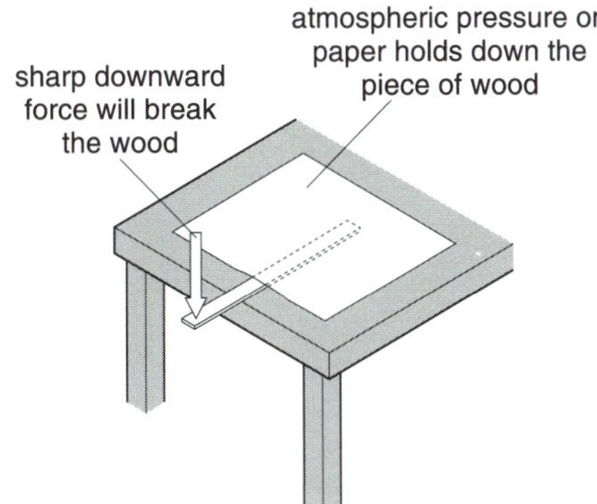


(a)

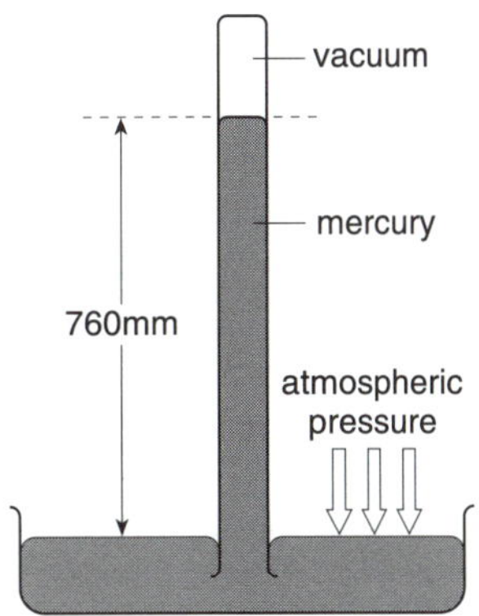


(b) Fortin barometer

**Figure 2.5** Atmospheric pressure

and so

$$\text{force} = 100 \times 1 = 100\text{kN}$$

In terms of apples this is about 100 000, which is a large force. It is little wonder that the wood breaks before the paper lifts.

## 2.5.1 Fortin barometer

Atmospheric pressure can be measured using a mercury barometer – the **Fortin barometer**. It consists of a vertical glass tube, from which all the air has been removed, immersed in a bath of mercury (Figure 2.5b). Atmospheric pressure pushing down on the open surface pushes mercury up the tube. The height of the mercury column is a measure of atmospheric pressure. It is normally measured in mm and the long-term average value at sea level is 760mm.

The pressure–head equation links together atmospheric pressure and the height of the mercury column, but remember the fluid is now mercury and not water:

$$\text{atmospheric pressure} = \rho g h$$

A typical value for $h$ is 760mm of mercury. so

$$\begin{aligned}\text{atmospheric pressure} &= 13.6 \times 1000 \times 9.81 \times 0.76 \\ &= 101\ 400\text{N/m}^2 \text{ or } 101.4\text{kN/m}^2\end{aligned}$$

Atmospheric pressure can be measured using any liquid and not just mercury. If water is used the height of the water column would be quite different. Using the pressure–head equation again:

$$\text{atmospheric pressure} = \rho g h$$

This time the fluid is water and so

$$101\ 400 = 1000 \times 9.81 \times h$$

$$h = 10.34\text{m}$$

This is a very tall water column and there would be practical difficulties if this was used for routine measurement of atmospheric pressure. This is the reason why a very dense liquid like mercury is used to make measurement more manageable.

Atmospheric pressure is also used as a unit of measurement for pressure both for meteorological purposes and in hydraulics. This is known as the **bar**. For convenience 1bar pressure is rounded off to 100kN/$m^2$. A more commonly used term in meteorology is the **millibar** (mbar). So

$$1\text{mbar} = 0.1\text{kN/m}^2 = 100\text{N/m}^2$$

To summarise, there are several ways of expressing atmospheric pressure:

$$\begin{aligned}\text{atmospheric pressure} &= 1\text{bar}\\ &= 100\text{kN/m}^2\\ &= 10\text{m of water}\\ &= 760\text{mm of mercury}\end{aligned}$$

## Example: Calculating pressure head

A pipeline is operating at a pressure of 3.5bar. Calculate the pressure in metres head of water.

We know that

$$1\text{bar} = 100\text{kN/m}^2 = 100\ 000\text{N/m}^2$$

and so

$$3.5\text{bar} = 350\text{kN/m}^2 = 350\ 000\text{N/m}^2$$

Using the pressure–head equation:

$$p = \rho g h$$

$$350\ 000 = 1000 \times 9.81 \times h$$

Calculating $h$

$$h = 35.67\text{m}$$

Rounding this off

$$3.5\text{bar} = 36\text{m of water (approximately)}$$

## 2.6 Measuring pressure

### 2.6.1 Gauge and absolute pressures

Pressure-measuring devices work in the atmosphere with normal atmospheric pressure all around them. Rather than add atmospheric pressure each time to the pressure on the gauge it is common practice to assume that atmospheric pressure is equal to zero and so it becomes the baseline (or zero point) from which all pressure measurements are made. It is rather like setting sea level as the zero from which all ground elevations are measured (Figure 2.6). Such pressure measurements are called **gauge pressures.** Gauge pressure can be either positive (above atmospheric pressure) or negative (below atmospheric pressure).

In some applications in mechanical engineering, **absolute pressure** is used. This is the pressure measured using a vacuum as the datum or zero point. Thus all absolute pressures are measured from this point and all have a positive value.

To summarise: *Gauge pressures are pressures measured above or below atmospheric pressure. Absolute pressures are pressures measured above a vacuum.* To change from one to the other:

absolute pressure = gauge pressure + atmospheric pressure

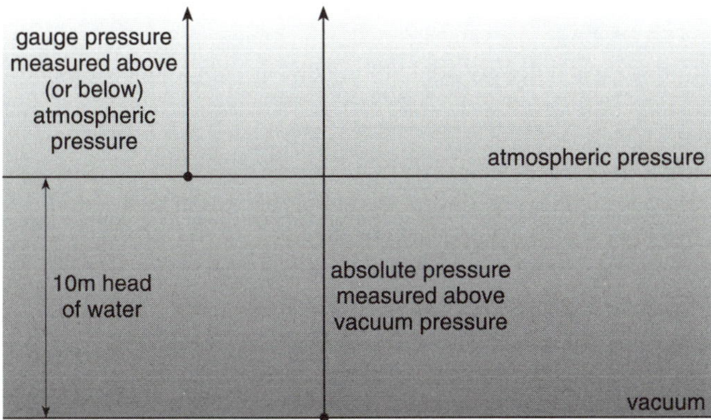


**Figure 2.6** Gauge and absolute pressures

Note that, if only the word 'pressure' is used, it is reasonable to assume that this means gauge pressure.

### 2.6.2 Bourdon gauges

Pressure can be measured in several ways. The most common instrument used is the **Bourdon gauge** (Figure 2.7a). This is located at some convenient point on a pipeline or pump to record pressure, usually in $kN/m^2$ or bar. It is a simple device and works on the same principle as a party toy. When you blow into this toy, the coil of paper unfolds and the feather rotates. Inside a Bourdon gauge there is a similar curved tube which tries to straighten out under pressure and causes a pointer to move through a gearing system across a scale of pressure values.

### 2.6.3 Piezometers

This is another device for measuring pressure. A vertical tube is connected to a pipe so that water can rise up the tube because of the pressure in the pipe (Figure 2.7a). This is called a **piezometer** or **standpipe.** The height of the water column in the tube is a measure of the pressure in the pipe, i.e. the pressure head. The pressure in $kN/m^2$ can be calculated using the pressure–head equation $p = \rho gh$.

### Example: Calculating the height of a standpipe for pressure measurement

Calculate the height of a standpipe needed to measure a pressure of $200kN/m^2$ in a water pipe.

Using the pressure–head equation

$$p = \rho gh$$

$$200\ 000 = 1000 \times 9.81 \times h$$

Note in the equation that pressure and density are both in newtons, not kilonewtons. So

$$h = 20.4m$$

A very high tube would be needed to measure this pressure! For this reason high pressures are normally measured by a Bourdon gauge or a manometer.

### 2.6.4 Manometers

It is not always convenient to use a vertical standpipe particularly when measuring high pressures (see example in box). An alternative is to use a **U-tube manometer**

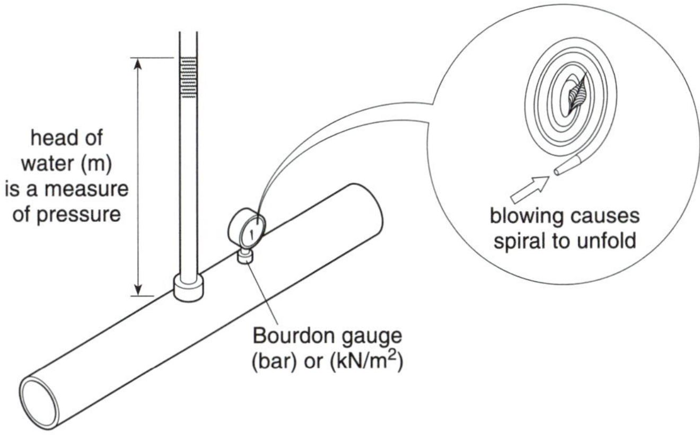


(a) Bourdon gauge and piezometer

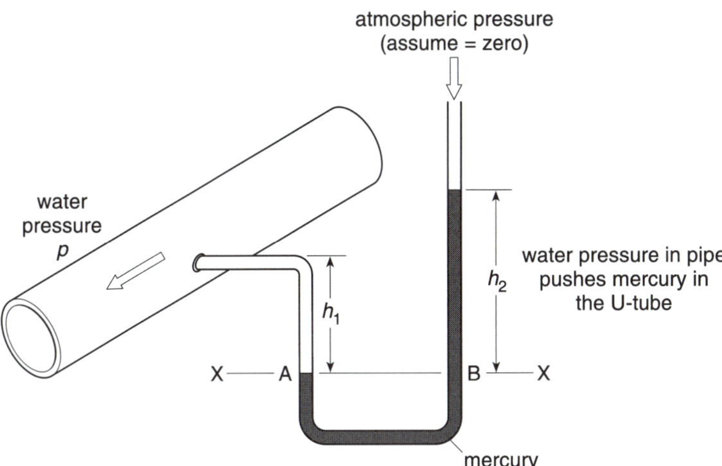


(b) U-tube manometer

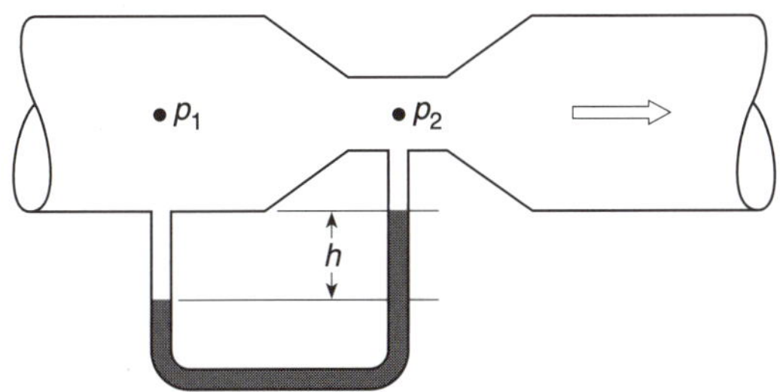


(c) Venturi flow meter

**Figure 2.7 Measuring pressure**

(Figure 2.7b). The bottom of the U-tube is filled with a different liquid which does not mix with that in the pipe. When measuring pressures in a water system, oil or mercury is used. Mercury is very useful because high pressures can be measured with a relatively small tube (see section 2.5).

To measure pressure, a manometer is connected to a pipeline and mercury is placed in the bottom of the U bend. The basic assumption is that as the mercury in the two limbs of the manometer is not moving then the pressures in the two limbs must be the same. If they were not then the mercury would move. So if a horizontal line X–X is drawn through the liquid surface in the first limb and extended to the second limb then it can be assumed that:

pressure at point A = pressure at point B

This is the fundamental assumption on which all manometer calculations are based. It is then a matter of adding up all the components that make up the pressures at A and B to work out a value for the pressure in the pipe.

First calculate the pressure at A:

$$\begin{aligned}\text{pressure at A} &= \text{water pressure at centre of pipe } (p)\\ &\quad + \text{pressure due to water column } h_1\\ &= p + \rho_{\text{water}} g h_1\\ &= p + (1000 \times 9.81 \times h_1)\\ &= p + 9810 \times h_1\end{aligned}$$

Now calculate the pressure at B:

$$\begin{aligned}\text{pressure at B} &= \text{pressure due to mercury column } h_2\\ &\quad + \text{atmospheric pressure}\end{aligned}$$

Remember that atmospheric pressure is assumed to be zero. So

$$\begin{aligned}\text{pressure at B} &= \rho_{\text{mercury}} g h_2 + 0\\ &= 1000 \times 13.6 \times 9.81 \times h_2\\ &= 133\,416 \times h_2\end{aligned}$$

Putting the pressure at A equal to the pressure at B:

$$p + 9810h_1 = 133\,416h_2$$

Rearranging this to determine $p$:

$$p = 133\,416h_2 - 9810h_1$$

Note that $p$ is in $N/m^2$. So the pressure in this pipeline can be calculated by measuring $h_1$ and $h_2$ and using the above equation.

Some manometers are used to measure pressure differences rather than actual values of pressure. One example of this is the measurement of the pressure difference in a venturi meter for pipe flow measurement (see section 4.9) (Figure 2.7c). In this case it is the drop (difference) in pressure as water passes through a narrow section of pipe that is important. By connecting one limb of the manometer to the main pipe and the other limb to the narrow section, the difference in pressure can be determined. It is not just the difference in the liquid columns on the manometer as is often thought. The pressure difference must be calculated using the principle described above for the simple manometer.

When solving manometer problems remember the principle on which all manometer calculations are based and not the formula for $p$. There are many different ways of arranging manometers, each resulting in a different formula for $p$. If you remember and apply the principle to each case then the pressure can be easily determined without having to remember several complicated formulae.

## Example: Measuring pressure using a manometer

A mercury manometer is used to measure the pressure in a water pipe (Figure 2.7b). Calculate the pressure in the pipe when $h_1 = 1.5$m and $h_2 = 0.8$m.

To solve this problem start with the principle on which all manometers are based:

pressure at A = pressure at B

The pressure at A is made up of the following:

pressure at A = water pressure in pipe ($p$)

+ pressure due to water column $h_1$

$$= p + \rho_{water} g h_1$$

$$= p + 1000 \times 9.81 \times 1.5$$

Also

pressure at B = pressure due to mercury column $h_2$

+ atmospheric pressure

$$= \rho_{mercury} g h_2 + 0$$

$$= 1000 \times 13.6 \times 9.81 \times 0.8$$

Note that as all the pressures are gauge pressures, atmospheric pressure is assumed to be zero.

Putting the pressure at A equal to the pressure at B:

$$p + 1000 \times 9.81 \times 1.5 = 1000 \times 13.6 \times 9.81 \times 0.8$$

Rearranging this to determine $p$:

$$p = (1000 \times 13.6 \times 9.81 \times 0.8) - (1000 \times 9.81 \times 1.5)$$

$$= 106\ 732 - 14\ 715$$

$$= 92\ 017\text{N/m}^2$$

$$= 92\text{kN/m}^2$$

## 2.7 Designing dams

An important use of hydrostatics is for the design of dams. The procedure is exactly the same for a small dam only a few metres high as it is for a major dam 40m or more in height and the same equations are used.

When starting a new design, engineers are always interested in the way structures can fall down so that they can find ways of making sure they do not fail in future. For a dam, the pressure of water stored behind it produces a horizontal force that could push it over if the dam was not strong enough to resist (Figure 2.8). So the total force resulting from the water pressure must first be calculated. The location of this force is also important. If it is near the top of the dam then the dam may fail by overturning. If it is near the base then it may fail by sliding.

The force on a dam is calculated from the water pressure (Figure 2.9a). Remember that pressure pushes in all directions and in this case it is the horizontal push on the dam that is important. At the water surface the pressure is zero, but 1.0m below the surface the pressure rises to 10kN/m$^2$ (approximately), and at 2.0m it reaches 20kN/m$^2$ and so on (remember the pressure–head equation $p = \rho g h$). A graph of the changes in pressure with depth is a straight line and together with the axes of the graph it forms a triangle. The pressure at the top of the triangle (the

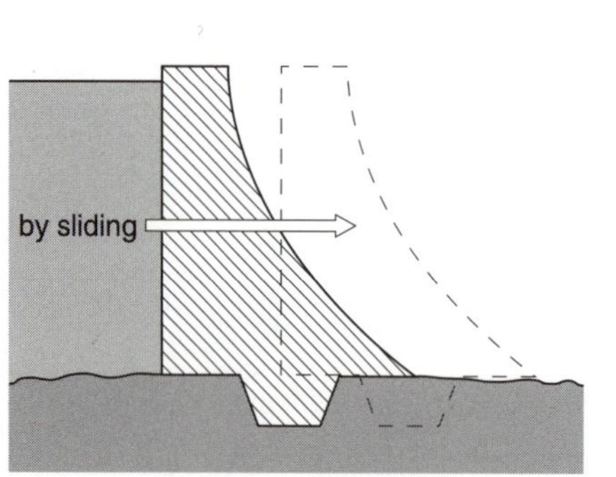


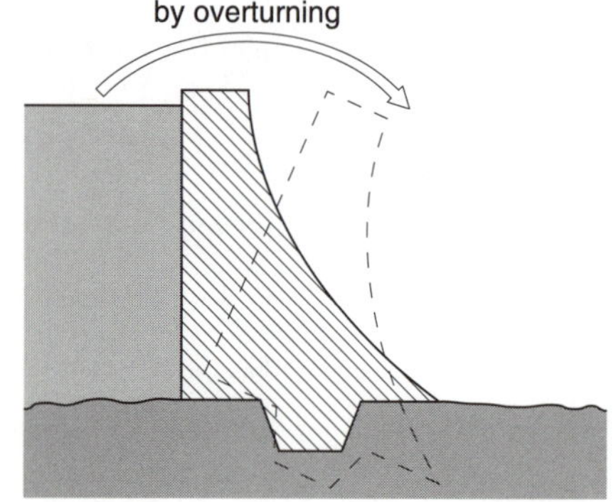


**Figure 2.8 Dams can fail by sliding and overturning**

water surface) is zero while at the base the pressure is maximum. This triangle is called the **pressure diagram** and shows how the pressure varies with depth on the upstream face of a dam.

The force on the dam could be calculated from the pressure and the area of the dam face using the equation $F = pa$. But the pressure is not constant; it varies down the face of the dam and so the question is: Which value of pressure should be used? One approach is to divide the dam face into lots of small areas and use the average pressure for each area. The force on each area is then calculated using the equation $F = pa$. But this means lots of calculations and it results in lots of forces. Another, much simpler method is to use a formula that has been derived from combining all the small forces mathematically into one larger force called the **resultant force** (Figure 2.9a). This single force has the same effect as the sum of all the smaller forces and is much easier to deal with:

$$\text{resultant force } (F) = \rho g a \bar{y}$$

where $\rho$ is density of water (kg/m$^3$), $g$ is gravity constant (9.81m/s$^2$), $a$ is area of the face of the dam (m$^2$) and $\bar{y}$ is the depth from the water surface to the centre of the area of the dam (m). For the mathematically minded a derivation of this formula can be found in most engineering hydraulics textbooks.

Returning to the pressure diagram, this can also be used to determine the resultant force. It is in fact equal to the area of the diagram, i.e. the area of the triangle. To see how this, and the formula for force, works, look at the example of how to calculate the force on a dam in the box.

The position of this force is also important. To determine the depth $D$ from the water surface to the resultant force $F$ (Figure 2.9b) on the dam the following formula can be used:

$$D = \frac{h^2}{12\bar{y}} + \bar{y}$$

where $h$ is height of the dam face in contact with the water (m) and $\bar{y}$ is depth from the water surface to the centre of the area of the dam (m). Like the force formula this one can also be derived from the principles of hydrostatics. The pressure diagram can also be used to determine $D$. The force is located at the centre of the diagram and as this is a triangle it is located two-thirds down from the apex (i.e. from the water surface).

Note that these formulae only work for simple vertical dams. When more complex shapes are involved then it is advisable to seek the help of a civil engineer.

### 2.7.1 The dam paradox

When calculating the force on a dam do not let the amount of water stored behind it confuse you. Remember that the force depends only on the depth of water and not on the amount of water being stored (Figure 2.9c). The force on dam 1 is exactly the same as on dam 2 even though the storage behind dam 2 is much greater than dam 1.

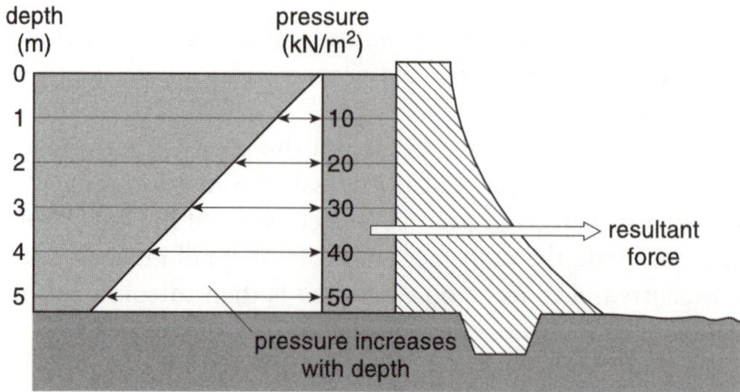


(a) The pressure diagram

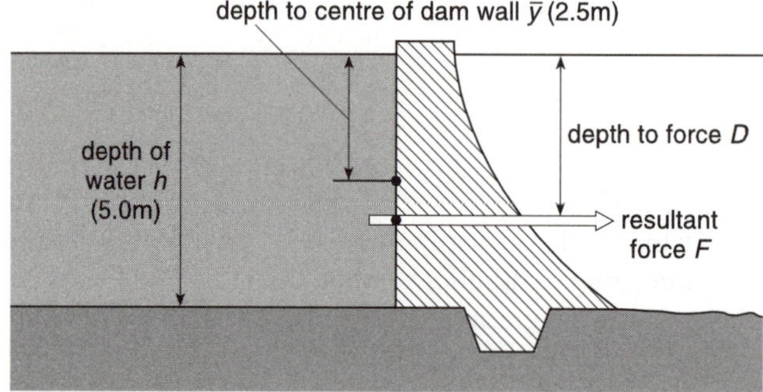


(b) Location of resultant force

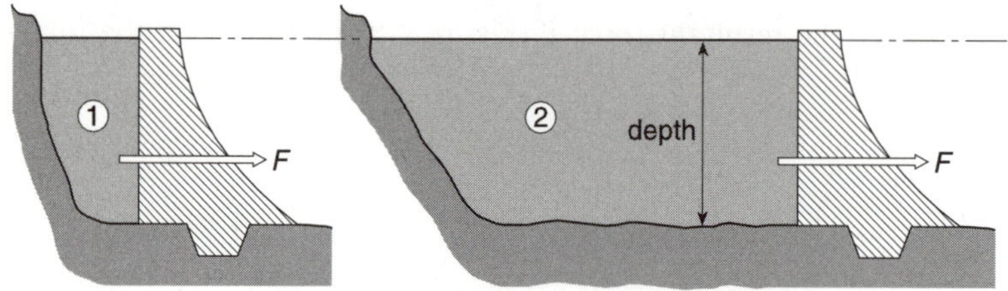


(c) The dam paradox

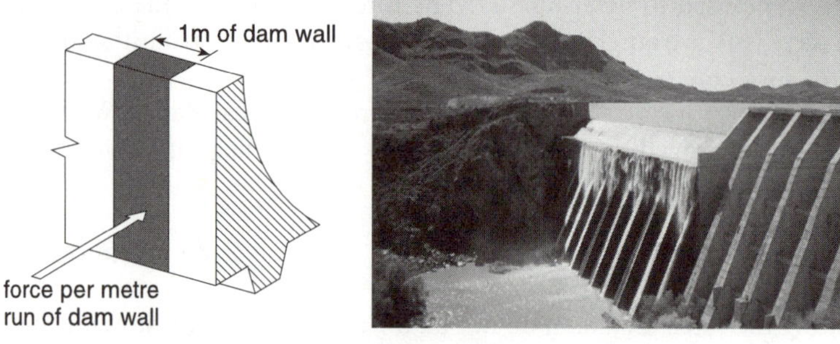


(d) Assume dam is 1.0m long

(e) Typical concrete dam

**Figure 2.9 Designing a dam**

## Example: Calculating the force on a dam

A farm dam is to be constructed to contain water up to 5m deep. Calculate the force on the dam and its position in relation to the water surface (Figure 2.9b).

Calculate the force

$$F = \rho g a \bar{y}$$

where $\rho = 1000\text{kg/m}^3$, $g = 9.81\text{m/s}^2$ and $a = b \times h = 1 \times 5 = 5\text{m}^2$. Note that, when the length of the dam is not given, assume $b = 1\text{m}$. The force is then the force per metre length of the dam (Figure 2.9d). Depth from water surface to dam centre is

$$\bar{y} = \frac{h}{2} = 2.5\text{m}$$

So

$$F = 1000 \times 9.81 \times 5 \times 2.5$$

$$= 122\ 625\text{N}$$

$$= 122.6\text{kN per m length of the dam}$$

Using the alternative method of calculating the area of the pressure diagram:

$$\text{area of triangle} = \frac{1}{2} \times \text{base} \times \text{height}$$

$$= \frac{1}{2} \times \rho g h \times h$$

$$= \frac{1}{2} \times 1000 \times 9.81 \times 5 \times 5$$

So

$$F = 122.6\text{kN per m length of the dam}$$

To locate the force use

$$D = \frac{h^2}{12\bar{y}} + \bar{y}$$

$$= \frac{5^2}{12 \times 2.5} + 2.5$$

$$= 3.33\text{m below the water surface}$$

Using the pressure diagram method, the force is located at the centre of the triangle which is two-thirds the depth from the apex (or the water surface):

$$D = \frac{2}{3} \times h = \frac{2}{3} \times 5$$

$$= 3.33\text{m below the water surface}$$

## 2.8 Forces on sluice gates

Sluice gates are used to control the flow of water from dams into pipes and channels (see section 7.2). They may be circular or rectangular in shape and are raised and lowered by turning a wheel on a threaded shaft (Figure 2.10a).

Gates must be made strong enough to withstand the forces created by hydrostatic pressure. The pressure also forces the gate against the face of the dam, which can make it difficult to lift easily because of the friction it creates. So the greater the pressure the greater will be the force required to lift the gate. This is the reason why some gates have gears and hand-wheels fitted to make lifting easier.

The force on a gate and its location can be calculated in the same way as for a dam. The force on any gate can be calculated using the same formula as was used for the dam:

$$F = \rho g a \bar{y}$$

The formula for calculating $D$, the depth to the resultant force, depends on the shape of the gate.

- For rectangular gates

$$D = \frac{d^2}{12\bar{y}} + \bar{y}$$

  where $d$ is depth of gate (m) and $\bar{y}$ is depth from water surface to centre of the gate (m). Note that $d$ is the depth of the gate (m) and *not* the depth of water behind the dam.
- For circular gates

$$D = \frac{r^2}{4\bar{y}} + \bar{y}$$

  where $r$ is radius of the gate (m).

The depth $D$ from the water surface to the force $F$ must not be confused with $\bar{y}$. $D$ is the depth to the point where the resultant force acts on the gate and this is always greater than $\bar{y}$.

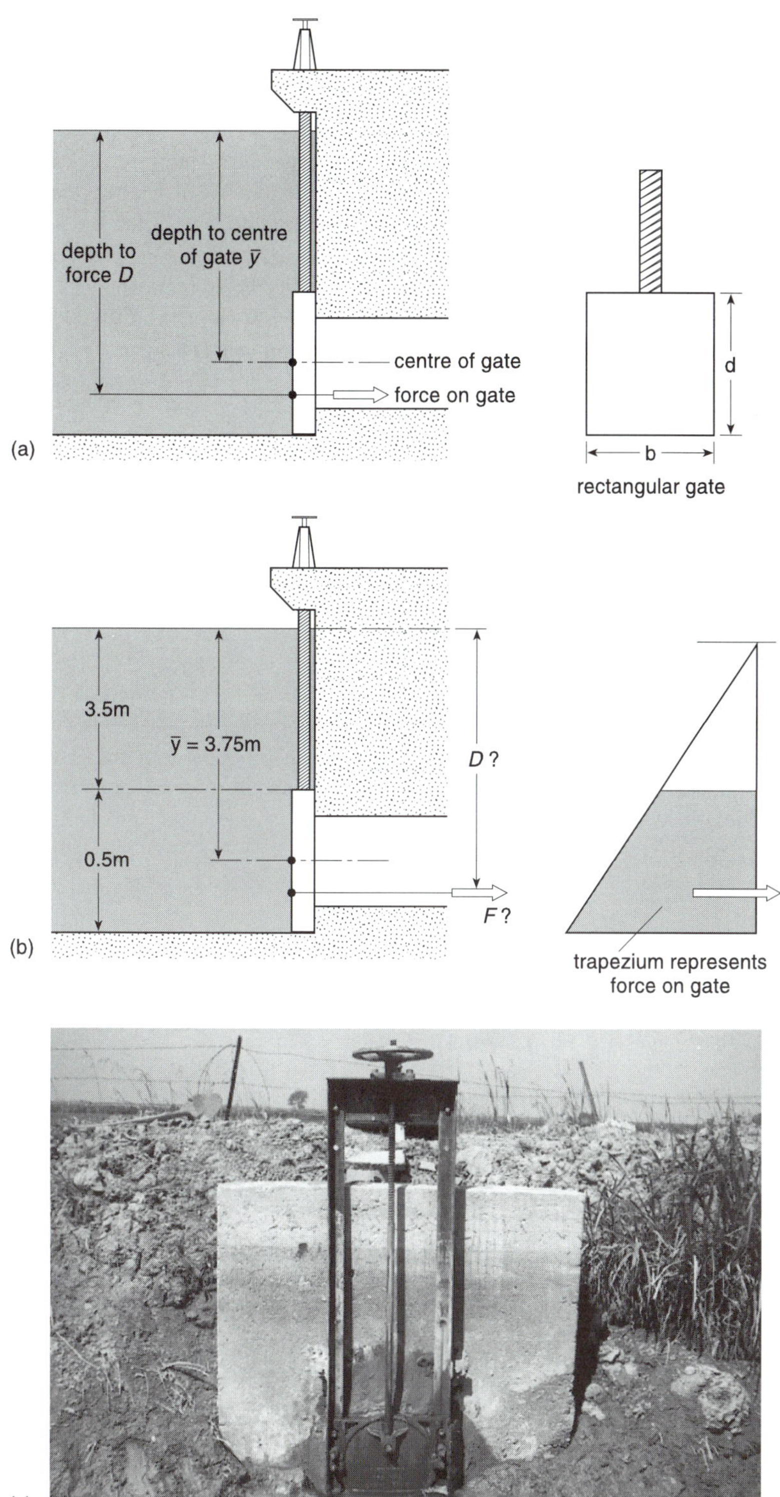


**Figure 2.10** Forces on sluice gates

The force and its location can also be obtained from the pressure diagram but in this case it is only that part of the diagram in line with the gate that is of interest. The force on the gate can be calculated from the area of the trapezium and its location is at the centre of the trapezium. This can be found by using the principle of moments. But if this is not understood the centre can be found by cutting out a paper shape of the trapezium and freely suspending it from each corner in turn and drawing a vertical line. The point were all the lines cross is the centre. A common mistake is to assume that the depth $D$ is two-thirds of the depth from the water surface. It is true for a simple dam but not for a sluice gate.

The above equations cover most hydraulic sluice gate problems but occasionally gates of different shapes may be encountered and they may also be at an angle rather than vertical. It is possible to work out the forces on such gates but these are best left to an engineer. An example of calculating the force on a hydraulic gate and its location is shown in the box.

## Example: Calculating the force on a sluice gate

A rectangular sluice gate controls the release of water from a reservoir. If the gate is 0.5m × 0.5m and located 3.5m below the water surface calculate the force on the gate and its location below the water surface (Figure 2.10b).

First calculate the force $F$ on the gate:

$$F = \rho g a \bar{y}$$

where

$$a = \text{area of the gate} = 0.5 \times 0.5 = 0.25\text{m}^2$$

$$\bar{y} = \text{depth from water surface to the centre of the gate}$$

$$= 3.5 + 0.25 = 3.75\text{m}$$

$$F = 1000 \times 9.81 \times 0.25 \times 3.75$$

$$= 9197\text{N} \quad \text{or} \quad 9.2\text{kN}$$

Next calculate depth from water surface to where force $F$ is acting:

$$D = \frac{d^2}{12\bar{y}} + \bar{y}$$

$$= \frac{0.25}{12 \times 3.75} + 3.75$$

$$= 3.76\text{m}$$

## 2.9 Archimedes principle

We return now to Archimedes who first set down the rules of hydrostatics. His most famous venture was in the baths in Greece around the year 250BC when he was reported to have run out into the street naked shouting 'Eureka' at the discovery of an experimental method of detecting the gold content of the crown of the King of Syracuse. He had realised that when he got into his bath, the water level rose around him because his body was displacing the water and that this was linked to the feeling of weight loss – that uplifting feeling that everyone experiences in the bath. As the baths were usually public places he probably noticed as well that smaller people displaced less water than larger people. It is at this point that many people draw the wrong conclusion. They assume that this has something to do with a person's weight. This is quite wrong; it is only to do with their volume. To explain this, let us return to the crowns.

Perhaps the King had two crowns that looked the same in every way but one was made of gold and he suspected that someone had short-changed him by making the other of a mixture of gold and some cheaper metal. The problem that he set Archimedes was to tell him which was the gold one. Weighing them on a normal balance in air would not have provided the answer because a clever forger would make sure that both crowns were the same weight. If however, he could measure their densities he would then know which was gold because the density of gold has a fixed value (19 300kg/m$^3$) and this would be different to the crown of mixed metals. But to determine their densities their volumes must first be known. If the crowns were simple shapes such as cubes then it would be easy to calculate. But crowns are not simple shapes and it would have been almost impossible to measure them accurately enough for calculation purposes. This is where immersing them in water helps.

When he weighed the crowns in water he observed that they had different weights. Putting this another way, each crown experienced a different loss in weight due to the buoyancy effect of the water. It is this *loss in weight* that was the key to solving the mystery. By measuring the loss in weight of the crowns, Archimedes was indirectly measuring their volumes.

To understand this, imagine a crown is immersed in a container full of water up to the overflow pipe (Figure 2.11a). The crown displaces the water, spilling it down the overflow where it is caught in another container. The volume of the spillage water can easily be measured and it has exactly the same volume as the crown. But the most interesting point is that the weight of the spillage water (water displaced) is equal to the loss in weight of the crown. So by measuring the loss in weight, Archimedes was in fact measuring the weight of displaced water, i.e. the weight of an equal volume of water. As the density of water is a fixed value (9810N/m$^3$) it is a simple matter to convert this weight of water into a volume and so determine the density of the crown.

This is the principle that Archimedes discovered: *When an object is immersed in water it experiences a loss in weight and this is equal to the weight of water it displaces.*

What Archimedes measured was not actually the density of gold but its relative density or specific gravity as it is more commonly known. This is the density of gold relative to that of water and he calculated this using the formula:

$$\text{specific gravity} = \frac{\text{weight of crown}}{\text{weight loss when immersed in water}}$$

This may not look like the formula for specific gravity in section 1.12.2 but it is the same. From section 1.12.2

$$\text{specific gravity} = \frac{\text{weight of an object}}{\text{weight of an equal volume of water}}$$

but Archimedes principle says that:

weight loss when immersed in water

= weight of an equal volume of water

So the two formulae are in fact identical and Archimedes was able to tell whether a crown was made of gold or not by some ingenious thinking and some simple calculations. The method works for all materials and not just gold and also for all fluids and not just water. Indeed, this immersion technique is now a standard laboratory method for measuring the volume of irregularly shaped objects and for determining their specific gravity.

Still not convinced? Try this example with numbers. A block of material has a volume of $0.2\text{m}^3$ and is suspended on a spring balance (Figure 2.11b) and weighs 3000N. When the block is lowered into the water it displaces $0.2\text{m}^3$ of water. As water weighs 10 000N/m$^3$ (approximately) the displaced water weighs 2000N (i.e. $0.2\text{m}^3 \times 10\,000\text{N/m}^3$). Now according to Archimedes the weight of this water should be equal to the weight loss of the block and so the spring balance should now be reading only 1000N (i.e. 3000N – 2000N).

To explain this, think about the space that the block ($0.2\text{m}^3$) will occupy when it is placed in the water (Figure 2.11b). The space is occupied by $0.2\text{m}^3$ of water weighing 2000N. Suppose that the water directly above the block weighs 1500N (note that any number will do for this argument). These two weights of water added together are 3500N and this is supported by the underlying water and so there is an upward balancing force of 3500N. The block is now lowered into the water and it displaces $0.2\text{m}^3$. The water under the block takes no account of this change and continues to push upwards with a force of 3500N and the downward force of the water above it continues to exert a downward force of 1500N. The block thus experiences a net upward force or a loss in weight of 2000N (i.e. 3500N – 1500N). This is exactly the same value as the weight of water that was displaced by the block. The reading on the spring balance is reduced by this amount from 3000N down to 1000N.

A simple but striking example of this apparent weight loss is to tie a length of cotton thread around a brick and to try to suspend it first in air and then in water. If

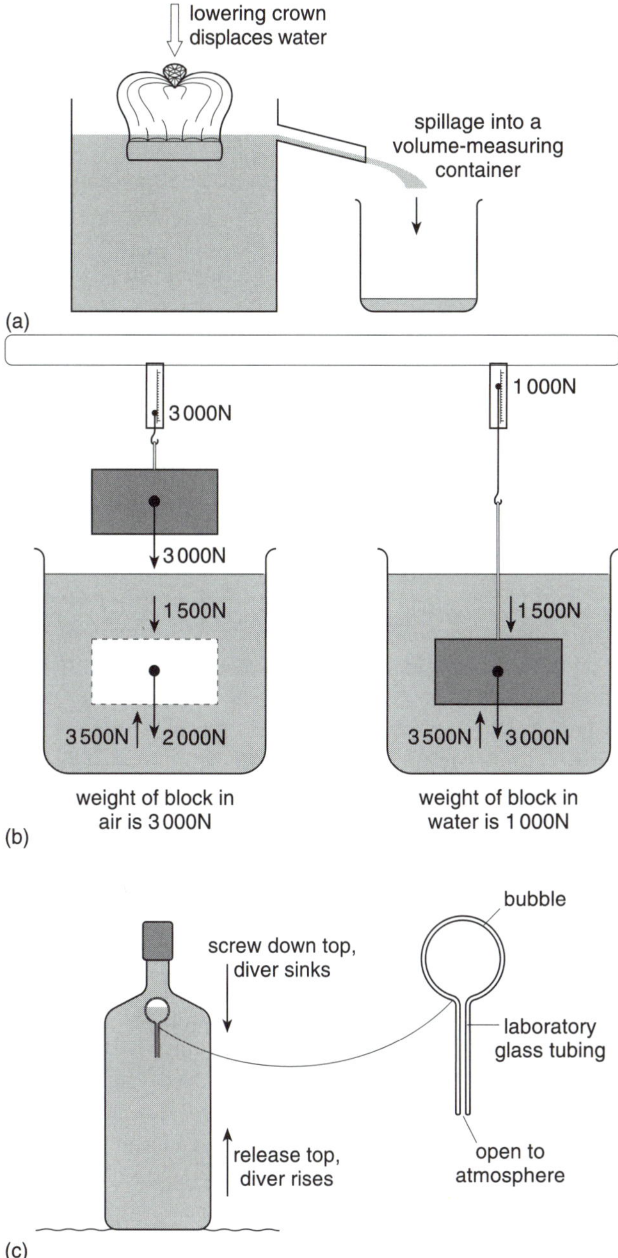


**Figure 2.11** Archimedes principle

you try to lift the brick in air the thread will very likely break. But the uplift force when the brick is in water means that the brick can now be lifted easily. It is this same weight loss that enables rivers to move great boulders during floods and the sea to move shingle along the beach.

### 2.9.1 Flotation

When an object such as a cork floats on water it is supported by the uplift force or buoyancy. It appears that the object has *lost* all of its weight. If the cork is held below the water surface and then released it rises to the surface. This is because the weight of the water displaced by the cork is greater than the weight of the cork itself and so the cork rises under the unbalanced force. Once at the surface the weight of the cork is balanced by the lifting effect of the water. In this case the water displaced by the cork *is not a measure of its volume but a measure of its weight.*

Another way of determining if an object will float is to determine its density. When the density is less than that of water it will float. When it is greater it will sink. A block of wood for example is half the density of water and so it floats half submerged. Icebergs, which have a density close to that of water, float with only one-tenth of their mass above the surface. The same principle also applies to other fluids. Hydrogen balloons, for example, rise in air because hydrogen is 14 times less dense than air.

Steel is six times denser than water and so it will sink. People laughed when it was first proposed that ships could be made of steel and would float. But today this is just taken for granted. Ships float because, even when loaded, much of their volume is filled with relatively light cargo and a lot of air space and so their average density is less than that of sea water.

Buoyancy is also affected by the density of sea water, which varies considerably around the world. In Bombay the sea is more salty than it is near Britain and so ships ride higher in the water in Bombay. This needs to be taken into account when loading a ship in Bombay that is bound for Britain. Once in British waters it will lie much lower in the water and this could be dangerous if it is overloaded.

The Cartesian diver is an interesting example of an object that can either sink or float by slightly varying its density a little above or below that of water (Figure 2.11c). The diver comprises a small length of glass tubing, sealed and blown into a bubble at one end and open at the other. You can make one easily in a laboratory using a bunsen burner and a short length of glass tubing. Next find a bottle with a screw top, fill it to the top with water and put the diver into the water. The diver will float because the air bubble ensures the average density is less than that of water. Now screw down the top and the diver will sink. This is because this action increases the water pressure, which compresses the air in the diver and increases its average density above that of water. Releasing the screw top allows the diver to rise to the surface again. This same principle is used to control submarines. When a submarine dives, its tanks are allowed to fill with water so that its average density is greater than that of water. The depth of submergence is determined by the extent to which its tanks are flooded. To make the submarine rise, water is blown out of its tanks using compressed air.

To summarise: *An object floats when it is less dense than water but sinks when it is more dense than water. When an object floats it displaces water equal to its weight.*

### 2.9.2 Applying the principle

Here are two little problems to test your understanding of Archimedes principle.

- A submarine is floating in a lock (Figure 2.12). It then submerges and sinks to the bottom. What happens to the water level in the lock? Does it rise or fall?

Archimedes principle says that when an object floats it displaces its own weight of water and when it sinks it displaces its own volume. Apply this to the submarine. When it is floating on the water surface, the submarine displaces its own weight of water, which will be substantial because submarines are heavy. But when the submarine sinks to the bottom it only displaces water equivalent to its volume. So the amount of water displaced by the floating submarine will be much greater than the volume of water displaced when it is submerged. This means that when the submarine dives the water level in the lock will drop (very slightly!).

- When ice is added to a tank of water, the water level rises. When the ice melts what happens to the water level? Does it rise, fall or stay the same?

Ice is a solid object that floats and so it should behave in the same way as any other solid object. When it melts however, it becomes part of the water and, in effect, it sinks.

Start by looking at 1.0 litre of water, which has a mass of 1kg and so weighs 10N. If this is turned into ice its volume will increase by approximately 8% to 1.08 litres of ice but remember it is still the same amount of water and so its weight does not change. It is still 10N of water. If the ice is now placed in the tank the water level will rise. The ice will float on the water because the density of the ice is slightly less than that of the water. Like any solid object that floats the ice displaces its own weight of water, which is still 10N. But 10N of water has a volume of 1.0 litre and so 1.0 litre of water is displaced. It has nothing to do with the volume of the ice – only its weight. When the ice melts it 'sinks' into the tank and now only displaces its own volume of water. The volume of the melted ice is still only 1.0 litre. As the

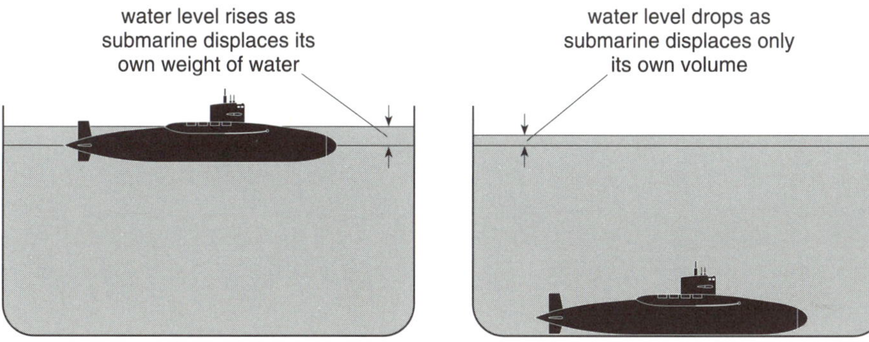
water level rises as submarine displaces its own weight of water
water level drops as submarine displaces only its own volume

**Figure 2.12** Applying Archimedes principle

displacement is the same in each case, i.e. 1.0 litre, the water level in the tank remains unchanged when the ice melts.

It is the volume of the ice that can be misleading in this problem as there is a significant change in volume when water freezes into ice. Do not be misled by this, just follow the principle of Archimedes and everything will work out right.

## 2.10 Some examples to test your understanding

1. Determine the pressure in $N/m^2$ for a head of (a) 14m of water and (b) 1.7m of oil. Assume the mass density of water is $1000kg/m^3$ and oil is $785kg/m^3$.
2. A storage tank 2.3m long by 1.2m wide and 0.8m deep is full of water. Calculate (a) the mass of water in the tank, (b) the pressure on the bottom of the tank, (c) the force on the end of the tank and (d) the position of this force below the water surface.
3. Calculate atmospheric pressure in $kN/m^2$ when the barometer reading is 750mm of mercury. Calculate the height of a water barometer needed to measure atmospheric pressure.
4. Calculate the pressure in $kN/m^2$ and metres head of water in a pipeline carrying water using a mercury manometer when $h_1 = 0.5$m and $h_2 = 1.2$m (Figure 2.7b). Assume the specific gravity of mercury is 13.6.
5. A vertical rectangular sluice gate 1.0m high by 0.5m wide is used to control the discharge from a storage reservoir. Calculate the horizontal force on the gate and its location in relation to the water surface when the top of the gate is located 2.3m below the water surface.
6. Calculate the force and its location below the water surface on a 0.75m diameter circular sluice gate when the top of the gate is located 2.3m below the water surface.

Chapter 3

# Hydrodynamics – when water starts to flow

## 3.1 Introduction

**Hydrodynamics** is the study of water flow. This is more complex than hydrostatics because several additional factors must be taken into account, namely, velocity, direction of flow and viscosity. Hydrodynamics provides the link between pressure, velocity and the size of pipes and channels that carry the flow. How large must a channel be to carry water from a dam to an irrigation scheme? What diameter of pipe is needed to supply water to a small town? What kind of pumps might be required and how large must they be? These are the practical problems of hydrodynamics.

In early times hydrodynamics, like many other developments, moved forward on a trial-and-error basis. If it fell down then it was built a bit stronger. But during the past 250 years or so more scientific approaches have been developed on which to base new designs. One approach was to carry out experiments in the laboratory and another was to develop theories of water flow using mathematics and physics.

### 3.1.1 Experimentation

This approach involved building physical models of hydraulic systems in a laboratory and testing them. Much of our current knowledge of water flow in pipes and open channels has come from this kind of experimentation and empirical formulae have been derived from the data collected to link flow with the size of pipes and channels needed to carry water. But there are still many problems which are not easily solved by empirical formulae and in such cases practical laboratory experiments are still used to find solutions. Harbours fall into this category and so do tidal power stations, complex river flooding problems and dam spillways. Small-scale models are built to test new designs and to investigate their influence both locally and in the surrounding area (Figure 3.1).

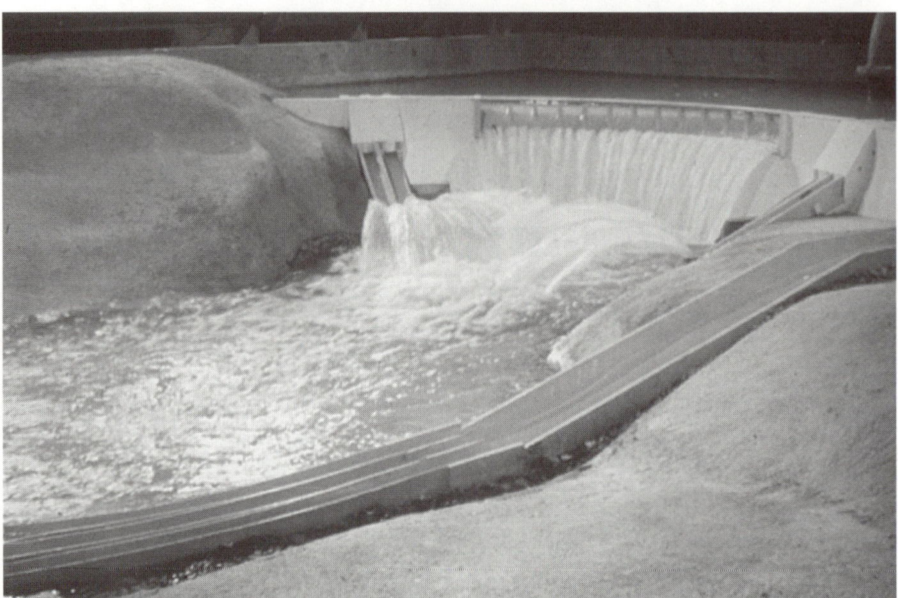

**Figure 3.1** Laboratory model of a dam spillway

## 3.2 Development of a theory

Another approach is to develop formulae that link flow to pipe and channel sizes based on an understanding of the physical principles involved. In the case of hydrostatics the fundamental approach works very well, but when water moves it is difficult to take account of all the new factors involved, in particular viscosity. The engineering approach, rather than the scientific one, is to try to simplify the problem by ignoring those aspects of the problem which are not so important. In the case of water, viscosity is usually ignored because its effects are very small. This not only simplifies problems but it also makes no real difference to the answers. In this regard engineering is as much an art as a science. The science is knowing what physical factors must be taken into account but the art of engineering is knowing which of the factors can be safely left out in order to simplify a problem without it seriously affecting the accuracy of the outcome.

Remember that engineers are not always looking for high levels of accuracy. This is engineering and not laboratory science. There are inherent errors in all data and so there is little point in calculating an answer to several decimal places when the data being used have not been recorded with the same precision. Electronic calculators have created much of this problem and many people still continue to quote answers to many decimal places simply because the calculator says so. The answer is only as good as the data going into a calculation and so another skill of the engineer is to know how accurate an answer needs to be. Unfortunately this is a skill that can only be learnt through practice and experience. This is the reason why a vital part of the training of young engineers always involves working with older, more experienced engineers to acquire this skill.

In addition to this there are the practical limitations set by the available materials. For example, commercially available pipes come in a limited range of sizes, e.g. 50mm, 75mm, 100mm diameter. If an engineer calculates that a 78mm diameter pipe is needed he or she is likely to choose the next size of pipe to make sure it will do the job properly, i.e. 100mm. So there is nothing to be gained in spending a lot of time refining the design process in such circumstances.

Simplifying problems so that they can be solved more easily, without loss of accuracy, is at the heart of hydrodynamics – the study of water movement.

## 3.3 Hydraulic tool box

From the development of theory have come *three* basic tools (equations), which are fundamental to solving many problems in hydrodynamics. They are not difficult to master and it is essential to develop a good understanding of them.

- Discharge and continuity
- Energy
- Momentum

## 3.4 Discharge and continuity

**Discharge** refers to the volume of water flowing along a pipe or channel each second. Volume is measured in cubic metres ($m^3$) and so discharge is measured in cubic metres per second ($m^3/s$). Alternative units are litres per second (litre/s) and cubic metres per hour ($m^3/h$). Although litre/s is not strictly an SI unit, it has wide acceptance in the water industry for pipe flow and pumping.

There are two ways of determining discharge. The first involves measuring the volume of water flowing in a system over a given time period. For example, water flowing from a pipe can be caught in a bucket of known volume (Figure 3.2a). If the time to fill the bucket is recorded then the discharge from the pipe can be determined using the following formula:

$$\text{discharge } (m^3/s) = \frac{\text{volume } (m^3)}{\text{time } (s)}$$

Discharge can also be determined by multiplying the velocity of the water by the area of the flow. To understand this, imagine water flowing along a pipeline (Figure 3.2b). In one second the amount of water flowing past X–X will be the shaded volume. This can be calculated by multiplying the cross-sectional area of the pipe by the length of the shaded portion. But the shaded length is numerically equal to the velocity $v$ and so the volume flowing each second (i.e. the discharge) is equal to the

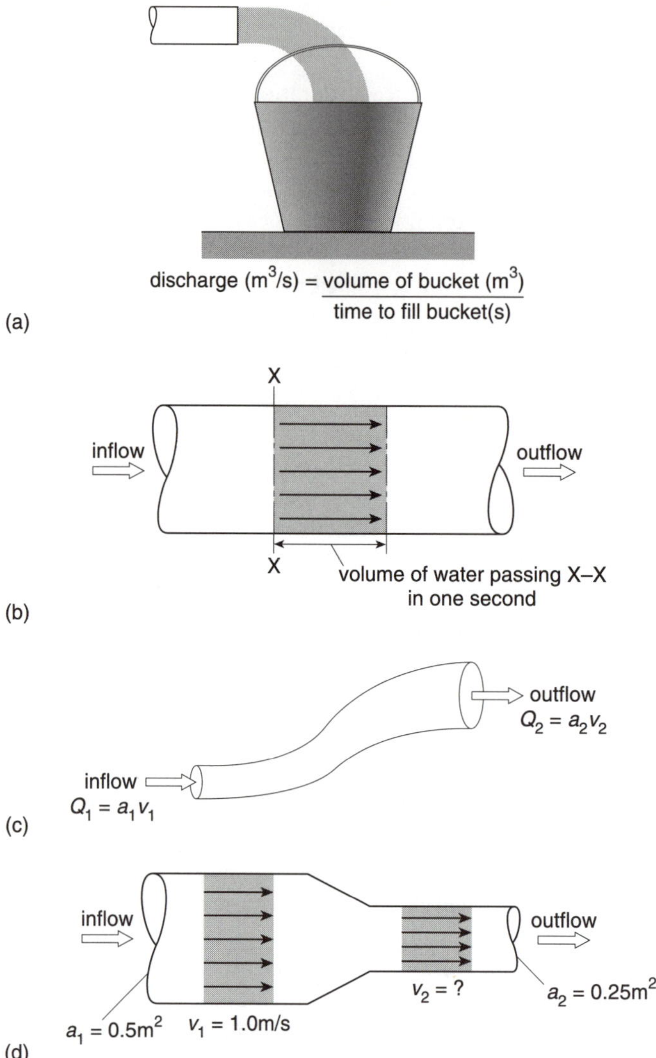


**Figure 3.2 Discharge and continuity**

pipe area multiplied by the velocity. Writing this as an equation:

$$\text{discharge } (Q) = \text{velocity } (v) \times \text{area } (a)$$

$$Q = va$$

The **continuity equation** builds on the discharge equation and simply means that water flowing into a system must be equal to the water flowing out of it (Figure 3.2c):

$$\text{inflow} = \text{outflow}$$

and so

$$Q_1 = Q_2$$

But from the discharge equation

$$Q = va$$

and so

$$v_1 a_1 = v_2 a_2$$

So the continuity equation links areas and velocities in a system. An example in the box shows how this works in practice for a pipeline that changes diameter.

**Example: Calculating velocity using the continuity equation**

A pipeline changes area from $0.5\text{m}^2$ to $0.25\text{m}^2$ (Figure 3.2d). If the velocity in the larger pipe is 1.0m/s calculate the velocity in the smaller pipe.

Using the continuity equation

$$\text{inflow} = \text{outflow}$$

and so

$$v_1 a_1 = v_2 a_2$$

$$1 \times 0.5 = v_2 \times 0.25$$

$$v_2 = 2\text{m/s}$$

Note how water moves much faster in the smaller pipe.

The simple equation of inflow equals outflow is only true when the flow is steady. This means the flow remains the same over time. But there are cases when inflow does not equal outflow. An example of this is a domestic storage tank found in most houses (Figure 3.3). The release of water from the tank may be quite different from the inflow. Dams are built on rivers to perform a similar function so that water supply can be more easily matched with water demand. If an additional term is added to the continuity equation to allow for the change in storage in the reservoir then the equation can still be used as follows:

$$\text{inflow} = \text{outflow} + \text{rate of increase (or decrease) in storage}$$

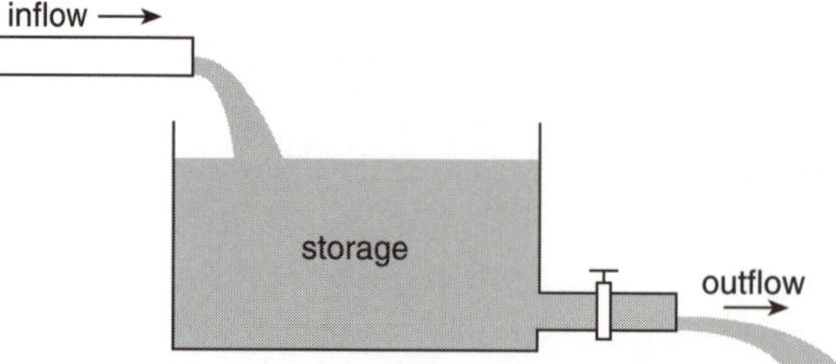


**Figure 3.3** Continuity when there is water storage

Hydrologists use this equation when studying rainfall and runoff from catchments and refer to it as the **water balance equation.**

## 3.5 Energy

This is the second of the basic tools and is the link between pressure and velocity in pipes and channels (see section 1.10.2 for more details about energy). Energy is the capacity to do useful work and water can store energy in three ways:

- Pressure energy
- Kinetic energy
- Potential energy

Energy for solid objects has the units of Nm. For fluids the units are a little different. It is common practice to measure energy in terms of **energy per unit weight** and so energy for fluids has units of Nm/N. This simplifies to metres (m) and so it looks like a pressure head, although strictly speaking it is energy.

### 3.5.1 Pressure energy

This is the energy available when water is under pressure. Imagine a gas bottle used in the home for cooking (Figure 3.4a). The gas is under pressure and when it is released it can do useful work. So pressure is a measure of the energy available to do that work. It is calculated as follows:

$$\text{pressure energy} = \frac{p}{\rho g}$$

where $p$ is pressure (kN/m$^2$), $\rho$ is mass density (kg/m$^3$) and $g$ is the gravity constant (9.81m/s$^2$).

Pressure energy is measured in metres (m) and is the same as the measurement of pressure head. Note that this is the familiar pressure–head equation presented in a different way (remember $p = \rho g h$).

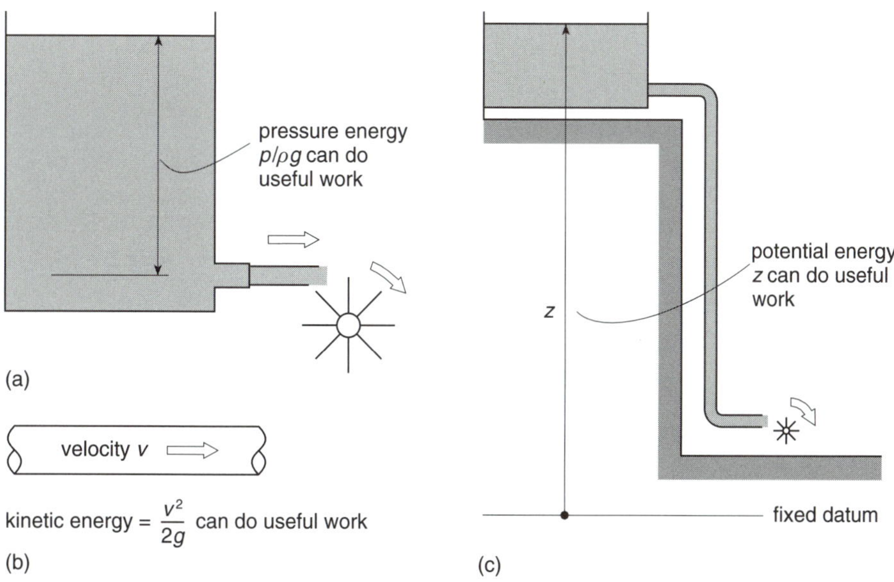


**Figure 3.4 Pressure, kinetic and potential energy**

### 3.5.2 Kinetic energy

When water is moving it has energy because of this movement and this is known as **kinetic energy** or **velocity energy**. The faster it moves the greater the kinetic energy (Figure 3.4b). It is calculated as follows:

$$\text{kinetic energy} = \frac{v^2}{2g}$$

where $v$ is velocity (m/s) and $g$ is the gravity constant (9.81 m/s$^2$).

Kinetic energy is also measured in metres and so it is sometimes referred to as **velocity head**. An example of how to calculate kinetic energy is shown in the box.

**Example: Calculating kinetic energy**

Calculate the kinetic energy in a pipeline when the flow velocity is 3.7m/s.

We have

$$\text{kinetic energy} = \frac{v^2}{2g} = \frac{3.7^2}{2 \times 9.81} = 0.7\text{m}$$

As this can also be thought of as a velocity head, calculate the equivalent pressure in kN/m$^2$.

To calculate head as a pressure in $kN/m^2$ use:

$$\begin{aligned}\text{pressure} &= \rho g h\\ &= 1000 \times 9.81 \times 0.7\\ &= 6867\text{N/m}^2 = 6.87\text{kN/m}^2\end{aligned}$$

### 3.5.3 Potential energy

This is energy related to the location of water. If, for example, a tank of water is placed on the ground (Figure 3.4c) there is little useful work this water can do. If it is placed on top of a building, like a domestic service tank in a house, then the flow can be much more usefully used. So water has energy because of its location. This is called **potential energy**. It is determined by the height of the water in metres above some fixed datum point:

$$\text{potential energy} = z$$

where $z$ is the height of the water in metres (m) above a fixed datum.

It is normal practice to relate height measurements to a fixed datum in this way. It is similar to using sea level as the fixed datum for measuring changes in land elevation.

### 3.5.4 Energy equation

The different forms of energy in a system can be added together (all the dimensions are the same) to determine the total energy. So:

$$\text{total energy} = \frac{p}{\rho g} + \frac{v^2}{2g} + z$$

This is one of the best-known equations in hydraulics and is called the **Bernoulli equation** in recognition of the contribution to the study of fluid behaviour by the Swiss mathematician Daniel Bernoulli (1700–1782). Indeed it was Bernoulli who is said to have put forward the name of hydrodynamics to describe water flow.

Two aspects of energy are very helpful in hydraulics. The first is that energy can be changed from one form to another (see section 1.10.2). This means that pressure energy can be changed to kinetic energy and to potential energy and vice versa. The second is that the total energy is the same at different points in a water system even though the components of energy may be different. This is only strictly true for an ideal fluid, i.e. no friction or energy losses in the flow. But it is a reasonable assumption to make in many situations although not so reasonable for long pipelines where energy losses can be significant and so cannot be ignored. But for now, assume that water is an ideal fluid.

So when water flows along a pipeline between two points 1 and 2, the total energy at point 1 will be the same as the total energy at point 2 (Figure 3.5):

total energy at point 1 = total energy at point 2

and so

$$\frac{p_1}{\rho g} + \frac{v_1^2}{2g} + z_1 = \frac{p_2}{\rho g} + \frac{v_2^2}{2g} + z_2$$

Although the total energy is the same, the component parts may be different. This is because pressure, velocity and elevation of the pipe may change from point 1 to 2.

The following examples show just how useful this equation can be.

## 3.6 Using energy and continuity

Several practical examples of the use of energy and continuity are described below.

### 3.6.1 Pressure and elevation changes

An important application of the energy equation to pipelines explains why pressure changes when there are changes in ground elevation. Pipelines tend to follow the natural ground contours up and down the hills. Such changes in elevation cause direct changes in pressure in the pipe (Figure 3.5). When the ground level rises the pressure drops and when the ground level falls the pressure increases. This can be explained using the energy equation. Consider total energy at two points 1 and 2 along the pipeline some distance apart and at different elevations. Assuming no energy losses between these two points the total energy in the pipeline at point 1 is equal to the total energy at point 2:

$$\frac{p_1}{\rho g} + \frac{v_1^2}{2g} + z_1 = \frac{p_2}{\rho g} + \frac{v_2^2}{2g} + z_2$$

$z_1$ and $z_2$ are measured from some chosen horizontal datum.

Normally pipelines would have the same diameter and so the velocity at point 1 is the same as the velocity at point 2. This means that the kinetic energy at points 1 and 2 are also the same. The above equation then simplifies to:

$$\frac{p_1}{\rho g} + z_1 = \frac{p_2}{\rho g} + z_2$$

Rearranging this to bring the pressure terms and the potential terms together:

$$\frac{p_1}{\rho g} - \frac{p_2}{\rho g} = z_2 - z_1$$

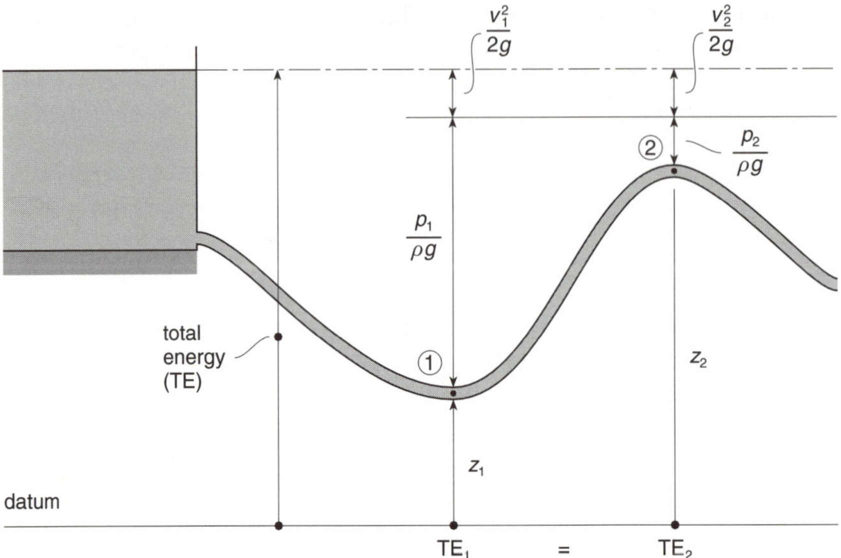


**Figure 3.5 Pressure changes with elevation**

This means that

changes in pressure (m) = changes in ground level (m)

Here $p_1$ and $p_2$ represent a pressure difference between points 1 and 2 (measured in metres) which is a direct result of the change in ground level from $z_1$ to $z_2$. So when a pipeline goes uphill by 10m, the pressure will drop by 10m head. Conversely when a pipeline goes downhill by 10m, the pressure will increase by 10m head. So there is a direct link between pressure and ground elevation.

A numerical example of how to calculate changes in pressure due to changes in elevation is shown in the box.

## Example: Calculating pressure changes due to elevation changes

A pipeline is constructed along undulating ground (Figure 3.5). Calculate the pressure at point 2 when the pressure at point 1 is $150\text{kN/m}^2$ and point 2 is 7.5m above point 1.

Assuming no energy loss along the pipeline this problem can be solved using the energy equation:

total energy at 1 = total energy at 2

$$\frac{p_1}{\rho g} + \frac{v_1^2}{2g} + z_1 = \frac{p_2}{\rho g} + \frac{v_2^2}{2g} + z_2$$

As the pipe diameter is the same throughout then the velocity is the same and so is the kinetic energy. The equation then simplifies to

$$\frac{p_1}{\rho g} + z_1 = \frac{p_2}{\rho g} + z_2$$

Rearranging this gives

$$\frac{p_1}{\rho g} - \frac{p_2}{\rho g} = z_2 - z_1$$

All elevation measurements are made from the same datum level and so

$$z_2 - z_1 = 7.5\text{m}$$

This means that

$$\frac{p_1 - p_2}{\rho g} = 7.5\text{m}$$

and so

$$p_1 - p_2 = 1000 \times 9.81 \times 7.5 = 73575\text{N/m}^2 = 73.6\text{kN/m}^2$$

But

$$\text{pressure at point } 1 = 150\text{kN/m}^2$$

and so

$$\text{pressure at point } 2 = 150 - 73.6 = 76.4\text{kN/m}^2$$

So the result is a drop in pressure at point 2 which is directly attributed to the elevation rise in the pipeline. Note that this has nothing to do with energy losses due to friction as is sometimes thought to be the case. Energy loss due to friction is important in pipes but it is a different issue. This is discussed in Chapter 4.

### 3.6.2 Measuring velocity

Another very useful application of the energy equation is for measuring velocity. This is done by stopping a small part of the flow and measuring the pressure change that results from this. When water flows around an object (Figure 3.6a) most of it is deflected around it but there is one small part of the flow that hits the object head-on and stops. Stopping the water in this way is called **stagnation** and the point at which this occurs is the **stagnation point**. Applying the energy equation to the main stream (point 1) and the stagnation point (point s):

$$\frac{p_1}{\rho g} + \frac{v_1^2}{2g} + z_1 = \frac{p_s}{\rho g} + \frac{v_s^2}{2g} + z_s$$

Assuming the flow is horizontal

$$z_1 = z_s$$

As the water stops

$$v_s = 0$$

and so

$$\frac{p_1}{\rho g} + \frac{v_1^2}{2g} = \frac{p_s}{\rho g}$$

Rearranging this

$$\frac{v_1^2}{2g} = \frac{p_s}{\rho g} - \frac{p_1}{\rho g}$$

and rearranging again gives

$$v_1 = \sqrt{2\left(\frac{p_s - p_1}{\rho}\right)}$$

So it is possible to calculate the mainstream velocity by creating a stagnation point and measuring $p_1$ and $p_s$. This idea is used extensively for measuring water velocity in pipes using a device known as a pitot tube (Figure 3.6b). The stagnation pressure $p_s$ on the end of the tube is measured together with the general pressure in the pipe $p_1$. The velocity is then calculated using the energy equation. One disadvantage of this device is that it does not measure the average velocity in a pipe but only the velocity at the particular point where the pitot tube is located. It is very useful, however, in experimental work for exploring the changes in velocity across the diameter of a pipe to produce velocity profiles.

Stagnation points also occur in channels and it is possible to see them when some object is placed in a flow. On a bridge pier (Figure 3.6c), for example, the water level rises a little just in front of the pier as a result of the change from kinetic energy to pressure energy as the flow stops. In this case the pressure rise is seen as a rise in water level. Unfortunately the change in level is small and difficult to measure accurately and so it is not a very reliable way of measuring velocity in channels.

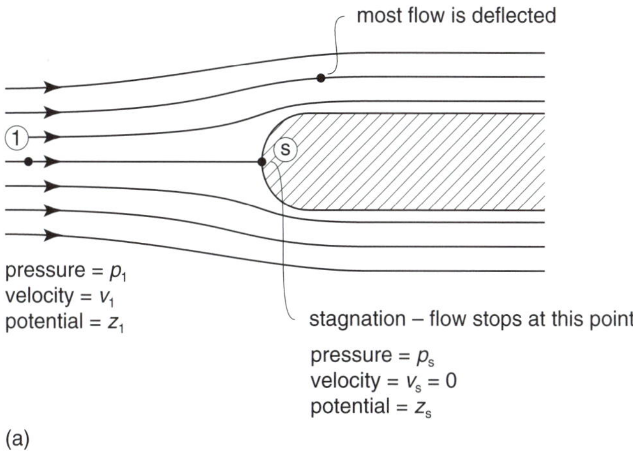


(a)

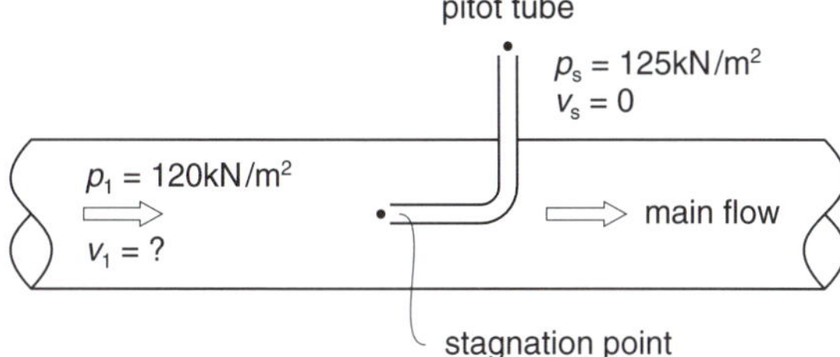


(b)

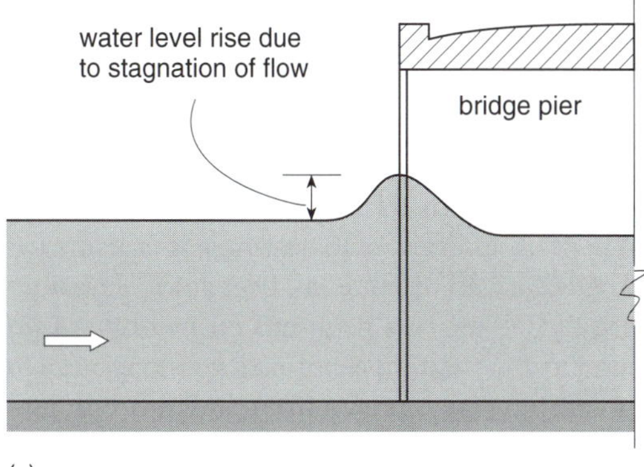


(c)

**Figure 3.6 Measuring velocity**

## Example: Calculating the velocity in a pipe using a pitot tube

Calculate the velocity in a pipe using a pitot tube when the normal pipe operating pressure is $120\text{kN/m}^2$ and the pitot pressure is $125\text{kN/m}^2$ (Figure 3.6b).
Although there is an equation for velocity given in the text it is a good idea at first to work from basic principles to build up confidence. This problem is solved using the energy equation. Point 1 describes the main flow and point s describes the stagnation point on the end of the pitot tube:

$$\frac{p_1}{\rho g} + \frac{v_1^2}{2g} + z_1 = \frac{p_s}{\rho g} + \frac{v_s^2}{2g} + z_s$$

At the stagnation point

$$v_s = 0$$

and as the system is horizontal

$$z_1 = z_s = 0$$

This reduces the energy equation to

$$\frac{p_1}{\rho g} + \frac{v_1^2}{2g} = \frac{p_s}{\rho g}$$

All the values in the equation are known except for $v_1$ and so this can now be determined:

$$\frac{120\,000}{1000 \times 9.81} + \frac{v_1^2}{2 \times 9.81} = \frac{125\,000}{1000 \times 9.81}$$

$$12.23 + \frac{v_1^2}{2 \times 9.81} = 12.74$$

$$\frac{v_1^2}{2 \times 9.81} = 12.74 - 12.23 = 0.51\text{m}$$

$$v_1 = \sqrt{2 \times 9.81 \times 0.51} = 3.16\text{m/s}$$

### 3.6.3 Orifices

A final application of the energy equation is to orifices. These can be openings in the side of a tank or they can be openings under sluice gates used to control water flow in channels (Figure 3.7a). They are usually rectangular or circular in shape. Using the energy equation it is possible to calculate the flow velocity from an orifice and when the area of the orifice is also known the discharge can be calculated as well.

Writing the energy equation for a tank and orifice, point 1 is chosen at the water surface in the tank and point 0 is at the orifice:

$$\frac{p_1}{\rho g}+\frac{v_1^2}{2g}+z_1=\frac{p_0}{\rho g}+\frac{v_0^2}{2g}+z_0$$

At the water surface the pressure is atmospheric and this is taken as zero. Also the downward velocity in the tank is very small and so the kinetic energy is also zero. All the initial energy is potential. At the orifice the jet comes out into the atmosphere and this is at atmospheric pressure which is zero. So the equation reduces to:

$$z_1=\frac{v_0^2}{2g}+z_0$$

Rearranging this equation:

$$\frac{v_0^2}{2g}=z_1-z_0$$

Put

$$z_1-z_0=h$$

Now rearrange this for $v_0$:

$$v_0=\sqrt{2gh}$$

This connection between the head available in a tank and the velocity of the jet is said to have been first made by Evangelista Torricelli (1608–1647) some considerable time before Bernoulli developed his energy equation. He was greatly influenced by Galileo Galilei (1564–1642) and applied Galileo's concepts of mechanics to water falling under the influence of gravity. Although the above equation is now referred to as Torricelli's law he did not include the $2g$ term. This was introduced much later by other investigators.

Torricelli sought to verify this law by directing a water jet from an orifice, vertically upwards (Figure 3.7b). He showed that the jet rose to almost the same height as the free water surface in the tank, showing that the potential energy in the tank and the velocity energy at the orifice are equal. So knowing the pressure head available in a pipe it is possible to calculate the height to which a water jet would rise if a nozzle was attached to it. This can be very useful for designing fountains!

The discharge from an orifice is calculated using the discharge equation:

$$Q=av$$

and so

$$Q=a\sqrt{2gh}$$

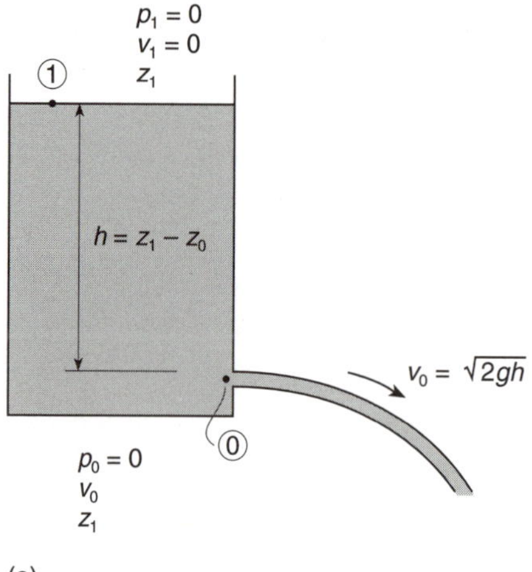


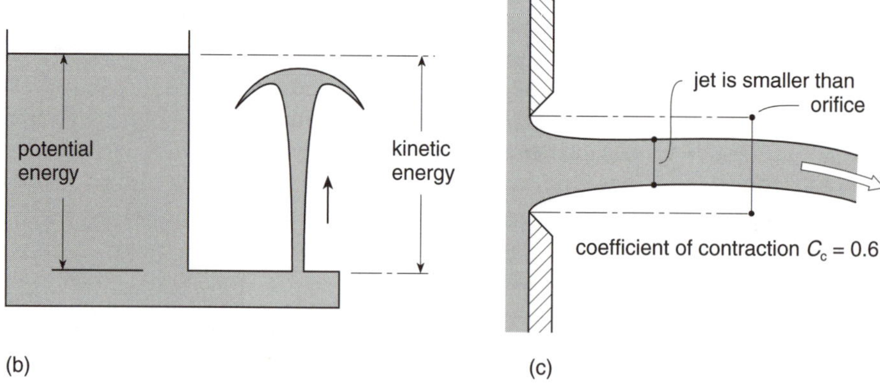


**Figure 3.7 Flow through orifices**

where $a$ is area of the orifice ($m^2$). This equation is not so accurate because the area of the jet of water is not the same as the area of the orifice. As the jet emerges and flows around the edge of the orifice it follows a curved path and so the jet ends up smaller than the orifice (Figure 3.7c). The contraction of the jet is taken into account by introducing a **coefficient of contraction** $C_c$. This has a value of approximately 0.6. So the discharge formula now becomes:

$$Q = C_c a \sqrt{2gh}$$

Although it might be interesting to work out the discharge from holes in tanks, a more useful application of Torricelli's law is for the design of hydraulic structures using underflow gates for both measuring and controlling discharges. (This is discussed in more detail in section 7.2.)

### 3.6.4 Pressure and velocity changes in a pipe

The energy equation can also be used to predict the results of changes in pressure, velocity and elevation in a pipeline. An example in the box shows just how versatile this equation can be.

#### Example: Calculating pressure changes using the energy equation

A pipeline carrying a discharge of $0.12\text{m}^3/\text{s}$ changes from 150mm diameter to 300mm diameter and rises through 7m (Figure 3.8). Calculate the pressure in the 300mm pipe when the pressure in the 150mm pipe is $350\text{kN/m}^2$.

This problem involves changes in pressure, kinetic and potential energy and its solution requires both the energy and continuity equations. The first step is to write down the energy equation for the two points in the system 1 and 2:

$$\frac{p_1}{\rho g} + \frac{v_1^2}{2g} + z_1 = \frac{p_2}{\rho g} + \frac{v_2^2}{2g} + z_2$$

The next step is put all the known values into the equation, identify the unknowns and then determine their values. Here $p_1$, $z_1$ and $z_2$ are known values but $p_2$ is unknown and so are $v_1$ and $v_2$. To determine $v_1$ and $v_2$ use the continuity equation

$$Q = va$$

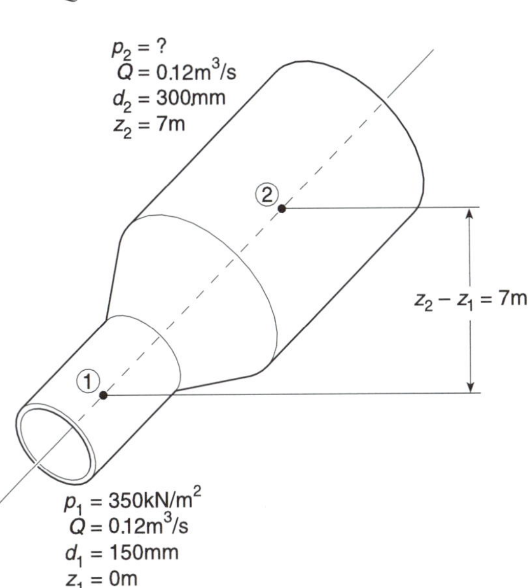


**Figure 3.8** Calculating pressure, velocity and elevation changes

Rearranging this to calculate $v$:

$$v = \frac{Q}{a}$$

and so

$$v_1 = \frac{Q}{a_1} \quad \text{and} \quad v_2 = \frac{Q}{a_2}$$

The pipe areas are not known but their diameters are known, so now calculate their cross-sectional areas:

$$a_1 = \frac{\pi d_1^2}{4} = \frac{\pi 0.15^2}{4} = 0.018\text{m}^2$$

$$a_2 = \frac{\pi d_2^2}{4} = \frac{\pi 0.3^2}{4} = 0.07\text{m}^2$$

Now calculate the velocities:

$$v_1 = \frac{Q}{a_1} = \frac{0.120}{0.018} = 6.67\text{m/s}$$

$$v_2 = \frac{Q}{a_2} = \frac{0.120}{0.07} = 1.71\text{m/s}$$

Putting the known values into the energy equation

$$\frac{350\ 000}{1000 \times 9.81} + \frac{6.67^2}{2 \times 9.81} + 0 = \frac{p_2}{\rho g} + \frac{1.71^2}{2 \times 9.81} + 7$$

Note that although pressures are quoted in kN/m$^2$ it is less confusing to work all calculations in N/m$^2$ and then convert back to kN/m$^2$. The equation simplifies to

$$35.68 + 2.26 = \frac{p_2}{\rho g} + 0.15 + 7$$

Rearranging this equation for $p_2$:

$$\frac{p_2}{\rho g} = 35.68 + 2.26 - 0.15 - 7 = 30.8\text{m head of water}$$

To determine this head as a pressure in kN/m$^2$ use the pressure–head equation:

$$\text{pressure} = \rho g h$$

$$p_2 = 1000 \times 9.81 \times 30.8$$

$$= 302\ 000\text{N/m}^2 = 302\text{kN/m}^2$$

## 3.7 Some more energy applications

### 3.7.1 When flow is constricted

When water flows through constrictions in pipes and channels it does not behave in the same way as solid objects do when they are moving through narrow openings. First, imagine a large crowd of people all walking along a corridor. Suddenly the corridor becomes narrower and typically what happens is that too many people try to squeeze through at the same time and so it becomes blocked (Figure 3.9a). Think now about water flowing in a pipe. When it is constricted it is often thought that a similar blockage will occur and this will slow down the water. But this is not so. Continuity and energy control this event. As the pipe becomes narrower, the area gets smaller but continuity tells us that the velocity must increase. It must do since there is the same total energy available to drive the flow and continuity must be maintained. So the flow passes through the constriction quickly and smoothly (Figure 3.9b). At the same time the pressure in the constriction drops as the increase in kinetic energy is gained at the expense of pressure energy. So a narrow pipe, or indeed any other constriction such as a partly open valve, does not throttle the flow, it just speeds it up so that it goes through much faster. An example of this occurs when opening a domestic water tap. The discharge through a partially open tap is almost the same as that through a fully open one. The total energy available is the same but the flow area is smaller when it is partially opened and so the water just flows through with a faster velocity.

This same principle also applies to flow in open channels. When flow is constricted it speeds up (kinetic energy increases) and the water level drops (pressure energy decreases). This can be seen in channels when water flows under bridges or over weirs (this is discussed more fully in Chapters 4 and 5).

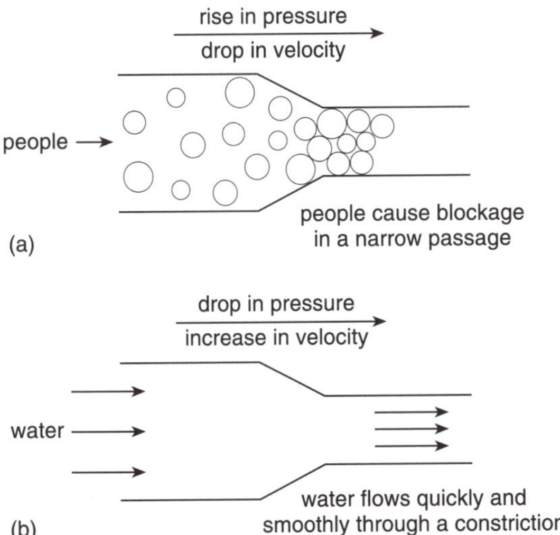


**Figure 3.9** People and water flow differently through narrow passages

Some people have suggested that the design of sports stadiums, which can easily become congested with people, could benefit from linking the flow of people to the flow of water. Some years ago there was a major accident at a football stadium in Belgium in which many people were crushed to death when those at the rear of the stadium suddenly surged forward in a narrow tunnel pushing those in front onto fixed barriers and crushing them. At the time it was suggested that stadiums should, in future, be designed with hydraulics in mind so the layout, size and shape of tunnels and barriers would allow people to 'flow' smoothly onto the terraces in a more orderly and safe manner. This is a dangerous analogy as people clearly do not behave in the same way as water does. People tend to get stuck in narrow passages and against solid barriers whereas water behaves much more sensibly, flowing around barriers and speeding up and slowing down when needed to get through some tight spots.

### 3.7.2 How aeroplanes fly

Aeroplanes rely on the energy equation to fly. Changes in energy around an aeroplane wing create the forces necessary to lift it into the air.

An aircraft wing is specially shaped so that the air flow path is longer over the wing than under it (Figure 3.10a). So when an aircraft is taking off the air moves faster over the wing than under it. This is necessary to maintain continuity of air flow around the wing. The result is an increase in kinetic energy over the wing. But the total energy around the wing does not change and so there is a corresponding reduction in the pressure energy above the wing. This means that the pressure above the wing is less than that below it and so the wing experiences a lift force. This is the force that can lift hundreds of tons of aeroplane into the air. It never ceases to amaze people and it works every time. Have you noticed that aeroplanes usually take off into the wind. This is because the extra velocity of the wind provides a larger change in pressure and so extra lift. This is particularly important at take-off when the aeroplane is at its heaviest and carrying its full fuel load.

The same principle is used in reverse on racing cars. In this case the wing is upside down and located on the back of the car. The velocity of the air flowing over it, due to the forward movement of the car, produces a downward thrust which holds the car firmly on the road. The faster the car the greater is the downthrust, which improves road holding and helps drivers to maintain high speeds even when cornering.

You can experience this lift force yourself (Figure 3.10b). Tear off a strip of paper approximately 20mm wide and 200mm long. Grip the paper firmly in your teeth and blow gently across the top of the paper. You will see the paper rise to a horizontal position. This is because the blowing action increases the velocity of the air and so reduces the pressure. The pressure below the paper is higher than above it and so the paper lifts – just like the aeroplane.

One way to feel the substantial force involved is to hold a spoon with its convex side close to the water jet running from a tap (Figure 3.10c). The spoon is not pushed away from the water jet as might be expected, but is drawn towards it. This is due to the increase in velocity of water flowing around the spoon which causes a drop in pressure. This draws the spoon into the jet with surprising force.

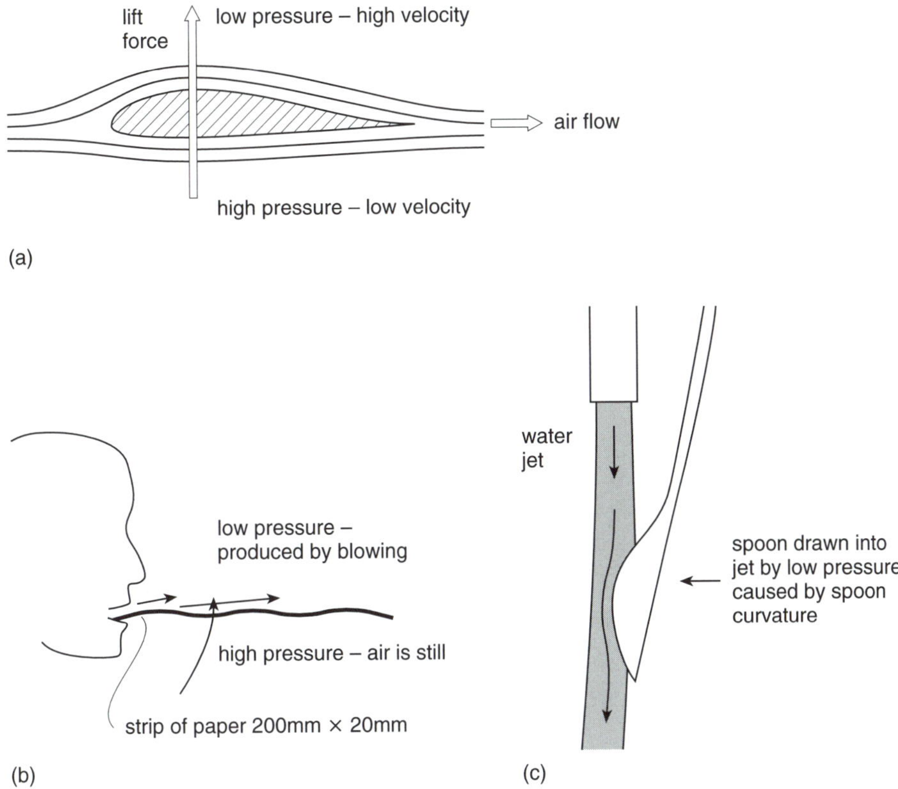


**Figure 3.10** How aeroplanes fly

### 3.7.3 Carburettors

Carburettors use changes in energy to put fuel into petrol engines (Figure 3.11a). When air is drawn into a carburettor it increases in velocity as it moves into the narrow section (or throat). As the total energy of the air remains the same the pressure energy in the throat drops below that of the surrounding atmosphere. The petrol in the carburettor is stored at atmospheric pressure and so fuel begins to flow from the higher (atmospheric) pressure in the tank to the lower pressure in the throat. It then mixes with the air and is drawn into the engine.

### 3.7.4 Fluid injectors

A device similar to a carburettor is used to inject one fluid into another such as the injection of fertiliser into irrigation water. The narrow section is located in the main irrigation pipeline, which causes the velocity to increase and the pressure to drop. Some of the flow passes from the main pipe upstream of the throat (where the

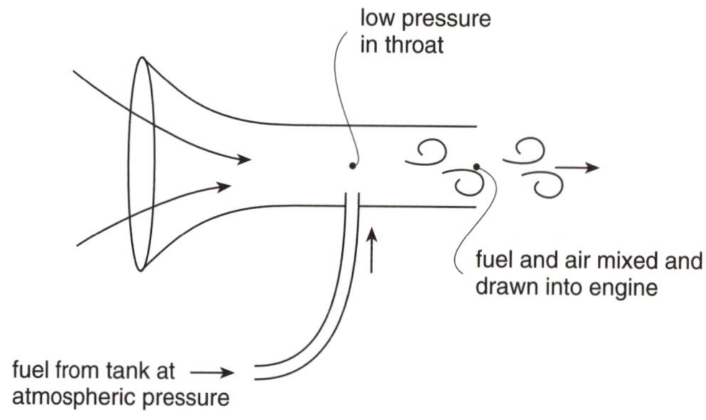


(a) Carburettor

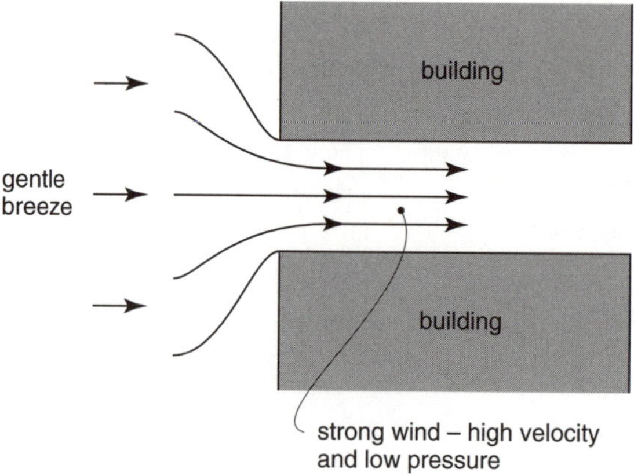


(b) Wind blowing between buildings

**Figure 3.11** Applying the energy equation

pressure is high) through the fertiliser tank and back into the pipe via the throat (where the pressure is low), taking some fertiliser with it. The turbulence just downstream of the throat, where the pipe expands again to its normal size, ensures that the fertiliser is well mixed in the flow.

### 3.7.5 Strong winds

Most people have noticed how suddenly the wind becomes much stronger in the gaps between buildings (Figure 3.11b). This is another example of the effect of changing energy. A narrow gap causes an increase in wind velocity and a corresponding drop in air pressure. The pressure drop can cause doors to bang because the pressure between the buildings is lower than the pressure inside them (remember the air inside is still and at normal atmospheric pressure).

### 3.7.6 A final comment

These are just some of the many examples that show how useful continuity and energy can be. But one very useful application for water that is described later is for flow measurement. Changing the energy in pipes and channels produces changes in pressure which can be more easily measured than velocity. Using the energy and continuity equations, the pressure change is used to calculate velocities and hence the discharge (see sections 4.9 and 7.7).

## 3.8 Momentum

The third basic tool of hydraulics is the momentum equation. Momentum is about movement and the forces that cause it (see section 1.11). It is the link between force, mass and velocity and is used to determine the forces created in pipes and on hydraulic structures.

The momentum equation is normally written as:

$$\text{force (N)} = \text{mass flow (kg/s)} \times \text{change in velocity (m/s)}$$

but

$$\text{mass flow (kg/s)} = \text{mass density (kg/m}^3) \times \text{discharge (m}^3\text{/s)}$$

$$= \rho Q$$

and

$$\text{velocity change} = v_2 - v_1$$

where $v_1$ and $v_2$ represent two velocities in a system, and so

$$\text{force} = \rho Q(v_2 - v_1)$$

This is now in a form that can be useful for calculating forces in hydraulics. An example of the use of this equation is shown in the box.

#### Example: Calculating the force on a plate from a jet of water

A jet of water with a diameter of 60mm and a velocity of 5m/s hits a vertical plate. Calculate the force of impact of the jet on the plate (Figure 3.12).

It is important to remember two points when dealing with momentum: (1) Forces and velocities are vectors and so their direction is as important as their magnitude. (2) The force of the water jet on the plate is equal to the force of the plate on the water. They are the same magnitude but in opposite directions (Newton's third law).

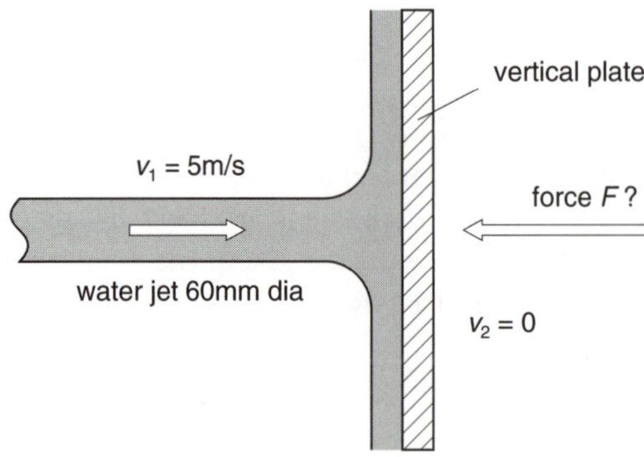


**Figure 3.12** Applying momentum

When forces are involved in a problem use the momentum equation

$$-F = \rho Q(v_2 - v_1)$$

Notice that flow and forces from left to right are all positive and those from right to left are negative. $F$ is the force of the plate on the water and is in the opposite direction to the flow and so it is negative. (Working out the right direction can be rather tricky sometimes and so working with the momentum equation does take some practice.)

Reversing all the signs in the above equation makes $F$ positive:

$$F = \rho Q(v_1 - v_2)$$

The next step is to calculate the discharge $Q$:

$$Q = va = v \times \frac{\pi d^2}{4}$$

$$= 5 \times \frac{\pi 0.06^2}{4} = 0.014\text{m}^3/\text{s}$$

For this problem $v_2 = 0$ because the velocity of the jet after impact *in the direction of the flow* is zero. So putting the known values into the momentum equation

$$F = 1000 \times 0.014 \times 5 = 70\text{N}$$

## 3.9 Real fluids

The assumption made so far is that water is an ideal fluid. This means it has no viscosity and there is no friction between the flow and the boundaries of pipes and channels. Sometimes these are reasonable assumptions to make. Ignoring viscosity (the internal friction of the fluid), for example, does not affect the design of pipes and channels because the influence of viscosity in water is very small. But there are many circumstances when the external friction between water and its boundaries cannot be ignored and so the behaviour of water as a real fluid needs to be properly understood.

### 3.9.1 Energy losses

When water flows along pipes and channels energy is lost from friction and as this can be a significant amount it needs to be taken into account in the energy equation. Writing the energy equation for points 1 and 2 along a pipeline carrying a real fluid needs an additional term $h_f$ to describe the energy loss between them:

$$\frac{p_1}{\rho g} + \frac{v_1^2}{2g} + z_1 = \frac{p_2}{\rho g} + \frac{v_2^2}{2g} + z_2 + h_f$$

The main issue in pipe flow problems (and also in open channel problems) is how to determine the **energy loss** term $h_f$ as this in turn determines the size of pipe or channel needed to carry a given flow. This idea is developed more fully in Chapters 4 and 5. Although $h_f$ is referred to as an energy loss it is sometimes called a **head loss** or **pressure loss**. All three names have the same meaning.

### 3.9.2 Cavitation

This is a special condition that is not taken account of by the energy equation. It occurs when water is moving very fast and as a consequence the pressure is very low. This often occurs in the suction side of centrifugal pumps and under partially closed valves (Figure 3.13a).

When a valve is nearly closed the velocity under the gate can be very high. This increases the kinetic energy but at the expense of the pressure energy. If the pressure drops below the vapour pressure of water (this is approximately 0.3m absolute) bubbles, called **cavities**, start to form in the water. They are very small but there are many of them and the water may have a cloudy or misty appearance. Cavities are not *air* bubbles as is often thought. The latter is just air entrainment as water draws in air when it is very turbulent. Cavities are different. They are small bubbles filled with *water vapour* and inside them the pressure is very low. As these bubbles move under the gate and into the pipe downstream, the velocity slows, the pressure rises and the bubbles begin to collapse. If they collapse in the main flow they do no harm, but if they are close to the pipe wall they can do a great deal of damage. Notice the way in which the cavities collapse (Figure 3.13b). A tiny needle jet of water rushes across the cavity and it is this which can do great damage even to steel and concrete because the pressure under the jet can be as high as 4000bar!

Most modern centrifugal pumps and turbines suffer from cavitation and this is discussed further in section 8.15.

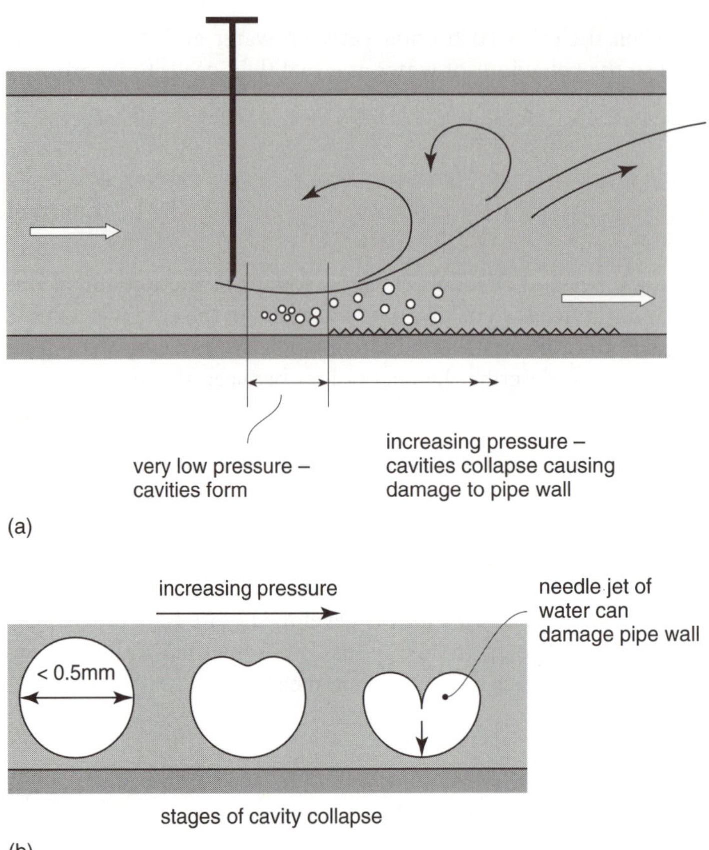
very low pressure – cavities form
increasing pressure – cavities collapse causing damage to pipe wall
(a)
increasing pressure
needle jet of water can damage pipe wall
< 0.5mm
stages of cavity collapse
(b)

**Figure 3.13** Cavitation

## 3.9.3 Boundary layers

In real fluids, like water, there is always friction between the water and the boundary and indeed between the layers of flow (the viscosity). Because of this, the flow near a boundary moves much more slowly than in the main stream and, although it is not possible to see it, at the boundary the fluid actually sticks to it and the velocity is zero. This slows down fluid layers close to the boundary, which in turn slows others. Gradually the slowing effect moves up through the fluid. The flow affected by the boundary in this way is called the **boundary layer**. The use of the word 'layer' can be misleading here as it implies a thin slice of the flow. This is not the case. It refers not just to the layer of flow immediately in contact with the boundary but to all the flow that is slowed down as a result of the friction from the boundary.

The effect of viscosity and boundary friction is to vary the water velocity across the flow. A graph of this change in velocity is called the **velocity profile** (Figure 3.14a). It varies from zero near the boundary to a maximum in the centre of a pipe or channel where the boundary has least effect. Compare this with the velocity profile for an ideal fluid where the velocity is the same across the entire flow.

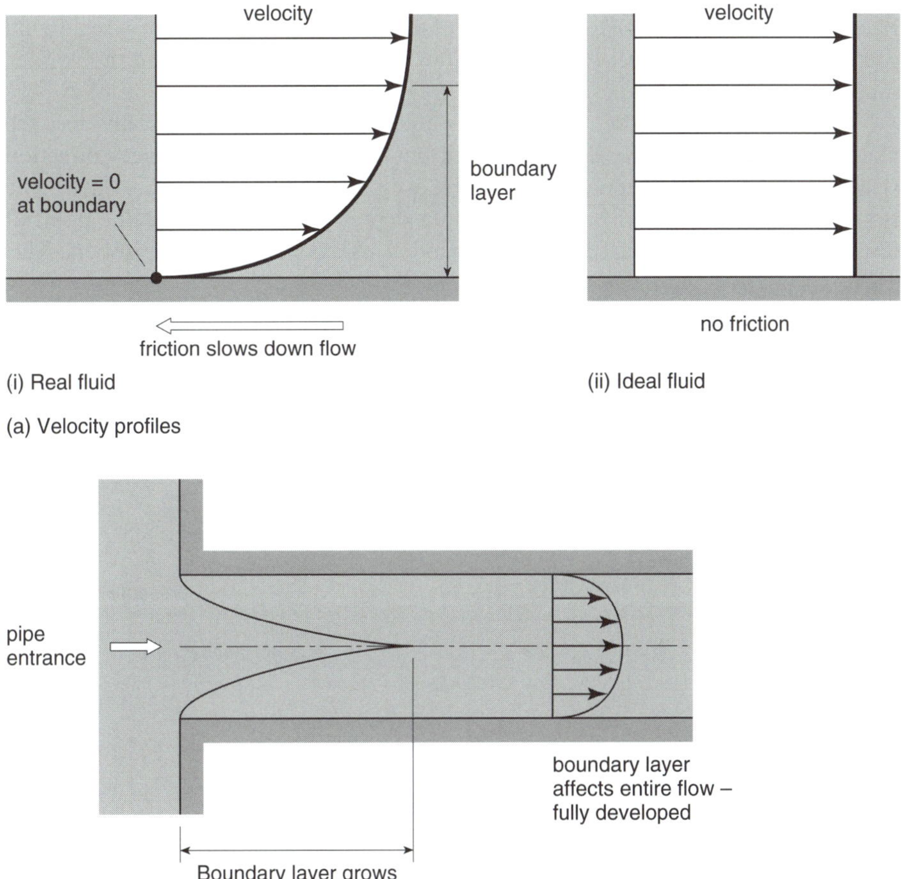


**Figure 3.14 Boundary effects**

When water enters a pipe, the boundary layer grows quickly over the first few metres until it meets in the middle of the pipe (Figure 3.14b). From this point onwards the pipe boundary influences the entire flow in the pipe. In channels the boundary effects of the bed and sides grow similarly over a few metres of channel and soon influence the entire flow. When the boundary layer fills the entire flow it is said to be **fully developed.** This fully developed state is the basis on which all the pipe and channel formulae are based in Chapters 4 and 5.

#### *3.9.3.1 The Earth's boundary layer*

The Earth's surface produces a boundary layer when the wind blows (Figure 3.15a). The wind is much slower near the ground where it is affected by friction between the air and the Earth's surface and its influence extends several metres above the

Earth's surface. For this reason it is important to specify the height at which wind speed is measured in meteorological stations. At 2m above the ground the wind is much slower than at 4m.

An interesting feature of the Earth's boundary layer is that not only does the wind slow down near the Earth's surface but it also gradually changes direction (Figure 3.15b). In the upper atmosphere, well beyond the boundary layer, the isobars (the lines of equal pressure) are in a depression circle around the point of lowest pressure and the direction of the wind is always parallel to the isobars. This

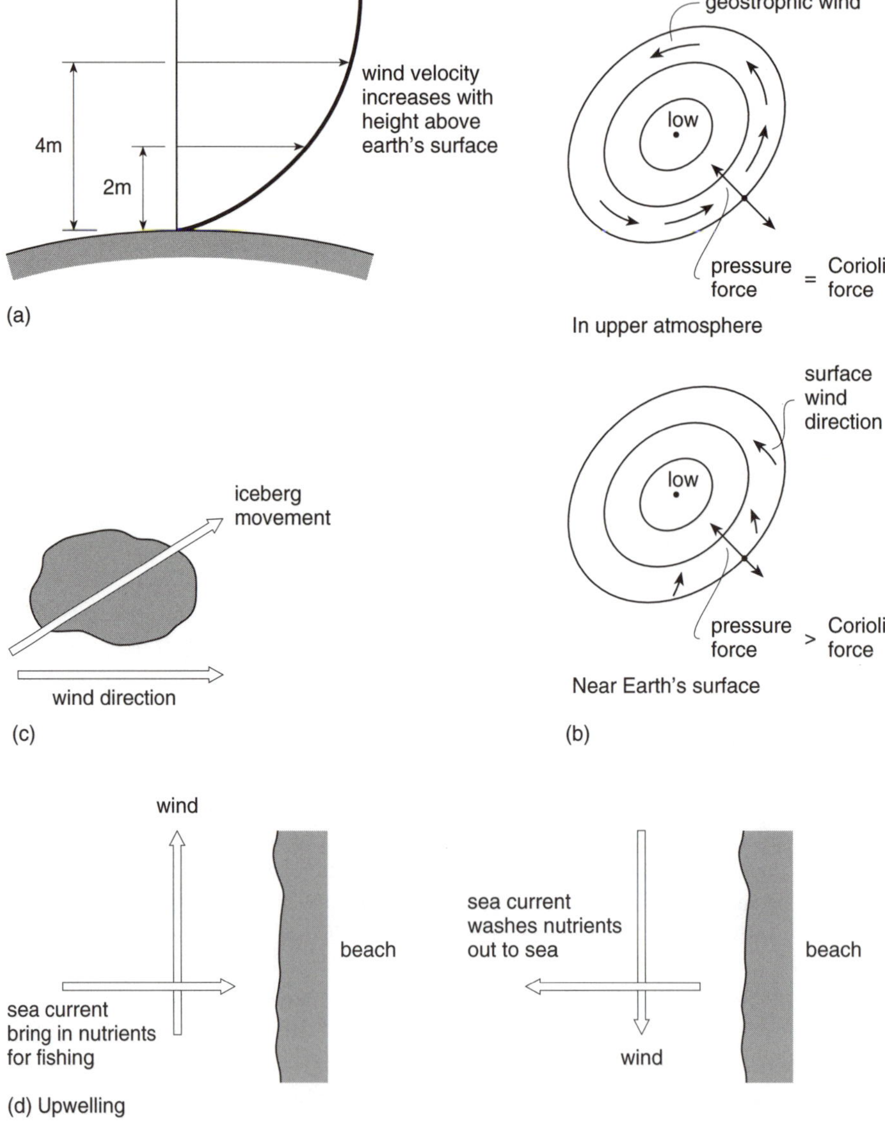


**Figure 3.15 Earth's boundary layer**

is because there is a balance between two important forces: the **Coriolis force**, which is a small but significant force that comes from the Earth's rotation, and the force trying to pull the air into the centre of the depression because of the difference in pressure. So the wind circulates around the centre of the depression and is known as the **geostrophic wind**. The Coriolis force does not affect us as individuals as we are too small but it does affect the movement of large masses such as the air and the sea. Nearer the Earth's surface, in the boundary layer, the wind slows down and this reduces the effect of the Coriolis force. The two forces are now out of balance and so the wind direction gradually changes as it is pulled in towards the centre of the depression. This is why the ground surface wind direction on weather maps is always at an angle to the isobars and points inwards towards the centre of the depression. This gradual twisting of the wind direction produces a spiral which is called the **Eckman spiral**.

Eckman first observed this spiral at sea. He noticed that, in a strong wind, icebergs do not drift in the same direction as the wind but at an angle to it (Figure 3.15c). Surface winds can cause strong sea water currents and although the surface current may be in the direction of the wind those currents below the surface are influenced both by the boundary resistance from the sea bed and by the Coriolis force from the Earth's rotation. The effect is similar to that in the atmosphere. The lower currents slow down because of friction and gradually turn under the influence of the Coriolis force. So at the sea surface the water is moving in the same direction as the wind but close to the sea bed it is moving at an angle to the wind. As icebergs float over 90% submerged their movement follows the water current rather than the wind direction and so they move at an angle to the wind.

This spiral effect is vital to several fishing communities around the world and is referred to as upwelling (Figure 3.15d). In Peru when the surface wind blows along the coastline the boundary layer and the Coriolis force conspire to induce a current along the sea bed at right angles to the wind direction. This brings all the vegetative debris and plankton on which fish like to feed into the shallow waters of the shoreline and so the fishing is very successful. However, when the wind blows in the opposite direction the current is reversed and all the food is washed out to sea leaving the shallow coastal fishing grounds bare and the fishing industry devastated.

## 3.10 Drag forces

Boundary layers occur around all kinds of objects, e.g. water flow around ships and submarines, air flow around aircraft and balls thrown through the air. The boundary layer slows them down and this is referred to as a **drag force**. You can feel this force by putting your hand out of the window of a moving car or in a stream of flowing water.

Sir George Stokes (1819–1903), an eminent physicist in his day, was one of the first people to investigate drag by examining the forces on spheres falling through different fluids. He noticed that the spheres fell at different rates, not just because of the viscosity of the fluids but also because of the size of the spheres. He also found that the falling spheres eventually reached a constant velocity which he called the **terminal velocity**. This occurred when the force of gravity causing the balls to accelerate was balanced by the resistance resulting from the fluid viscosity and the size of the balls.

Stokes also demonstrated that for any object dropped in a fluid (or a stationary object placed in a flowing liquid, which is essentially the same) there were two types of drag: **surface drag** or skin friction which resulted from friction between a fluid and an object, and **form drag** which resulted from the shape and size of an object.

Flow around a bridge pier in a river provides a good example of the two types of drag. When the velocity is very low, the flow moves around the pier as shown in Figure 3.16a. The water clings to the pier and in this situation there is only surface drag and the shape of the pier has no effect. The flow pattern behind the pier is the same as the pattern upstream. But as the velocity increases, the boundary layer grows and the flow can no longer cling to the pier and so it separates (Figure 3.16b). It behaves like a car that is travelling too fast to get around a tight bend. It spins away from the pier and creates several small whirlpools which are swept downstream. These are called **vortices** or **eddies** and together they form what is known as the **wake**. The flow pattern behind the pier is now quite different from that in front and in the wake the pressure is much lower than in front. It is this difference in pressure that results in the **form drag**. It is additional to the surface drag and its magnitude depends on the shape of the pier. Going back to your hand through the car window, notice how the force changes when the back or the side of your hand is placed in the direction of the flow. The shape of your hand in the flow determines the form drag.

Form drag is usually more important than surface drag and it can be reduced by shaping a bridge pier so that the water flows around it more easily and separation is delayed or avoided. Indeed, if separation could be avoided completely then form drag would be eliminated and the only concern would be surface drag. Shaping piers to produces a narrow wake and reduce form drag is often called **streamlining** (Figure 3.16c). This is the basis of design not just for bridge piers but also for aircraft, ships and cars to reduce drag and so increase speed or reduce energy requirements.

Swimmers too can benefit from reducing drag. This is particularly important at competitive levels when a few hundredths of a second can mean the difference between a gold and a silver medal. About 90% of the drag on a swimmer is form drag and only 10% is surface drag. Some female swimmers try to reduce form drag by squeezing into a swimsuit 2 or 3 sizes too small for them in order to improve their shape in the water.

Although women swimmers may seem to have an advantage in having a more streamlined shape than bulky males, their shape does present some hydraulic problems. A woman's breasts cause early flow separation which increases turbulence and form drag. One swimwear manufacturer has found a solution to this by using a technique used by the aircraft industry to solve a similar problem. Aircraft wings often have small vertical spikes on their upper surface and these stop the flow from separating too early by creating small vortices, i.e. zones of low pressure close to the wing surface. This not only reduces form drag significantly but helps to avoid stalling (very early separation) which can be disastrous for an aircraft. The new swimsuit has tiny vortex generators located just below the breasts

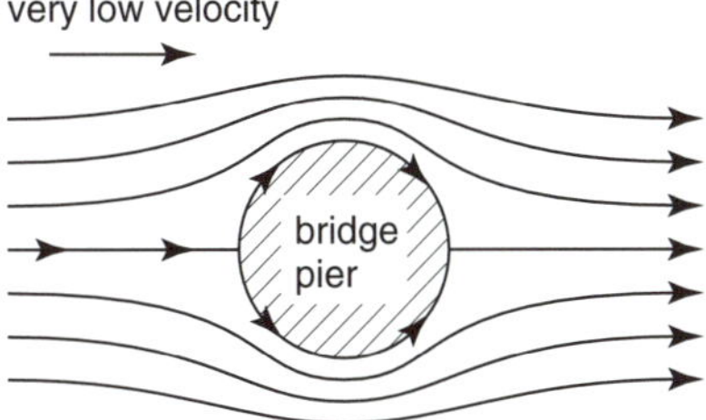


(a) Surface drag only – no form drag

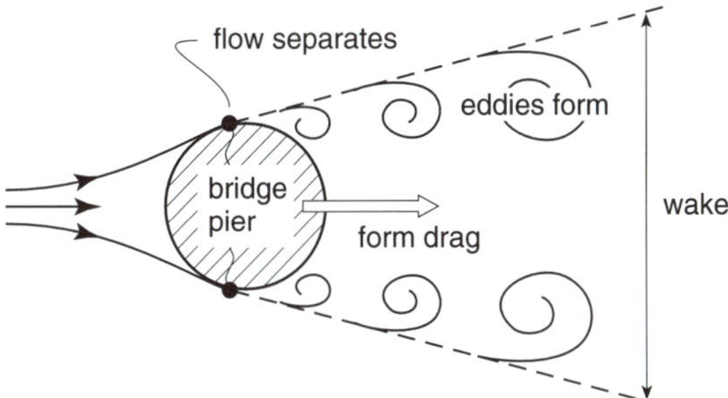


(b) Increasing velocity causes separation to occur

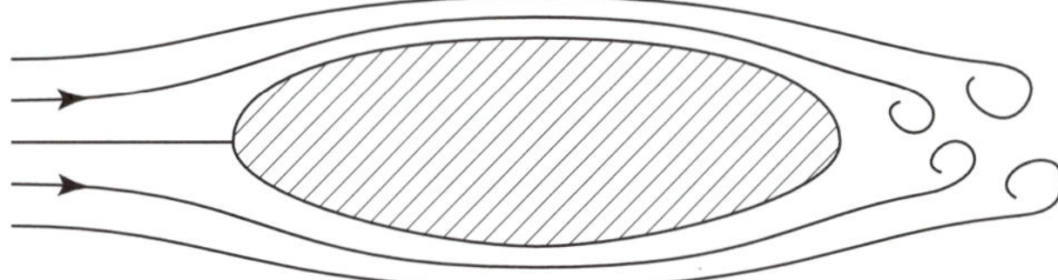

(c) Form drag reduced by streamlining

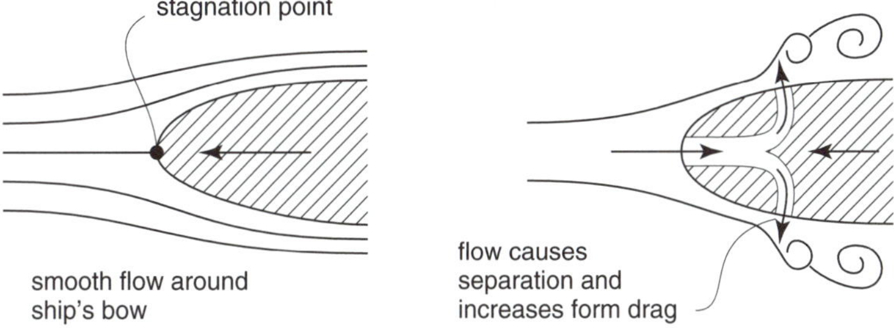


(d) Using form drag to stop tankers

**Figure 3.16 Boundaries and drag**

which cause the boundary layer to cling to the swimmer and not separate, thus reducing the form drag. The same manufacturer has also developed a ribbed swimsuit that creates similar vortices all along the swimmer's body to try to stop the flow from separating. The manufacturer claims a 9% reduction in drag for the average female swimmer over a conventional swimsuit.

Dolphins probably have the best-known natural shape and skin for swimming. Both their form drag and surface drag are very low and this enables them to move through the water with incredible ease and speed. This is something that human beings have been trying to emulate for many years.

There is a way of calculating drag force:

$$\text{drag force} = \tfrac{1}{2}C\rho a v^2$$

where $\rho$ is fluid density (kg/m$^3$), $a$ is cross-sectional area (m$^2$), $v$ is velocity (m/s) and $C$ is drag coefficient. $C$ is dependent on the shape of the body, the velocity of the flow and the density of the fluid.

### 3.10.1 Stopping super-tankers

Super-tankers are large ships which are designed for low drag so that they can travel the seas with only modest energy requirements to drive them. The problem comes when they want to stop. When the engines are stopped they can continue to travel for several kilometres before drag forces finally stop them. How then do you put on the brakes on a super-tanker? One way is to increase the form drag by taking advantage of the stagnation point at the bow of the ship to push water through an inlet pipe in the bow and out at the sides of the ship (Figure 3.16d). This flow at right angles to the movement of the ship causes the boundary layer to separate and so greatly increases the form drag. It is as if the ship is suddenly made much wider and this upsets its streamlined shape.

## 3.11 Eddy shedding

Eddies that form in the wake around bridge piers can also cause other problems besides drag. Eddies are not shed from each side of the pier at the same time but alternately, first from one side, then from the other. Under the right flow conditions large eddies can form and the rhythmic eddy shedding can induce a lateral force which can push an object back and forth causing a slow rhythmic vibration (Figure 3.17a). This problem is not just confined to bridge piers. It can happen to tall chimneys and to bridge decks in windy conditions. The vibration can become so bad that structures can collapse.

A famous suspension bridge, the Tacoma Narrows Bridge in the USA, was destroyed in the 1930s because of this problem (Figure 3.17b). In order to protect traffic from high winds blowing down the river channel, the sides of the bridge were boarded up. Unfortunately the boarding deflected the wind around the bridge deck,

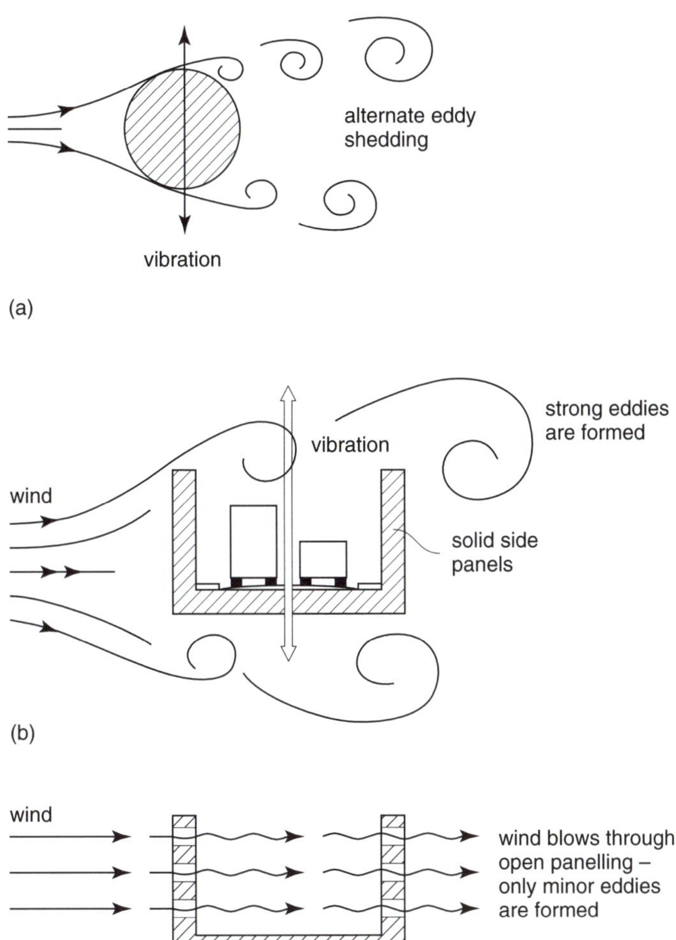


**Figure 3.17** Eddy shedding problems

the air flow separated forming large eddies and this set the bridge deck oscillating violently up and down. The bridge deck was quite flexible as it was a suspension bridge and could in fact tolerate quite a lot of movement, but this was so violent that eventually it destroyed the bridge.

The solution to the problem was quite simple, but it was not appreciated at the time. If the side panels had been removed this would have stopped the large eddies from forming and there would have been no vibration (Figure 3.17c). So next time you are on a suspension bridge and a strong wind is blowing and you are feeling uncomfortable, be thankful that the engineers have decided not to protect you from the wind by boarding up the sides.

A similar problem can occur around tall chimneys when eddies are shed in windy conditions. To avoid large eddies forming, a perforated sleeve or a spiral collar is placed around the top of the chimney. This breaks up the flow into lots of small eddies which are usually quite harmless.

## 3.12 Making balls swing

Sports players soon learn how useful boundary layers can be when they realise that balls can be made to move in a curved path and so confuse their opponents. A good example of this is the way some bowlers are able to make a ball 'swing' (move in a curved path) in cricket.

When a ball is thrown (for cricket enthusiasts this means bowled) the air flows around it and at some point it separates (Figure 3.18). When the separation occurs at the same point all around the ball then it moves along a straight path. However, when it occurs asymmetrically there is a larger pressure on one side of the ball and so it starts to move in a curved path (i.e. it swings). The bowler's task is to work out how to do this.

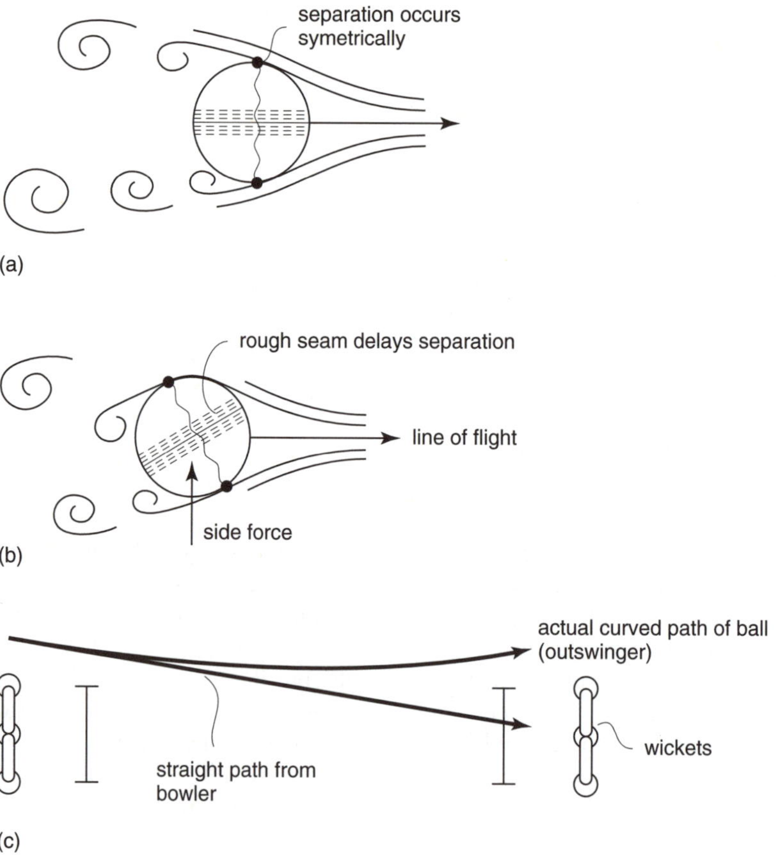


**Figure 3.18** Making balls swing

Laboratory experiments have shown that as air flows around a ball it can be either laminar or turbulent. (These are two different kinds of flow that are described in section 4.3.1.) When it is turbulent the air clings to the ball more easily than when it is laminar. So the bowler tries to make the air flow turbulent on one side of the ball and laminar on the other. This is done by making one side very smooth and the other side very rough. In cricket, this situation is helped by a special stitched seam around the middle of the ball which ensures that the ball is rough enough to create turbulent conditions. The ball can be bowled so that the polished side of the ball is facing the batsman and the seam is at an angle to the main direction of travel. The air flow on the smooth side separates earlier than on the rough side and so the ball swings towards the turbulent side. The cross force can be up to 0.8N depending on how fast the ball is travelling and may cause a swing of up to 0.6m in 20m – the length of a cricket pitch. This can be more than enough to deceive a batsman who may be expecting a straight ball. This is why bowlers seem to spend so much of their time polishing the ball on their trousers prior to their run up in order to get it as smooth as possible on one side to get the maximum swing. The swing may be in or out depending on how the bowler holds the ball. However, not all the surprise is with the bowler. An observant batsman may know what is coming by looking to see how the bowler is holding the ball and so anticipate the swing.

Sometimes strange things happen which even puzzle those who understand hydraulics. Just occasionally bowlers have noticed that a ball that was meant to swing in towards the batsman swings away from him instead. What happens is that when a ball is bowled fast enough the entire air flow around the ball turns turbulent and so the separation occurs much earlier. The stitched seam around the ball now acts as a ramp causing the air to be pushed away, creating a side force in the opposite direction to what was expected. This causes great delight for the bowler but can give the batsman a great shock. But most batsmen can relax as this special 'reverse swing' only occurs when the ball reaches 130 to 150km/h and only a few bowlers can actually reach this velocity. But, some unscrupulous bowlers have discovered a way of doing this at much lower velocities. By deliberately roughening the ball on one side (which is not allowed) and polishing it on the other (which is allowed) they can bowl reverse swing at much lower velocities. This caused a major row in cricket in the early 1990s when a bowler was accused of deliberately roughening the ball. But some bowlers can achieve very high bowling speeds and produce reverse swing without resorting to such tactics. It is of course allowed for the ball to scuff or become rough naturally through play but this can take some time.

Causing a ball to spin at the same time as propelling it forward can also add to the complexities of air flow and also to the excitement of ball sports. Perhaps the most famous ball swing in recent years resulted in the goal scored by the Brazilian footballer, Roberto Carlos, in 1997. The goal area was completely blocked by the opposing team players. He seemed to aim the ball towards the corner flag but the ball followed a curved path around the players and into the goal. He achieved this amazing feat by striking the ball on its edge, causing it to spin in an anticlockwise direction which induced a sideways force. This, together with the boundary layer effect and a great deal of skill (and a little luck), produced one of the best goals ever scored.

## 3.13 Some examples to test your understanding

1. To measure the discharge in a pipe a 10 litre bucket is used to catch the flow at its outlet. If it takes 3.5s to fill the bucket, calculate the discharge in $m^3/s$. Calculate the velocity in the pipe when the diameter is 100mm.
2. A main pipeline 300mm in diameter is carrying a discharge of $0.16m^3/s$ and a smaller pipe of diameter 100mm, which takes $0.04m^3/s$, is joined to it to form a T junction. Calculate the velocity in the 100mm pipe and the discharge and velocity in the main pipe downstream of the junction.
3. A fountain is to be designed for a local park. A nozzle diameter of 50mm is chosen and the water velocity at the nozzle will be 8.5m/s. Calculate the height to which the water will rise. The jet passes through a circular opening 2m above the nozzle. Calculate the diameter of the opening so that the jet just passes through without interference.
4. A pipeline of 500mm diameter carrying a discharge of $0.5m^3/s$ at a pressure of $55kN/m^2$ reduces to 300mm diameter. Calculate the velocity and pressure in the 300mm pipe.

Chapter 4

# Pipes

## 4.1 Introduction

Both pipes and channels are used to carry water. They are clearly different in appearance but they are also very different in how they behave hydraulically. Pipes are completely enclosed, circular in section and usually flow full of water. In contrast, channels are open to the atmosphere and can have many different shapes and sizes. Pipes can also flow uphill and downhill but open channels can only flow downhill under the influence of gravity. But pipes do sometimes flow only partly full though this is not so common. An example is when they are used for gravity flow sewers which take sewage from houses and factories into the main sewerage system. The flow in such cases only partly fills the pipes and so hydraulically they behave like open channels and not pipes. The reason pipes are used for this purpose is that sewers are usually buried below ground to avoid public health problems. It would be difficult to bury an open channel!

## 4.2 A typical pipe flow problem

A typical pipe flow problem might involve supplying water to a town from a storage reservoir (Figure 4.1). A pipeline connects the reservoir to a smaller storage tank just outside the town, which then supplies the individual houses. The discharge ($Q$ m$^3$/s) required is determined by the water demand of the users and the number of houses being supplied with water. The design problem is to select the right size of pipe to use to ensure that sufficient discharge is supplied to the storage tank.

As this is dealing with a real fluid there is significant friction and so the choice of pipe size depends on the energy available in the system to overcome the friction in the pipe as water flows from the main storage reservoir (point 1) to the town storage tank (point 2). Water always flows from a place where the energy is high to

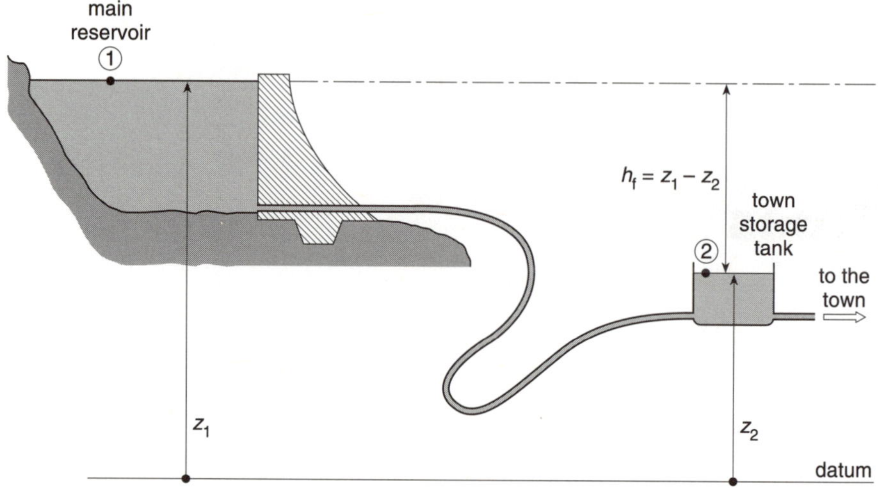


**Figure 4.1 A typical pipe flow problem**

one where the energy is low and so the energy equation can be very helpful in solving this problem.

The initial energy in the system is determined by the water level in the main reservoir at 1 and the final energy is determined by the water level in the tank at 2. Writing the energy equation for these two points including the energy loss term, which cannot be ignored in a real pipeline because of the friction losses:

$$\frac{p_1}{\rho g} + \frac{v_1^2}{2g} + z_1 = \frac{p_2}{\rho g} + \frac{v_2^2}{2g} + z_2 + h_f$$

Points 1 and 2 have been chosen with care so that the equation can be simplified. For point 1, $p_1$ is the pressure at the reservoir water surface. The pressure here is atmospheric and, as all the pressures are gauge pressures, this has a value of zero. For point 2, $p_2$ is also at the water surface and is also zero. The water velocities $v_1$ and $v_2$ in the two tanks are very small and so the kinetic energy terms are also very small and can be assumed to be zero. This leaves just the potential energy terms $z_1$ and $z_2$ and the energy loss term $h_f$ so the equation simplifies down to:

$$h_f = z_1 - z_2$$

Here $z_1 - z_2$ is the difference in water levels between the reservoir and the storage tank and this represents the energy available, and $h_f$ is the energy loss due to friction between the flowing water and the pipe. So there is a balance between the energy available and the energy that is lost through friction. The next step is to find a formula to link $h_f$ with the pipe so that the pipe size can be determined. Much of the research work on pipe flow over the past 150 years has concentrated on finding such a formula.

## 4.3 A formula for pipe friction

Some of the early research work on pipe friction was done by Osborne Reynolds (1842–1912), a mathematician and engineer working at the University in Manchester in the UK. He measured the pressure loss in pipes of different lengths and diameters at different discharges with some interesting results. At low flows he found that the energy loss varied directly with the velocity. So when the velocity was doubled the energy loss also doubled. But at high flows the energy loss varied as the square of the velocity. So when the velocity was doubled the energy loss increased four-fold. Clearly, Reynolds was observing two quite different types of flow. This thinking led to Reynolds' classic experiment that established the difference between what are now referred to as **laminar** and **turbulent** flow and formulae that would enable the energy loss to be calculated for each flow type from a knowledge of the pipes themselves.

### 4.3.1 Laminar and turbulent flow

Reynolds' experiment involved setting up a glass tube through which he could pass water at different velocities (Figure 4.2). A thin jet of coloured dye was injected into the flow so that the flow patterns were visible.

When the water was moving slowly the dye remained in a thin line as it followed the flow path of the water down the pipe. This was described as **laminar flow**. It was as though the water was moving as a series of very thin layers – like a pack of cards – each one sliding over the other, and the dye had been injected between two of the layers. This type of flow rarely exists in nature and so is not of great practical concern in hydraulics. However, it can be observed occasionally under very special conditions. Examples include smoke rising in a thin column from a chimney on a very still day or a slow flow of water from a tap that looks so much like a glass rod that you feel you could get hold of it. Blood flow in our bodies is usually laminar.

The second and more common type of flow he identified was **turbulent flow**. This occurred when water was moving faster. The dye was broken up as the water whirled around in a random manner and was dissipated throughout the flow. Turbulence was a word introduced by Lord Kelvin (1824–1907) to describe this kind of flow behaviour.

There are very clear visual differences between laminar and turbulent flow but what was not clear was how to predict which one would occur in any given set of circumstances. Velocity was obviously important. As velocity increased so the flow would change from laminar to turbulent flow. But it was obvious from the experiments that velocity was not the only factor. It was Reynolds who first suggested that the type of flow depended not just on velocity ($v$) but also on mass density ($\rho$), viscosity ($\mu$) and pipe diameter ($d$). He put these factors together in a way that is now called the **Reynolds number** in recognition of his work:

$$\text{Reynolds number} = R = \frac{\rho v d}{\mu}$$

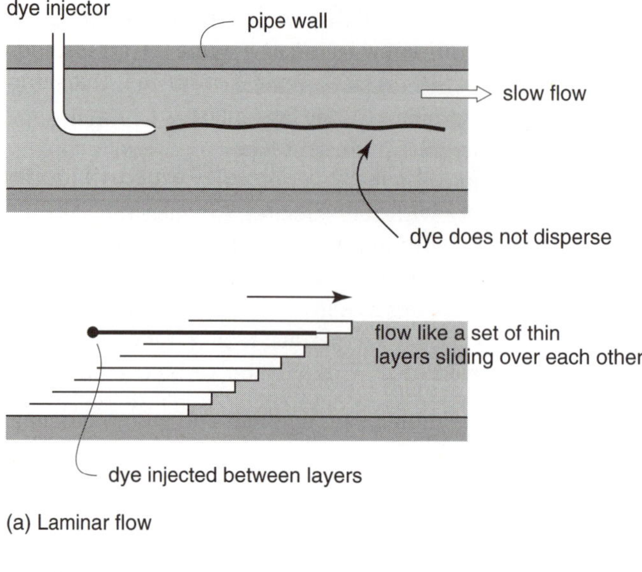


(a) Laminar flow

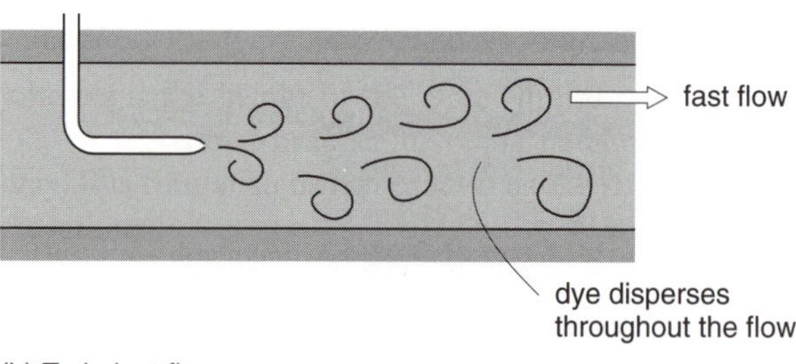


(b) Turbulent flow

**Figure 4.2 Laminar and turbulent flow**

Note that the Reynolds number $R$ has no dimensions. All the dimensions cancel out. Reynolds found that he could use this number to predict reliably when laminar and turbulent flow would occur:

$R < 2000$ flow would always be laminar

$R > 4000$ flow would always be turbulent

Between $R = 2000$ and 4000 he observed a very unstable zone as the flow seemed to jump from laminar to turbulent and back again as if the flow could not decide which of the two conditions it preferred. This is a zone to avoid as both the pressure and flow fluctuate widely in an uncontrolled manner.

The Reynolds number also shows just how important is viscosity in pipe flow. Low Reynolds number ($R < 2000$) means that viscosity ($\mu$) is large compared with the term $\rho v d$. So viscosity is important in laminar flow and cannot be ignored. High Reynolds number ($R > 4000$) means that viscosity is small compared with the $\rho v d$ term and so it follows that viscosity is less important in turbulent flow. This is the reason why engineers ignore the viscosity of water when designing pipes and channels as it has no material effect on the solution. Ignoring viscosity also greatly simplifies pipeline design.

It has since been found that the Reynolds number is very useful in other ways besides telling us the difference between laminar and turbulent flow. It is used extensively in hydraulic modelling (physical models – not mathematical models) for solving complex hydraulic problems. When a problem cannot be solved using some formula, another approach is to construct a small-scale model in a laboratory and test it to see how it performs. The guideline for modelling pipe systems (or indeed any fully enclosed system) is to ensure that the Reynolds number in the model is similar to the Reynolds number in the real situation. This ensures that the forces and velocities are similar so that the model, as near as possible, produces similar results to those in the real pipe systems.

Although it is useful to know that laminar flow exists it is not important in practical hydraulics for designing pipes and channels and so only turbulent flow is considered in this book. Turbulent flow is very important to us in our daily lives. Indeed it would be difficult for us to live if it were not for the mixing that takes place in turbulent flow which dilutes fluids. When we breathe out, the carbon dioxide from our lungs is dissipated into the surrounding air through turbulent mixing. If it did not disperse in this way we would have to move our heads to avoid breathing in the same gases that we had just breathed out. Car exhaust fumes are dispersed in a similar way, otherwise we could be quickly poisoned by the intake of concentrated carbon monoxide.

### 4.3.2 A design formula

Several formulae have been developed to link energy loss with the pipe for turbulent flow but one of the most commonly used today is that devised by Julius Weisbach (1806–1871) and Henry Darcy (1803–1858). It is now referred to as the **Darcy–Weisbach equation:**

$$h_f = \frac{\lambda l v^2}{2gd}$$

where $\lambda$ is a friction factor, $l$ is pipe length (m), $v$ is velocity (m/s), $g$ is gravity constant (9.81m/s$^2$) and $d$ is pipe diameter (m). This formula shows that energy loss depends on pipe length, velocity and diameter but also on the friction between the pipe and the flow as represented by $\lambda$.

- *Length* has a direct influence on energy loss. The longer the pipeline the greater the energy loss.
- *Velocity* has a great influence on energy loss because it is the square of the velocity that counts. When the velocity is doubled (say by increasing the discharge), the energy loss increases four-fold. It is usual practice in water

supply systems to keep the velocity below 1.6m/s. This is done primarily to avoid excessive energy losses but it also helps to reduce water hammer problems (see section 4.11).

- *Pipe diameter* has the most dramatic effect on energy loss. As the pipe diameter is reduced so the energy losses increase, not only because of the direct effect of $d$ in the formula but also because of its effect on the velocity $v$ (remember the discharge equation $Q = va$). The overall effect of reducing the diameter by half (say from 300mm to 150mm) is to increase $h_f$ by 32 times. See box for an illustration of this.
- *Pipe friction* $\lambda$ unfortunately is not just a simple measure of pipe roughness; it depends on several other factors which are discussed more fully in the next section.

Note that care is needed when using the Darcy–Weisbach formula as some textbooks, particularly American, use $f$ as the friction factor and not $\lambda$. They do not have the same value. The link between them is $\lambda = 4f$.

## Example: Effects of pipe diameter in energy loss

A pipeline 1000m long carries a flow of 100 litre/s. Calculate the energy loss when the pipe diameter is 0.3m, 0.25m, 0.2m and 0.15m and $\lambda = 0.04$.

The first step is to calculate the velocities for each pipe diameter using the discharge equation

$$Q = va$$

and so

$$v = \frac{Q}{a}$$

Use this equation to calculate velocity $v$ for each diameter and then use the Darcy–Weisbach equation to calculate $h_f$. The results are shown in Table 4.1.

Notice the very large rise in head loss as the pipe diameter is reduced. Clearly the choice of pipe diameter is a critical issue in any pipeline system.

**Table 4.1 Effect on head loss of changing pipe diameter**

| *Diameter (m)* | *Pipe area (m²)* | *Velocity (m/s)* | *Head loss $h_f$ (m)* |
|---|---|---|---|
| 0.30 | 0.07 | 1.43 | 13.6 |
| 0.25 | 0.049 | 2.04 | 33.3 |
| 0.20 | 0.031 | 3.22 | 103.7 |
| 0.15 | 0.018 | 5.55 | 418.6 |

## 4.4 The λ story

It would be convenient if $\lambda$ was just a constant number for a given pipe which depended only on its roughness and hence its resistance to the flow. But few things are so simple and $\lambda$ is no exception.

Some of the earliest work on pipe friction was done by Paul Blazius in 1913. He carried out a wide range of experiments on different pipes and different flows and came to the conclusion that $\lambda$ depended only on the Reynolds number and, surprisingly, the roughness of the pipe seemed to have no effect at all on friction. From this he developed a formula for $\lambda$:

$$\lambda = \frac{0.316}{R^{0.25}}$$

Another investigator was Johann Nikuradse who may well have been puzzled by the Blazius results. He set up a series of laboratory experiments in the 1930s with different pipe sizes and flows and he roughened the inside of the pipes with sand grains of a known size in order to create different but known roughness. His data showed that values of $\lambda$ were independent of Reynolds number and depended only on the roughness of the pipe.

Clearly, either someone was wrong – or they were both right but each was looking at something different.

### 4.4.1 Smooth and rough pipes

It is now known that both investigators were right but they were looking at different aspects of the same problem. Blazius was looking at flows with relatively low Reynolds numbers (4000 to 100 000) and his results refer to what are now called **smooth pipes**. Nikuradse's experiments dealt with high Reynolds number flows (greater than 100 000) and his results refer to what are now called **rough pipes**. The results of both Blazius and Nikuradse are shown graphically in Figure 4.3a. This is a graph with a special logarithmic scale for Reynolds number so that a wide range of values can be shown on the same graph. It shows how $\lambda$ varies with both Reynolds number and pipe roughness which is expressed as the height of the sand grains ($k$) divided by the pipe diameter ($d$). The Blazius formula produces a single line on this graph and it is almost a straight line.

The terms 'rough' and 'smooth' refer as much to the flow conditions in pipes as to the pipes themselves and so paradoxically it is possible for the same pipe to be described as both rough and smooth. Roughness and smoothness are also relative terms. How the inside of a pipe feels to the touch is not a good guide to its smoothness in hydraulic terms. Pipes that are smooth to the touch can still be quite rough hydraulically. However, a pipe that feels rough to touch will be very rough hydraulically and very high energy losses can be expected.

As there are two distinct types of flow then there must be some point or zone where the flow changes from one to the other. This is indeed the case. It is not a specific point but a zone known as the **transition zone** when $\lambda$ depends on both Reynolds number and pipe roughness (Figure 4.3a). This zone was successfully investigated by C.F. Colebrook and C.M. White working at Imperial College in London in the 1930s and they developed a formula to cover this flow range. This is not quoted here but it is used to develop the design chart for pipes shown later in this chapter in Figure 4.7.

The transition zone between smooth and rough pipe flow should *not* be confused with the transition zone from laminar to turbulent flow, as is often done.

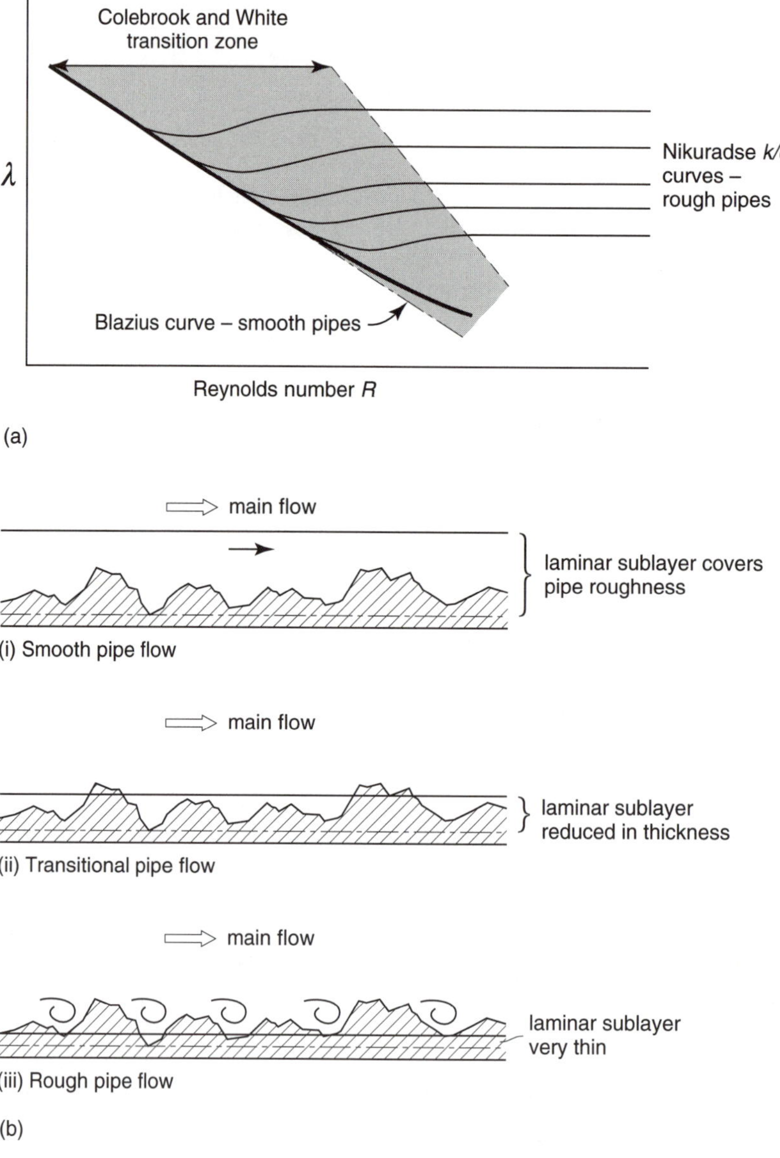


**Figure 4.3** The $\lambda$ story

The flow is fully turbulent for all smooth and rough pipes and the transition is from smooth to rough pipe flow.

To summarise the different flows in pipes:

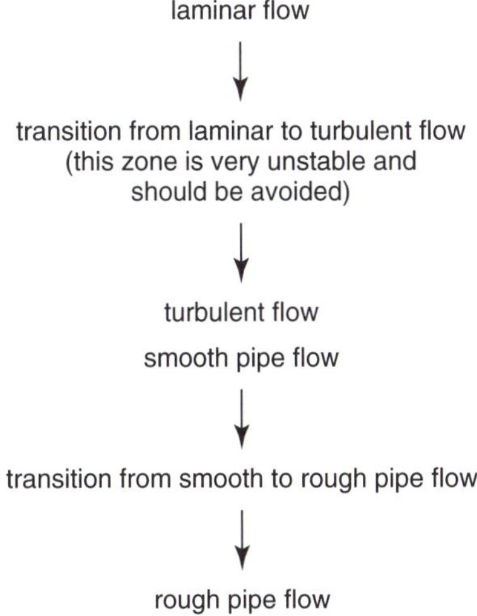


### 4.4.2 An explanation

Since those early experiments, modern scientific techniques have enabled investigators to look more closely at what happens close to a pipe wall. This has resulted in a physical explanation for smooth and rough pipe flow (Figure 4.3b). Investigators have found that even when the flow is turbulent there exists a very thin layer of fluid – less than 1mm thick – close to the boundary that is laminar. This is called the **laminar sublayer.** At low Reynolds numbers the laminar sublayer is at its thickest and completely covers the roughness of the pipe. The main flow is unaffected by the boundary roughness and is influenced mainly by viscosity in the laminar sublayer. It seems that the layer covers the roughness like a blanket and protects the flow from the pipe wall. This is the **smooth pipe flow** that Blazius investigated. As Reynolds number increases, the laminar sublayer becomes thinner and roughness elements start to protrude into the main flow. The flow is now influenced both by viscosity and pipe roughness. This is the **transition zone**. As Reynolds number is further increased the sublayer all but disappears and the roughness of the pipe wall takes over and dominates the friction. This is the **rough pipe flow** that Nikuradse investigated.

Commercially manufactured pipes are not artificially roughened with sand like experimental pipes, rather they are manufactured as smooth as possible to reduce energy losses. For this reason they tend to come within the transition zone where $\lambda$ varies with both Reynolds number and pipe roughness.

In practice, pipe manufacturers usually provide values of $\lambda$ for their products and so there is usually no need to use the graph in Figure 4.3. Often manufacturers go further than this to simplify pipe selection and present energy loss formulae in the form of graphs or nomographs. Figure 4.7 is an example of this.

## 4.5 Hydraulic gradient

One way of showing energy losses in a pipeline is to use a diagram (Figure 4.4a). The total energy is shown as a line drawn along the pipe length and marked e—e—e. This line always slopes downwards in the direction of the flow to show that energy is continually being lost through friction. It connects the water surfaces in the two tanks. Note that it is not necessarily parallel to the line of the pipe. This usually just follows the natural ground surface profile.

Although total energy is of interest, pressure is more important because this determines how strong the pipes must be to avoid bursts. For this reason a second line is drawn below the energy line, but parallel to it, to represent the pressure (pressure energy) and is marked h—h—h. This shows the pressure change along the pipeline. Imagine that a standpipe is attached to the pipe. Water would rise up to this line to represent the pressure head (Figure 4.4a). The difference between the two lines is the kinetic energy. Notice how both the energy line and the hydraulic gradient are straight lines. This shows that the rate of energy loss and the pressure loss are uniform (at the same rate). The slope of the pressure line is called the **hydraulic gradient**. It is calculated as follows:

$$\text{hydraulic gradient} = \frac{h_f}{l}$$

where $h_f$ is change in pressure (m) and $l$ is the pipe length over which the pressure change takes place (m).

The hydraulic gradient has no dimensions as it comes from dividing a head difference in metres by a length in metres. However, it is often expressed in terms of metres head per metre length of pipeline. As an example a hydraulic gradient of 0.02 means for every one metre of pipeline there will be a pressure loss of 0.02m. This may also be written as 0.02m/m or as 2m/100m of pipeline. This reduces the number of decimal places that must be dealt with and means that for every 100m of pipeline 2m of head is lost through friction. So if a pipeline is 500m long (there are five 100m lengths) the pressure loss over 500m will be $5 \times 2 = 10$m head.

The hydraulic gradient is not a fixed line for a pipe; it depends on the flow (Figure 4.4b). When there is no flow the gradient is horizontal but when there is full flow the gradient is at its maximum. Adjusting the outlet valve will produce a range of gradients between these two extremes.

The energy gradient can only slope downwards in the direction of flow to show how energy is lost, but the hydraulic gradient can slope upwards as well as downwards. An example of this is a pipe junction when water flows from a smaller pipe into a larger one (Figure 4.4c). As water enters the larger pipe the velocity reduces and so does the kinetic energy. Although there is some energy loss when the flow expands (this causes the energy line to drop suddenly) most of the loss of kinetic energy is recovered as pressure energy and so the pressure rises slightly.

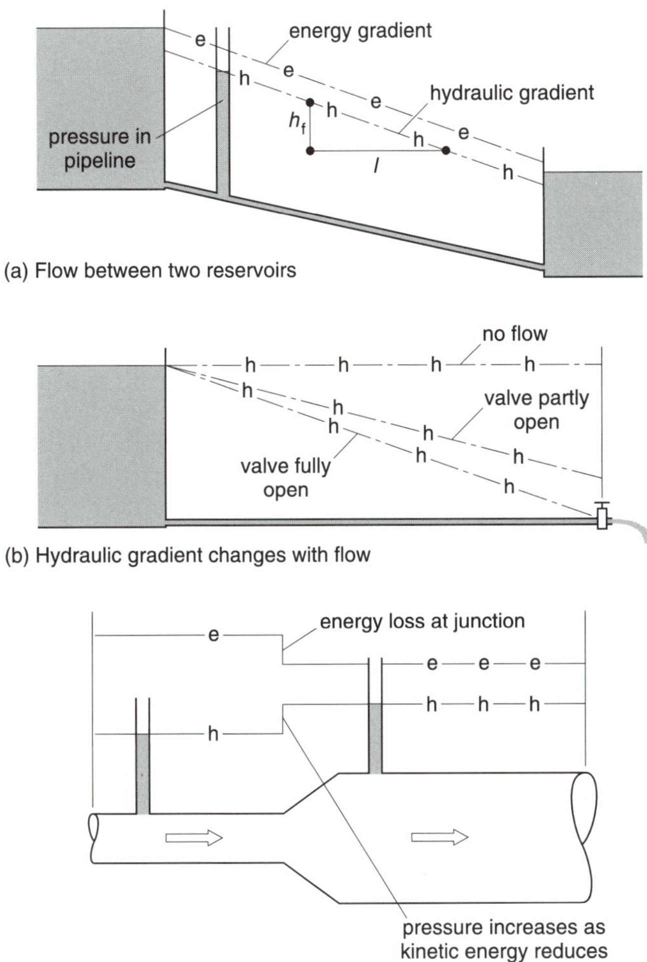


**Figure 4.4** Hydraulic gradient

Two more points of detail about the energy and hydraulic gradients must be considered (Figure 4.4a). At the first reservoir the energy gradient starts at the water surface but the hydraulic gradient starts just below it. This is because the kinetic energy increases as water enters the pipe and so there is a corresponding drop in the pressure energy. As the flow enters the second reservoir the energy line is just above the water surface. This is because there is a small loss in energy as the flow expands from the pipe into the reservoir. The hydraulic gradient is located just below the water level because there is still some kinetic energy in the flow. When it enters the reservoir this changes back to pressure energy. The downstream water level represents the final energy condition in the system.

Normally pipelines are located well below the hydraulic gradient. This means that the pressure in the pipe is always positive – see the standpipe in Figure 4.4a. Even though it may rise and fall as it follows the natural ground profile, water will flow as long as it is always below the hydraulic gradient and provided the outlet is below the inlet. There are limits to how far below the hydraulic gradient a pipeline can be located. The further below the higher will be the pressure in the pipe and so there is a risk that the pressure may exceed the limits set by the pipe manufacturer.

## 4.6 Energy loss at pipe fittings

Although there is an energy loss at the pipe connection with the reservoir in Figure 4.4a this is usually very small in comparison with the loss in the main pipeline and so it is often ignored. Similar losses occur at pipe bends, reducers, pipe junctions and valves, and although each one is small, together they can add up. Normal practice is simply to increase the energy loss in the main pipeline by 10% to allow for all these minor losses rather than try to calculate each one individually.

## 4.7 Siphons

Siphons occur when a pipeline rises above the hydraulic gradient. Normally pipes are located well below the hydraulic gradient. This ensures that the pressure in a pipeline is always positive and so well above atmospheric pressure. So water flows freely under gravity provided the outlet is lower than the inlet (Figure 4.4a). But when part of a pipeline is located above the hydraulic gradient, even though the outlet is located below the inlet, water will not flow without some help (Figure 4.5a). This is because the pressure in the section of pipe above the hydraulic gradient is negative.

### 4.7.1 How they work

Before water will flow, all the air must be taken out of the pipe to create a vacuum. When this happens atmospheric pressure on the open water surface pushes water into the pipe to fill the vacuum and once it is full of water it will begin to flow. Under these conditions the pipe is working as a **siphon**. Taking the air out of a pipeline is known as **priming**. Sometimes a pump is needed to extract the air but if the pipeline can be temporarily brought below the hydraulic gradient the resulting positive pressure will push the air out and it will prime itself. This can be done by closing the main valve at the end of the pipeline so that the hydraulic gradient rises to a horizontal line at the same level as the reservoir surface. An air valve on top of the siphon then releases the air. Once the pipe is full of water, the main valve can then be opened and the pipeline flows normally.

Note that an air valve can be a simple gate valve which is opened manually to release air and then closed to stop air from re-entering the pipe. There are also automatic valves that release trapped air. This can accumulate in normal pipelines running under positive pressures as well as in siphons. In such cases it is good

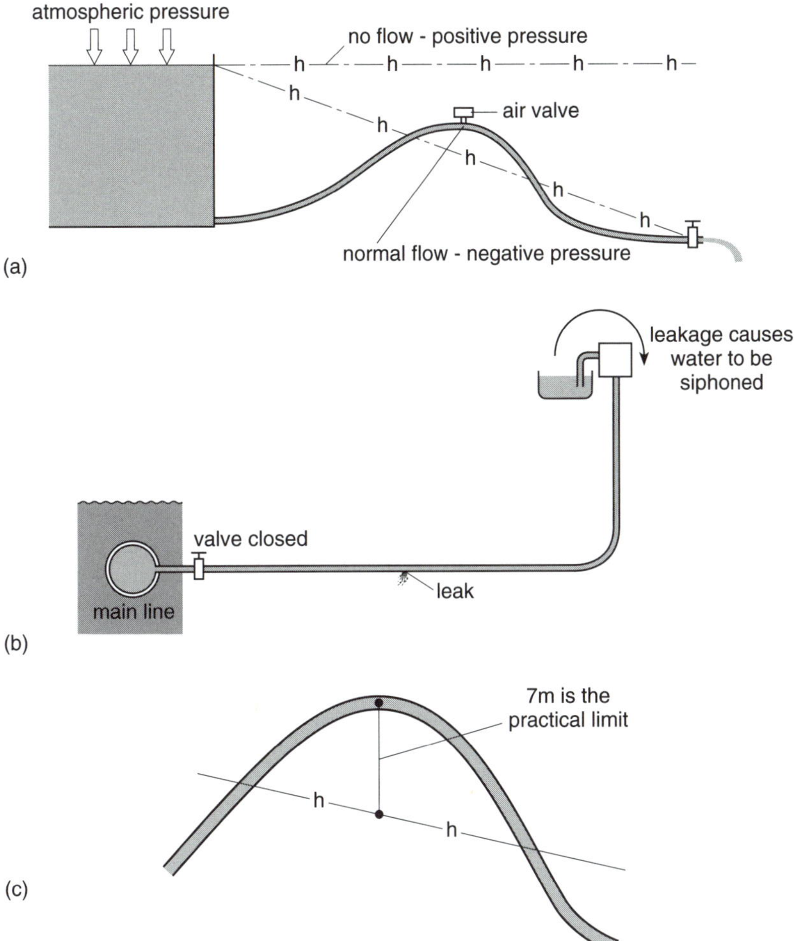


**Figure 4.5** Siphons

practice to include an air valve whenever there is a high spot as this is where the air normally accumulates.

A simple and very practical use of siphons is for getting petrol out of a car's fuel tank. By putting a flexible tube into the tank and sucking out all the air from the tube (making sure not to get a mouthful of petrol) the fuel begins to flow. Note that the outlet from the tube must be lower than the liquid level in the tank otherwise the siphon will not work.

Another very practical use for siphons is in leakage detection in domestic water mains (sometimes called rising mains) from the supply outside in the street to a house (Figure 4.5b). This can be important for those on a water meter who pay high prices for their water. A leaky pipe in this situation would be very costly. A pan full of water is used to seal the tap inside the house and the main valve to the house is closed. The house tap is then turned on. If there is any leakage in the main pipe then water will be siphoned back out of the pan into the main. The rate of flow will indicate the extent of the leakage.

Siphons can be very useful in situations where the land topography is undulating between a reservoir and the water users. It is always preferable to locate a pipe below the hydraulic gradient by putting it in a deep trench but this may not always be practicable. But in situations where siphoning is unavoidable there is a limit of approximately 7m to the height that water can be siphoned (Figure 4.5c) and this is set by atmospheric pressure. Remember atmospheric pressure drives a siphon and this is limited to 10m head of water. So 7m is a safe practical limit. When pipelines are located in mountainous regions then the limit needs to be lower than this due to the reduced atmospheric pressure.

The pressure inside a working siphon is less than atmospheric pressure and so it is negative when it is referred to as a gauge pressure (measured above or below atmospheric pressure as the datum) e.g. −7m head. Sometimes such pressures are quoted as absolute pressures (measured above vacuum pressure as the datum). So −7m gauge pressure is the same as +3m absolute pressure. This is calculated as follows:

$$\text{gauge pressure} = -7\text{m head}$$

$$\begin{aligned}\text{absolute pressure} &= \text{atmospheric pressure} + \text{gauge pressure}\\ &= 10 - 7\\ &= 3\text{m head absolute}\end{aligned}$$

## 4.8 Selecting pipes in practice

The development of $\lambda$ is an interesting story but for all practical purposes once a pipe manufacturer has supplied the values it is just a matter of using them in the Darcy–Weisbach formula to determine an appropriate pipe size to carry a given discharge or alternatively determining the discharge for a given pipe size. Two examples of the use of the Darcy–Weisbach formula are shown in the boxes.

### Example: Calculating pipe diameter using the Darcy–Weisbach equation

A 2.5km long pipeline connects a reservoir to a smaller storage tank outside a town which then supplies water to individual houses (Figure 4.6a). Determine the pipe diameter when the discharge required between the reservoir and the tank is $0.35\text{m}^3/\text{s}$ and the difference in their water levels is 30m. Assume the value of $\lambda$ is 0.03.

This problem can be solved using the energy equation. The first step is to write down the equation for two points in the system. Point 1 is at the water surface of the main reservoir and point 2 is at the surface of the tank. Friction losses are important in this example and so these must also be included

$$\frac{p_1}{\rho g}+\frac{v_1^2}{2g}+z_1=\frac{p_2}{\rho g}+\frac{v_2^2}{2g}+z_2+h_f$$

This equation can be greatly simplified because $p_1$ and $p_2$ are both at atmospheric pressure and are zero. The water velocities $v_1$ and $v_2$ in the two tanks are very small and so the kinetic energy terms are also very small and can be assumed to be zero. This leaves just the potential energy terms $z_1$ and $z_2$ and the energy loss term $h_f$ so the equation simplifies to:

$$h_f = z_1 - z_2$$

Using the Darcy–Weisbach formula for $h_f$:

$$h_f = \frac{\lambda l v^2}{2gd}$$

and so

$$\frac{\lambda l v^2}{2gd} = z_1 - z_2$$

Diameter *d* is unknown but so is the velocity in the pipe. So first calculate velocity $v$ using the continuity equation:

$$Q = v\mathrm{a}$$

$$v = \frac{Q}{a}$$

Calculate area *a*:

$$a = \frac{\pi d^2}{4}$$

and use this value to calculate

$$v = \frac{4Q}{\pi d^2} = \frac{4 \times 0.35}{3.14 \times d^2} = \frac{0.446}{d^2}$$

Note that as *d* is not known it is not yet possible to calculate a value for $v$ and so this must remain as an algebraic expression for the moment. Putting all the known values into the Darcy–Weisbach formula:

$$\frac{0.03 \times 2500 \times 0.198}{2 \times 9.81 \times d \times d^4} = 30$$

Rearranging this to calculate $d$:

$$d^5 = \frac{0.03 \times 2500 \times 0.198}{2 \times 9.81 \times 30} = 0.025$$

Calculating the fifth root of 0.025 to find $d$:

$$d = 0.47\text{m} = 470\text{mm}$$

The nearest pipe size to this would be **500mm**. So this is the size of pipe needed to carry this flow between the reservoir and the tank.

This may seem rather involved mathematically but another, and perhaps simpler, way of approaching the problem is to guess the size of pipe and then put this into the equation and see if it gives the right value of discharge. This is the way most engineers approach the problem as it allows them to put in available pipe sizes. The outcome will show if the chosen size was too small or too large. A second or third guess will usually produce the right answer.

A final, and perhaps the easiest, way of all is to use pipe design charts. These are discussed in section 4.8.1. Try using this approach to see if you get the same answer.

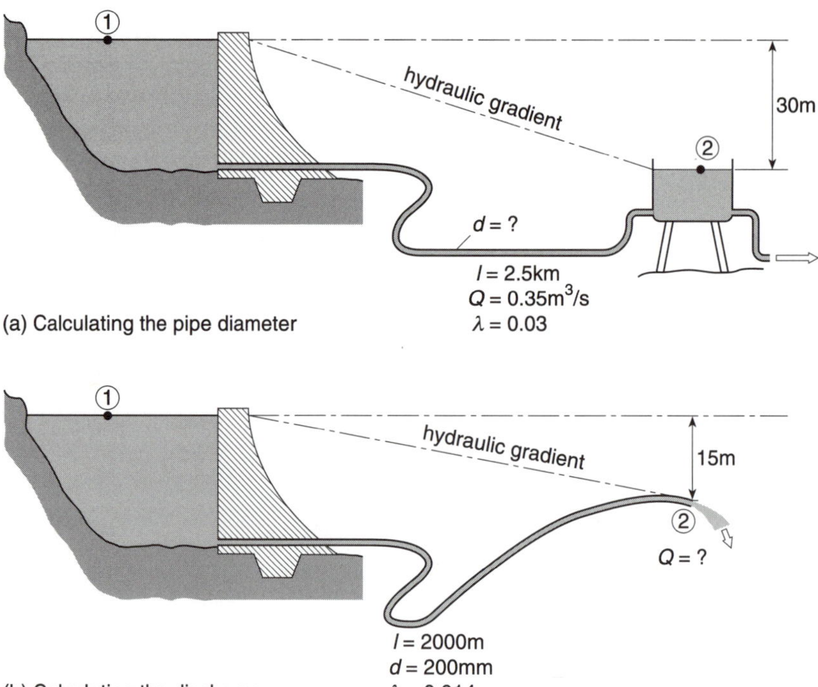


**Figure 4.6 Calculating discharge**

## Example: Calculating discharge from a pipeline

A 200mm diameter pipeline 2000m long is connected to a reservoir and its outlet is 15m below the reservoir water level and discharges freely into the atmosphere. Calculate the discharge from the pipe when the friction factor $\lambda$ is 0.014 (Figure 4.6b).

To solve this problem use the energy equation between point 1 at the surface of the reservoir and point 2 just inside the water jet emerging from the pipe outlet.

$$\frac{p_1}{\rho g} + \frac{v_1^2}{2g} + z_1 = \frac{p_2}{\rho g} + \frac{v_2^2}{2g} + z_2 + h_f$$

This equation can be greatly simplified because $p_1$ is at atmospheric pressure and so is zero and $p_2$ is very near atmospheric pressure because the position of 2 is in the jet as it emerges from the pipe into the atmosphere. If it was not at atmospheric pressure then the jet would flow laterally under the pressure. It does not do this and so the pressure must be the same as the atmosphere. Therefore $p_2$ is zero. The water velocity $v_1$ is zero in the reservoir and $v_2$ at the outlet is very small in comparison with the potential energy of 30m and so this can be assumed to be zero also. This leaves just the potential energy terms $z_1$ and $z_2$ and the energy loss term $h_f$ so the equation simplifies to:

$$z_1 - z_2 = \frac{\lambda l v^2}{2gd}$$

Put in the known values to calculate velocity $v$:

$$15 = \frac{0.014 \times 2000 \times v^2}{2 \times 9.81 \times 0.2}$$

$$v^2 = \frac{15 \times 2 \times 9.81 \times 0.2}{0.014 \times 2000} = 2.1$$

$$v = 1.45\text{m/s}$$

Using the continuity equation to calculate discharge:

$$Q = va$$

Calculate area $a$:

$$a = \frac{\pi d^2}{4} = \frac{\pi 0.2^2}{4} = 0.031\text{m}^2$$

$$Q = 1.45 \times 0.031 = 0.045\text{m}^3/\text{s or 45 litre/s}$$

Pipe selection is, in fact, made easier than this because many manufacturers provide design charts which link energy losses directly with pipe sizes and discharges (and not just velocity as the Darcy–Weisbach formula does).

When information is not available from manufacturers there are many other sources. An excellent and widely used source is *Charts for the Hydraulic Design of Channels and Pipes* (Hydraulics Research, 1983). This is a book of design charts based on the Colebrook–White equation. The equation best describes the transitional flow between smooth and rough pipe flow referred to in section 4.4.1, which covers all commercially available pipes. An example of one of these charts is shown in Figure 4.7. It does not use $\lambda$ values but expresses friction as the height of the roughness on the inside of a pipe. So for this chart, surface roughness is $k = 0.03$mm, which is a typical value for UPVC and asbestos cement pipes. The chart's range of flows is considerable: from less than 0.1 litre/s to 20 000 litre/s (or 20m$^3$/s) with pipe diameters from 0.025m to 2.5m. This is more than enough for any designer.

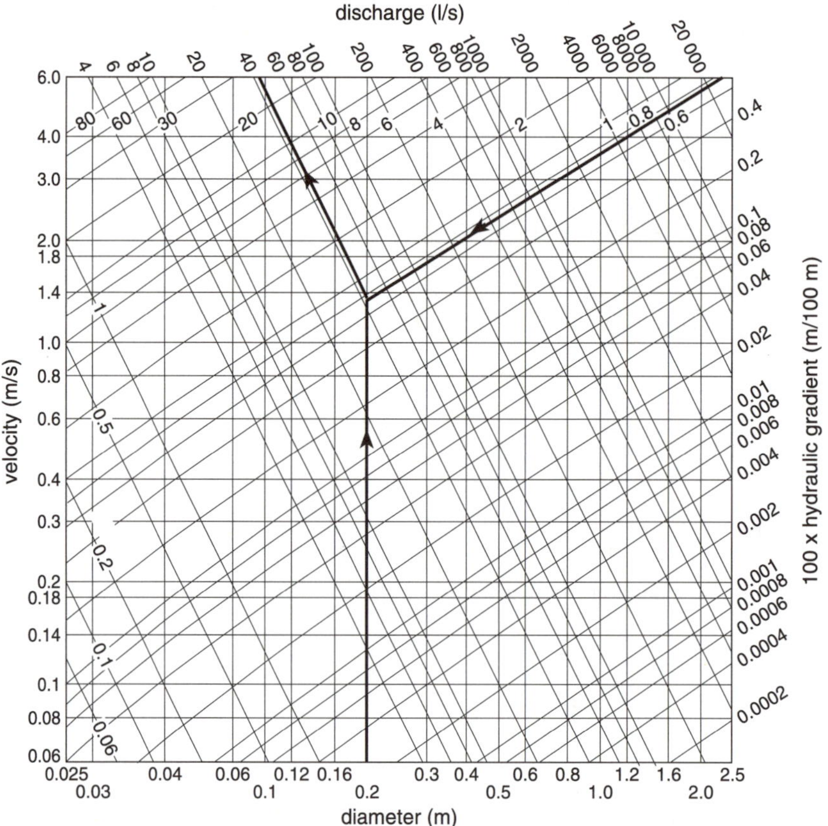


**Figure 4.7** Typical pipe design chart (redrawn with permission of HR Wallingford Ltd)

### 4.8.1 Using hydraulic design charts

The example in the box shows how a hydraulic design chart (Figure 4.7) is used, but for practice try to solve earlier examples using the chart.

#### Example: Calculating discharge from a pipeline using a design chart

Using the same example as for the Darcy–Weisbach equation, a 200mm diameter pipeline 2000m long is connected to a reservoir and the outlet is 15m below the reservoir water level (Figure 4.6b). Calculate the discharge from the pipe when the pipe roughness value $k$ is 0.03mm.

The design chart uses the hydraulic gradient to show the rate of head loss in a pipeline. So the first step is to calculate the hydraulic gradient from the information given above.

The pipe is 2000m long and the head loss from the reservoir to the pipe outlet is 15m. So

$$\text{hydraulic gradient} = \frac{h}{l}$$

$$= \frac{15}{2000} = 0.0075$$

$$= 0.75\text{m}/100\text{m}$$

Using the chart locate the intersection of the lines for a hydraulic gradient of 0.75m/100m and a diameter of 200mm. This locates the discharge line and the value of the discharge:

$$Q = 0.045 \text{ litre/s}$$

The chart can also be used in reverse to determine the diameter of a pipe and head loss for a given discharge.

There are four important practical points to note from the examples.

The first point refers to the first worked example, which showed how mathematically cumbersome it can be to determine the diameter by calculation. The easier way is to do what most engineers do: they guess the diameter and then check by calculation that their chosen pipe is the right one. This might seem a strange way of approaching a problem but it is quite common in engineering. It always helps to know approximately the answer to a problem before beginning to solve it. An experienced engineer usually knows what answer to expect – the calculation then becomes just a way of confirming this. (This is one of the basic unwritten laws of engineering.) This foresight is important because when a pipe size is calculated there is no point in wondering if the answer is correct. There will not be any answers available to the real problems in the field as there are in this textbook and there may not be anyone around to ask if it is the right answer. You need to know that you have the right answer and this comes largely from experience of similar design problems. New designers are unlikely to have this experience but they have to start somewhere and one way is to rely initially on the experience of others and to learn from them.

The second point to note is that there is no one unique pipe diameter that must be used in any given situation. If, for example, calculations show that a 100mm pipe is sufficient then any pipe larger than this will also carry the flow. The question of which one is the most acceptable is usually determined by several design criteria. One is that the velocity should not exceed 1.6m/s. Another might be a limit on the head that can be lost through friction. A third could be a limit on the pipe sizes available. There are only certain standard sizes that are manufactured and not all these may be readily available in some countries.

The third point to consider is the value for pipe roughness. It is easy to choose the value for a new pipe but how long will this value be maintained. What will the value be in say 10 years from now when the pipe will still be in use? The roughness will undoubtedly increase through general wear and tear. If there have been limescale deposits or algae slime build-up on the inside of the pipe or the pipe has been misused and damaged then the roughness will be significantly greater. So when choosing the most appropriate value for design it is important to think ahead to what the roughness might be later in the life of the pipe. This is where engineering becomes an art and all the engineer's experience is brought to bear in selecting the right roughness value. If it is too low then the pipe may not give good, long service; if it is too high then this will result in the unnecessary expense of having pipes that are too big for the job to be done.

The final point, and often the most important to consider, is cost. Small-diameter pipes are usually cheaper than larger-diameter ones but they require more energy to deliver the discharge because of the greater friction. The trade-off between the two must take account of both capital and operating costs if a realistic comparison is to be made between alternatives.

### 4.8.2 Sizing pipes for future demand

Pipe sizes are often selected using a discharge based on present water demands and little thought is given to how this might change in the future. Also there is always a temptation to select small pipes to satisfy current demand simply because they are less expensive than larger ones. These two factors can lead to trouble in the future. If demand increases and higher discharges are required from the same pipe, the energy losses will rise sharply and so a lot more energy is needed to run the system.

As an example, a 200mm diameter pumped pipeline, 500m long supplies a small town with a discharge of 50 litre/s. Several years later the demand doubles to

100 litre/s. This increases the velocity in the pipe from 1.67 to 3.34m/s (i.e. it doubles) and the energy loss rises from 5m to 20m (i.e. a four-fold increase). This increase in head loss plus the extra flow means that eight times more energy is needed to operate the system and extra pumps may be needed to provide the extra power required. A little extra thought at the planning stage and a little more investment at the beginning could save a lot of extra pumping cost later. The only realistic way to assess the cost of a pipeline is, as mentioned earlier, to consider both the capital and the running costs over the economic life of a scheme, say 10 to 15 years.

## 4.9 Measuring discharge in pipes

Discharges in pipelines can be measured using a **venturi meter** or an **orifice plate** (Figure 4.8). Both devices rely on changing the components of the total energy of flow from which discharge can be calculated (see section 3.5). The venturi meter was developed by an American, Clemens Herschel (1842–1930), who was looking for a way to measure water abstraction from a river by industrialists. Although the principles of this measuring device were well established by Bernoulli it was Herschel who, being troubled by unlicensed and unmeasured abstractions of water by pipelines from a canal by paper mills, developed it into the device used today.

A venturi meter (Figure 4.8a) comprises a short, narrow section of pipe (throat) followed by a gradually expanding tube. This causes the flow velocity to increase (remember continuity) and so the kinetic energy increases also. As the total energy remains the same throughout the system it follows that there must be a corresponding reduction in pressure energy. By measuring this change in pressure using a pressure gauge or a manometer and using the continuity and energy equations, the following formula for discharge in the pipe can be obtained:

$$Q = C_d a_1 \sqrt{\frac{2gH}{m^2 - 1}}$$

where $a_1$ is area of main pipe ($m^2$), $a_2$ is area of venturi throat ($m^2$), $m = a_1/a_2$, $H$ is the head difference between pipe and throat (m), $g$ is gravity constant (9.81m/s$^2$) and $C_d$ is coefficient of discharge.

As with previous formulae, in practice, there are some minor energy losses in a venturi and so a coefficient of discharge $C_d$ is introduced to obtain the true discharge. Care is needed when using this formula. Some textbooks quote the formula in terms of $a_2$ rather than $a_1$ and this changes several of the terms. It is the same formula but it can be confusing. The safest way is to avoid the formula and work directly from the energy and continuity equations. A derivation of the formula and an example of calculating discharge working from energy and continuity are shown in the boxes.

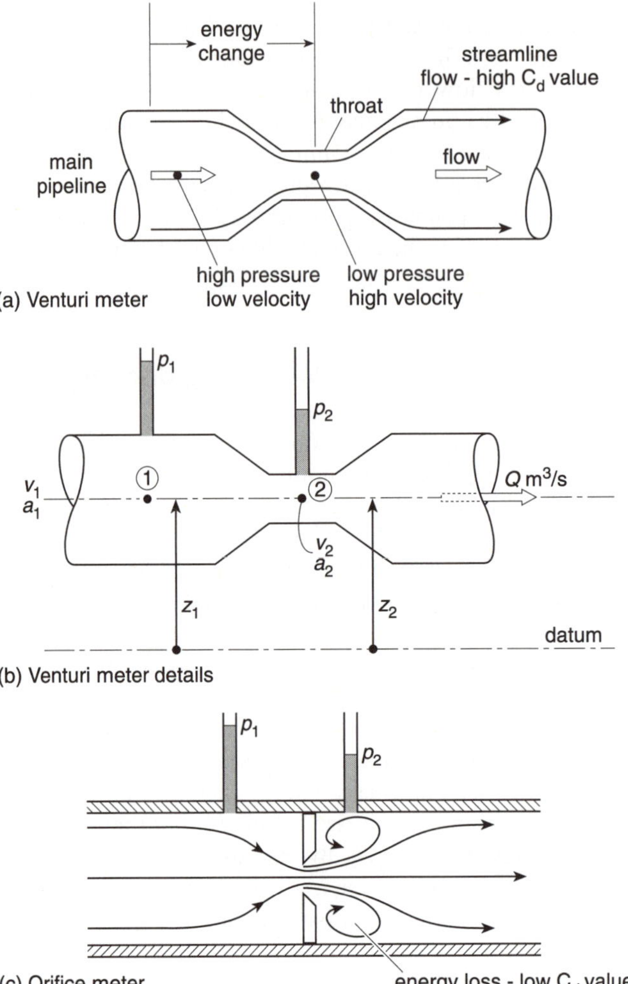


**Figure 4.8 Measuring discharge in pipelines**

## Derivation: Formula for discharge in a venturi meter

First write down the energy equation for the venturi meter. Point 1 is in the main pipe and point 2 is located in the throat of the venturi (Figure 4.8b). It is assumed that there is no energy loss between the two points. So

$$\frac{p_1}{\rho g}+\frac{v_1^2}{2g}+z_1=\frac{p_2}{\rho g}+\frac{v_2^2}{2g}+z_2$$

As the venturi is horizontal

$$z_1=z_2$$

and so

$$\frac{p_1}{\rho g} + \frac{v_1^2}{2g} = \frac{p_2}{\rho g} + \frac{v_2^2}{2g}$$

Now rearranging this equation so that all the pressure terms and all the velocity terms are brought together:

$$\frac{p_1}{\rho g} - \frac{p_2}{\rho g} = \frac{v_2^2}{2g} - \frac{v_1^2}{2g}$$

The left-hand side of this equation is the pressure difference between points 1 and 2 which can be measured using pressure gauges or a differential manometer. This is a manometer with one limb connected to the pipe and the other limb connected to the throat (see section 2.6.4).

At this point it is not possible to calculate the velocities because both $v_1$ and $v_2$ are unknown. A second equation is needed to do this – the continuity equation. Writing the continuity equation for points 1 and 2 in the venturi:

$$a_1 v_1 = a_2 v_2$$

Rearranging this:

$$v_2 = \frac{a_1}{a_2} v_1$$

Now $a_1$ and $a_2$ are the cross-sectional areas of the pipe and venturi respectively and can be calculated from the pipe and venturi throat diameters respectively. Substituting for $v_2$ in the energy equation:

$$\frac{p_1}{\rho g} - \frac{p_2}{\rho g} = \left(\frac{a_1^2}{a_2^2}\right) \frac{v_1^2}{2g} - \frac{v_1^2}{2g}$$

$$\frac{p_1}{\rho g} - \frac{p_2}{\rho g} = \frac{v_1^2}{2g} \left(\frac{a_1^2 - a_2^2}{a_2^2}\right)$$

Putting

$$H = \frac{p_1}{\rho g} - \frac{p_2}{\rho g}$$

where $H$ is the difference in head between the pipe (point 1) and the venturi throat (point 2) and rearranging the equation for $v_1$ gives

$$v_1 = \sqrt{2gH} \left(\frac{a_2}{\sqrt{a_1^2 - a_2^2}}\right)$$

Using the continuity equation to calculate discharge

$$Q = a_1 v_1$$

and so

$$Q = \sqrt{2gH}\left(\frac{a_1 a_2}{\sqrt{a_1^2 - a_2^2}}\right)$$

Put

$$m = \frac{a_1}{a_2}$$

and so

$$Q = a_1\sqrt{\frac{2gH}{m^2 - 1}}$$

Introducing a coefficient of discharge $C_d$:

$$Q = C_d a_1\sqrt{\frac{2gH}{m^2 - 1}}$$

## Example: Calculating discharge using a venturi meter

A 120mm diameter venturi meter is installed in a 250mm diameter pipeline to measure discharge. Calculate the discharge when the pressure difference between the pipe and the venturi throat is 2.5m of head of water and $C_d$ is 0.97 (Figure 4.8b).

Although there is a formula for discharge it can be helpful to work from first principles. Not only does this reinforce the principle but it also avoids possible errors in using a rather involved formula which can easily be misquoted. So this example is worked from the energy and continuity equations.

The first step is to write down the energy equation:

$$\frac{p_1}{\rho g} + \frac{v_1^2}{2g} + z_1 = \frac{p_2}{\rho g} + \frac{v_2^2}{2g} + z_2$$

As the venturi is horizontal

$$z_1 = z_2$$

and so

$$\frac{p_1}{\rho g} + \frac{v_1^2}{2g} = \frac{p_2}{\rho g} + \frac{v_2^2}{2g}$$

Now rearrange this equation so that all the pressure terms and all the velocity terms are brought together:

$$\frac{p_1}{\rho g} - \frac{p_2}{\rho g} = \frac{v_2^2}{2g} - \frac{v_1^2}{2g}$$

But

$$\frac{p_1}{\rho g} - \frac{p_2}{\rho g} = 2.5\text{m}$$

Remember that the pressure terms are in metres head of water and it is the difference that is important and not the individual pressures. So

$$\frac{v_2^2}{2g} - \frac{v_1^2}{2g} = 2.5\text{m}$$

It is not possible to solve this equation directly as both $v_1$ and $v_2$ are unknown. So use continuity to obtain another equation for $v_1$ and $v_2$:

$$a_1 v_1 = a_2 v_2$$

Rearranging this:

$$v_2 = \frac{a_1}{a_2} v_1$$

The next step is to calculate the areas $a_1$ and $a_2$. Area of pipe is

$$a_1 = \frac{\pi d_1^2}{4} = \frac{\pi 0.25^2}{4} = 0.05\text{m}^2$$

Area of venturi is

$$a_2 = \frac{\pi d_2^2}{4} = \frac{\pi 0.12^2}{4} = 0.011\text{m}^2$$

So

$$v_2 = \frac{0.05}{0.011} v_1 = 4.55 v_1$$

Substitute this value for $v_2$ in the energy equation:

$$\frac{4.55^2 v_1^2}{2g} - \frac{v_1^2}{2g} = 2.5\text{m}$$

$$20.7v_1^2 - v_1^2 = 2.5 \times 2 \times 9.81$$

$$19.7v_1^2 = 49.05$$

$$v_1 = \sqrt{\frac{49.05}{19.7}} = 1.58\text{m/s}$$

To calculate $Q$:

$$Q = C_d v_1 a_1 = 0.97 \times 1.58 \times 0.05 = 0.077\text{m}^3/\text{s}$$

In the case of the venturi meter $C_d = 0.97$ which means that the energy losses are small and the energy theory works very well ($C_d = 1.0$ would mean the theory was perfect). For orifice plates the same theory and formula can be used but the value of $C_d$ is quite different at $C_d = 0.6$. The theory is not so good for this case because there is a lot of energy loss (Figure 4.8c). The water is not channelled smoothly from one section to another as in the venturi but is forced to make abrupt changes as it passes through the orifice and expands downstream. Such abruptness causes a lot of turbulence which results in energy loss. (The $C_d$ value is similar to that for orifice flow from a tank – see section 3.6.3.)

## 4.10 Momentum in pipes

The momentum equation is used in pipe flow to calculate forces on pipe fittings such as nozzles, pipe bends and valves. In more advanced applications it is used in the design of pumps and turbines where water flow creates forces on pump and turbine impellers.

To solve force and momentum problems a concept known as the **control volume** is used. This is a way of isolating part of a system being investigated so that the momentum equation can be applied to it. To see how this works an example is given in the box below showing how the force on a pipe reducer (or nozzle) can be calculated.

### Example: Calculating the force on a nozzle

A 100mm diameter fire hose discharges 15 litre/s from a 50mm diameter nozzle (Figure 4.9a). Calculate the force on the nozzle.

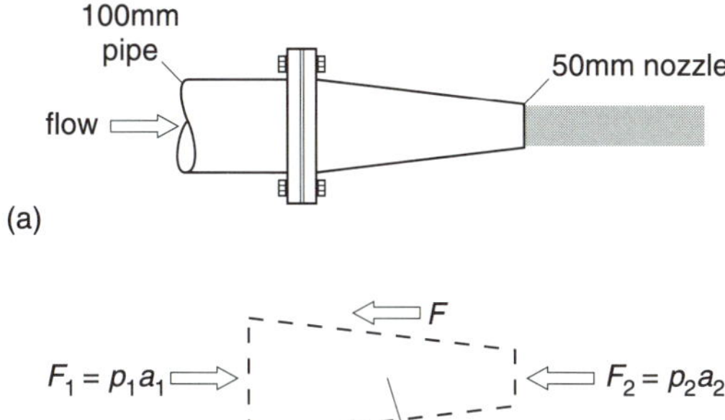


**Figure 4.9 Calculating the force on a nozzle**

To solve this problem all three hydraulic equations are needed; energy, continuity and momentum. The energy and continuity equations are needed to calculate the pressure in the 100mm pipe and momentum is then used to calculate the force on the nozzle.

The first step is to calculate the pressure $p_1$ in the 100mm pipe. Using the energy equation:

$$\frac{p_1}{\rho g} + \frac{v_1^2}{2g} + z_1 = \frac{p_2}{\rho g} + \frac{v_2^2}{2g} + z_2$$

$p_2$ is the pressure in the jet as it emerges from the nozzle into the atmosphere. The jet is at the same pressure as the atmosphere and so the pressure $p_2$ is zero. Because the nozzle and the pipe are horizontal $z_1$ and $z_2$ are equal to each other and so they cancel out. So the energy equation becomes

$$\frac{p_1}{\rho g} = \frac{v_2^2}{2g} - \frac{v_1^2}{2g}$$

The value of $p_1$ is unknown and so are $v_1$ and $v_2$. So the next step is to calculate the velocities from the discharge equation:

$$v_1 = \frac{Q}{a_1} \quad \text{and} \quad v_2 = \frac{Q}{a_2}$$

Area of pipe is

$$a_1 = \frac{\pi d_1^2}{4} = \frac{\pi 0.1^2}{4} = 0.0078\text{m}^2$$

Area of jet is

$$a_2 = \frac{\pi d_2^2}{4} = \frac{\pi 0.05^2}{4} = 0.0019\text{m}^2$$

Next calculate the velocities:

$$v_1 = \frac{Q}{a_1} = \frac{0.015}{0.0078} = 1.92\text{m/s}$$

$$v_2 = \frac{Q}{a_2} = \frac{0.015}{0.0019} = 7.9\text{m/s}$$

Putting all the known values into the energy equation:

$$\frac{p_1}{\rho g} = \frac{7.9^2}{2 \times 9.81} - \frac{1.92^2}{2 \times 9.81} = 3.18 - 0.19 = 2.99\text{m}$$

$$p_1 = 2.99 \times 1000 \times 9.81 = 29\ 332\text{N/m}^2$$

The final step is to calculate the force $F$ on the nozzle using the momentum equation. To do this the concept of the *control volume* isolates that part of the system being investigated (Figure 4.9b). All the forces that help to maintain the control volume are then identified. $F_1$ and $F_2$ are forces due to the water pressure in the pipe and the jet and $F$ is the force on the reducer itself. Although the force $F_2$ is shown acting against the flow remember that there is an equal and opposite force acting in the direction of the flow (Newton's third law). Using the momentum equation

$$F_1 - F_2 - F = \rho Q(v_2 - v_1)$$

$F$ is the force on the nozzle but at this stage $F_1$ and $F_2$ are also unknown. So the next step is to calculate $F_1$ and $F_2$ using known values of pressure and pipe area. Now

$$F_1 = p_1 \times a_1 = 29\ 332 \times 0.0078 = 228.8\text{N}$$

and

$$F_2 = p_2 \times a_2$$

but $p_2$ is zero and so

$$F_2 = 0$$

Finally all the information for the momentum equation is available to calculate $F$:

$$228.8 - F - 0 = 1000 \times 0.015(7.9 - 1.92)$$

$$F = 228.8 - 89.7 = 139\text{N}$$

As this is a fire hose, it would require a firm grip to hold it in place. If a fireman let go of the nozzle, the unbalanced force of 139N would cause it to shoot forward rapidly and this could do serious injury if it hit someone. A larger nozzle and discharge would probably need two firemen to hold and control it.

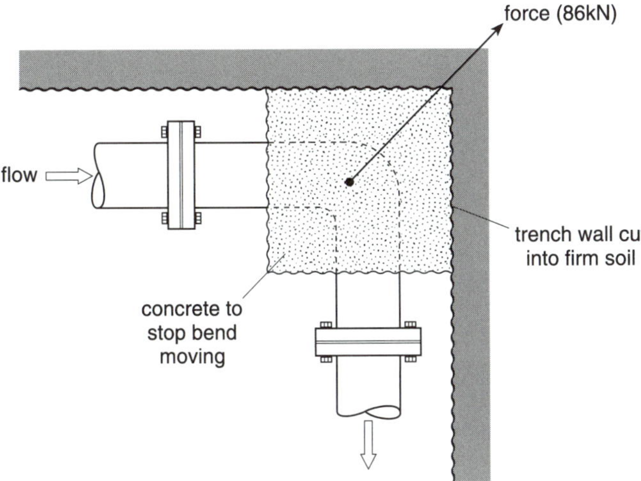


**Figure 4.10 Force on a pipe bend**

Forces also occur at pipe bends and this is not always appreciated. For example, a 90° bend on a 0.5m diameter pipe operating at 30m head carrying a discharge of $0.3m^3/s$ would produce a force of 86kN. This is a large thrust (over 8 tonnes) – which means that the bend must be held firmly in place if it is not to move and burst the pipe (Figure 4.10). A good way to deal with this is to bury the pipe below ground and encase the bend in concrete to stop it moving. The side of the trench must also be very firm for the concrete to push against it.

## 4.11 Water hammer

Most people will already have experienced this but may not have realised that it can be a serious problem. When a domestic water tap is turned off quickly, there is sometimes a loud banging noise in the pipes. The noise is the result of a high-pressure wave that moves rapidly through the pipes as a result of the rapid closure of the tap. This is known as **water hammer** and although it may not be too serious in domestic plumbing it can have disastrous consequences in larger pipelines and may result in bursts.

Water hammer occurs when flowing water is suddenly stopped. It behaves in a similar way to traffic flowing along a road when suddenly one car stops for no clear reason (Figure 4.11a). The car travelling close behind then crashes into it and the impact causes the cars to crumple. The next one crashes into the other two and so on until there is quite a pile-up. Notice that all the cars do not crash at the same time. A few seconds pass between each impact and so it takes several seconds before they all join the pile-up. If you are watching this from a distance it would appear as if there was a wave moving up the line of cars as each joins the pile-up. The speed of the wave is equal to the speed at which successive impacts occur. It is worth pointing out that cars are designed to collapse on impact so as to absorb the kinetic energy. If they were built more rigidly then all the energy on impact would be transferred to the driver and the passengers and not even seat belts would hold you in such circumstances.

Now imagine water flowing along a pipeline at the end of which is a valve that is closed suddenly (Figure 4.11b). If water was not compressible then it would behave like a long solid rod and would crash into the valve with such enormous force (momentum change) that it would probably destroy the valve. Fortunately, water is compressible and it behaves in a similar manner to the vehicles, it squashes on impact. Think of the flow being made up of small *parcels* of water. The first parcel hits the valve and compresses (like the first car); the second crashes into the first and compresses and so on until all the water is stopped (Figure 4.11b). This does not happen instantly but takes several seconds before all the water feels the impact and stops. The result is a sudden, large pressure rise at the valve and a pressure wave which travels rapidly along the pipe. This is referred to as a **shock wave** because of its suddenness.

The pressure wave is not just one-way. Once it reaches the end of a pipeline it reflects back towards the valve again. It is like a coiled spring that moves back and forth and gradually stops. This oscillating motion can go on for several minutes in a pipe until friction slowly reduces the pressure back to the normal operating level.

The extent of the pressure rise depends on how fast the water was travelling (velocity) and how quickly the valve was closed. It does not depend on the initial pipeline pressure as is often thought. It can be calculated using a formula developed by Nicholai Joukowsky (1847–1921) who carried out the first successful analysis of this problem:

$$\Delta h = \frac{cv}{g}$$

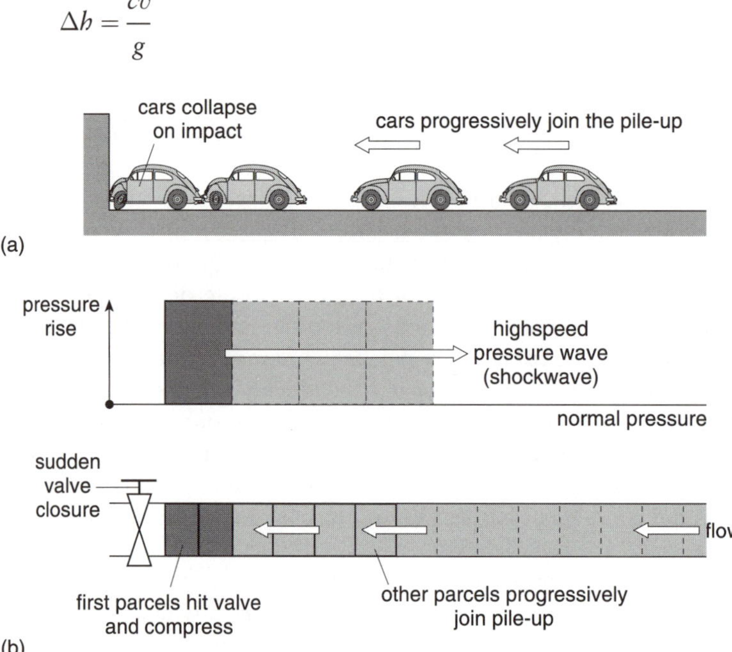


**Figure 4.11** Water hammer

where $\Delta h$ is rise in pressure (m), $c$ is velocity of the shock wave (m/s), $v$ is water velocity (m/s) and $g$ is gravity constant ($9.81 m/s^2$).

The shock wave travels at very high velocity between 1200 and 1400m/s. It depends on the diameter of the pipe and the material from which the pipe is made, as some materials absorb the energy of compression of the water better than others. An example in the box shows just how high the pressure can rise.

## Example: Calculating pressure rise in a pipeline due to water hammer

Using the Joukowsky equation determine the pressure rise in a pipeline when it is suddenly closed. The normal pipeline velocity is 1.0m/s and the shock-wave velocity is 1200m/s. If the pipeline is 10km long determine how long it takes for the pressure wave to travel the length of the pipeline.

Using the Joukowsky equation

$$\Delta h = \frac{cv}{g} = \frac{1200 \times 1.0}{9.81}$$

pressure rise = 122m

So the pressure rise would be 122m head of water or 12.2bar. This is on top of the normal operating pressure of the pipe and could well cause the pipe to burst.

To calculate the time it takes to travel the length of the pipe:

$$\text{time} = \frac{\text{distance}}{\text{velocity}} = \frac{10\,000}{1200}$$

time to travel pipe length = 8s

It takes only 8s for the shock wave to travel the 10km length of the pipe and 16s for this to return to the valve.

The example, of course, is an extreme one as it is difficult to close a valve instantaneously. It is also wrong to assume that the pipe is rigid. All materials stretch when they are under pressure and so the pipe itself will absorb some of the pressure energy by expanding. All these factors reduce the pressure rise but they do not stop it. Even if the pressure rise is only half the above value (say 6bar) it is still a high pressure suddenly to cope with and this too is enough to burst the pipe. When pipes burst they usually open up along their length rather than around their circumference. They burst open rather like unzipping a coat.

Reducing water hammer problems is similar to reducing car crash problems. When cars are moving slowly then the impact is not as great. Also when the first car slows down gradually then the others are unlikely to crash into it. Similarly, when water is moving more slowly the pressure rise when a valve closes is reduced (see Joukowsky equation). This is one of the reasons why most pipeline designers restrict velocities to below 1.6m/s so as to reduce water hammer problems. Also, when valves are closed slowly, water slows down gradually and there is little or no pressure rise along the pipe. In summary to reduce the effects of water hammer:

- make sure water velocities are low (below 1.6m/s),
- close control valves slowly.

In some cases it is not always possible to avoid the sudden closure of a pipeline. For example, if a heavy vehicle drives over pipes laid out on the ground, such as might occur with fire hoses, it will squash them and stop the flow instantly. This will immediately cause the pressure to rise rapidly and this could burst the pipes. A similar situation can occur on farms where mobile irrigation machines use flexible pipes. It is easy for a tractor accidentally to drive over a pipe without realising that the resulting pressure rise can split open the pipeline and cause a lot of damage. In such situations where there are pipes on the ground and vehicles about, it is wise to use pipe bridges.

Some incidents are not always easy to foresee. On a sprinkler irrigation scheme in East Africa an elephant got into the farm and was walking through the crop. It trod on an aluminium irrigation pipe and squashed it flat resulting in an instantaneous closure. This caused a massive pressure rise upstream and several pipes were burst open!

## 4.12 Surge

Surge and water hammer are terms that are often confused because one is caused by the other. Surge is the large mass movement of water that sometimes takes place as a result of water hammer. It is much slower and can last for many minutes whereas water hammer may only last for a few seconds.

An example of the difference between the two can be most easily seen in a hydro-electric power station (Figure 4.12). Water flows down a pipeline from a large reservoir and is used to turn a turbine which is coupled to a generator that produces electricity. Turbines run at high speeds and require large quantities of water and so the velocities in the supply pipe can be very high. The demand for electricity can vary considerably over very short periods and problems occur when the demand falls and one or more of the turbines have to be shut down quickly. This is done by closing the valve on the supply pipe and this can cause water hammer. To protect a large part of the pipeline a **surge tank** is located as close to the power station as possible. This is a vertical chamber many times larger than the pipeline diameter. Water no longer required for the turbine is diverted into the tank and any water hammer shock waves coming up from the valve closure are absorbed by the tank. Thus water hammer is confined to the pipeline between the turbine and the tank and so only this length of pipe needs to be constructed to withstand the high water hammer pressures. Gradually the tank fills with water and the flow from the reservoir slows down and eventually stops. Usually, the

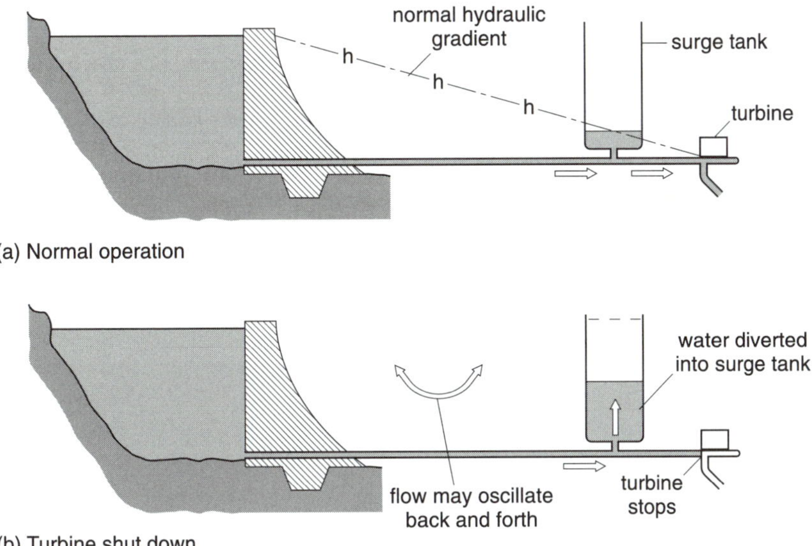


**Figure 4.12** Surge in pipelines

rushing water can cause the tank to overfill. In such cases water may flow back and forth between the tank and the reservoir for several hours. This slow but large movement of water is called a **surge** and although it is the result of water hammer it is quite different in character.

Surge can also cause problems in pumping mains and these are discussed more fully in section 8.13.

## 4.13 Some examples to test your understanding

1 A 150mm pipeline is 360m long and has a friction factor $\lambda = 0.02$. Calculate the head loss in the pipeline using the Darcy–Weisbach formula when the discharge is $0.05\text{m}^3/\text{s}$. Calculate the hydraulic gradient in m/100m of pipeline.

2 A pipeline 2.5km long and 150mm diameter supplies water from a reservoir to a small town storage tank. Calculate the discharge when the pipe outlet is freely discharging into the tank and the difference in level between the reservoir and the outlet is 15m. Assume $\lambda = 0.04$.

3 Water from a large reservoir flows through a pipeline 1.8km long and discharges into a service tank. The first 600m of pipe is 300mm in diameter and the remainder is 150mm in diameter. Calculate the discharge when the difference in water level between the two reservoirs is 25m and $\lambda = 0.04$ for both pipes.

4 A venturi meter is fitted to a pipeline to measure discharge. The pipe diameter is 300mm and the venturi throat diameter is 175mm. Calculate the discharge in $\text{m}^3/\text{s}$ when the difference in pressure between the pipe and the venturi throat is 400mm of water. Assume the coefficient of discharge is 0.97.

5 A pipeline is reduced in diameter from 500mm to 300mm using a concentric reducer pipe. Calculate the force on the reducer when the discharge is $0.35\text{m}^3/\text{s}$ and the pressure in the 500mm pipe is $300\text{kN/m}^2$.

6 A 500mm diameter pipeline is fitted with a 90° bend. Calculate the resultant force on the bend and its line of action if the normal operating pressure is 50m head of water and the discharge is $0.3\text{m}^3/\text{s}$. Calculate the resultant force when there is no flow in the pipe but the system is still under pressure.

7 Calculate the pressure rise in a 0.5m diameter pipeline carrying a discharge of $0.3\text{m}^3/\text{s}$ when a sluice valve is closed suddenly.

## Chapter 5

# Channels

## 5.1 Introduction

Natural rivers and man-made canals are referred to as **open channels**. They have many advantages over pipes and have been used for many centuries for water supply, for transport and for agriculture. The Romans made extensive use of channels and built their famous aqueducts for their sophisticated water supply schemes. Barge canals are still an important means of transporting heavy bulk materials in Europe and irrigation canals bring life and prosperity to the arid lands of North Africa, the Middle East, India and Australia as they have done for thousands of years.

## 5.2 Pipes or channels?

The choice between pipes and open channels is most likely to depend on which provides the cheapest solution in terms of both capital expenditure and the recurrent costs of operation and maintenance. However, there are advantages and disadvantages with each which may influence or restrict the final choice.

Channels, for example, are very convenient and economical for conveying large quantities of water over relatively flat land such as in large irrigation systems on river floodplains. It is hard to imagine some of the large irrigation canals in India and Pakistan being put into pipes. In hilly areas the cost of open channels can rise significantly because the alignment must follow the land contours to create a gentle downward slope for the flow. A more direct route would be too steep, causing erosion and serious damage to channels. Pipes would be more suitable in such conditions. They can be used in any kind of terrain and can take a more direct route. Water velocities too can be much higher in pipes because there is no risk of erosion.

Although there are obvious physical differences between channels and pipes, there are several important hydraulic differences between them:

- Open channels have a free or open water surface whereas pipes are enclosed and usually flow full.

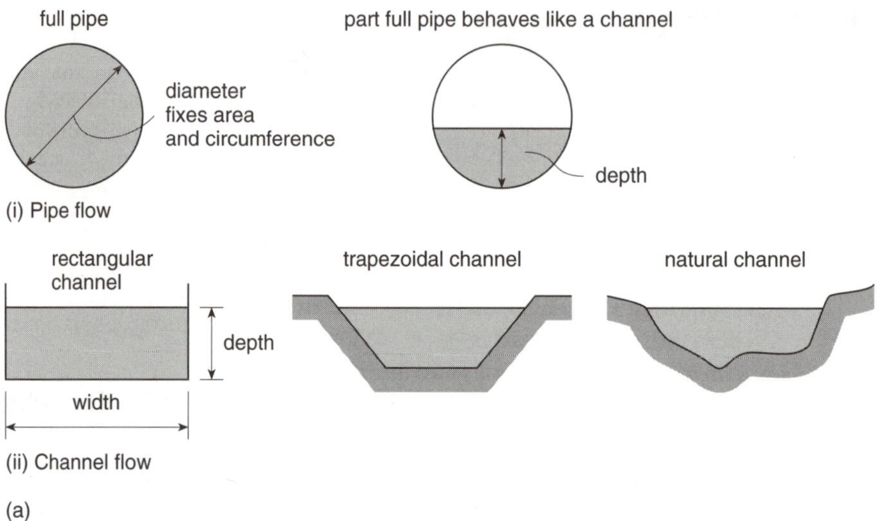

(b) A lined irrigation canal in Nigeria

**Figure 5.1 Channels can have many different shapes and sizes**

- Water can only flow downhill in channels but in pipes it can flow both uphill and downhill. Flow in pipes depends on a pressure difference between the inlet and outlet. As long as the pressure is higher at the inlet than at the outlet then water will flow even though the pipeline route may be undulating. Channels depend entirely on the force of gravity to make water move and so they can only flow downhill.
- Man-made channels can have many different shapes (circular, rectangular or trapezoidal) and sizes (different depths, widths and velocities). Natural river channels are irregular in shape (Figure 5.1). Pipes in contrast are circular in section and their shape is characterised by one simple dimension – the diameter. This fixes the area of the waterway and the friction from the pipe circumference.
- Water velocities are usually lower in channels than in pipes. This is because channels are often in natural soils that erode easily. So channels are usually much larger than pipes for the same flow.
- Channels need much more attention than pipes. They tend to erode and weeds grow in waterways and so regular cleaning is required. Water losses from seepage and evaporation can also be a problem.

These differences make channels a little more complicated to deal with than pipes but most open channel problems can be solved using the basic tools of hydraulics: discharge and continuity, energy and momentum.

The study of open channels is not just confined to channel shapes and sizes. It can also include waves, the problem of handling varying flood flows down rivers, and sediment transport associated with the scouring and silting of rivers and canals. Some of these issues are touched on in this chapter but waves are discussed more fully in Chapter 6.

## 5.3 Laminar and turbulent flow

Laminar and turbulent flow are not just confined to pipe flow, they can also occur in channels. But for all practical purposes, flow in rivers and canals is turbulent and, like pipes, laminar flow is unlikely to occur except for very special conditions. For example, laminar flow only occurs in a channel when the depth is less than 25mm and the velocity is less than 0.025m/s. This is not a very practicable size and velocity for any channel and so laminar flow in channels can be ignored. The only time when it is important is when more complex problems are being solved using hydraulic models built in the laboratory. Scaling down the size to fit in the laboratory may mean that the flow in the model becomes laminar. This change in flow will affect the results obtained from such a model and the engineer would take this into account in analysis.

## 5.4 Using the hydraulic tools

Continuity and energy are particularly useful tools for solving open channel flow problems. Momentum is also helpful for problems in which there are energy losses and where there are forces involved.

### 5.4.1 Continuity

Continuity is applied to open channels in much the same way as it is applied to pipes (Figure 5.2a). The discharge $Q_1$ passing point 1 in a channel must be equal to the discharge $Q_2$ passing point 2:

$$Q_1 = Q_2$$

Writing this in terms of velocity and area:

$$v_1 a_1 = v_2 a_2$$

The term 'discharge per metre width' ($q$) is often used to describe channel flow rather than the total discharge ($Q$). This is the flow in a 1.0m wide portion of a channel (Figure 5.2b).

To calculate the discharge per metre width ($q$) for a rectangular channel, use the continuity equation

$$Q = va$$

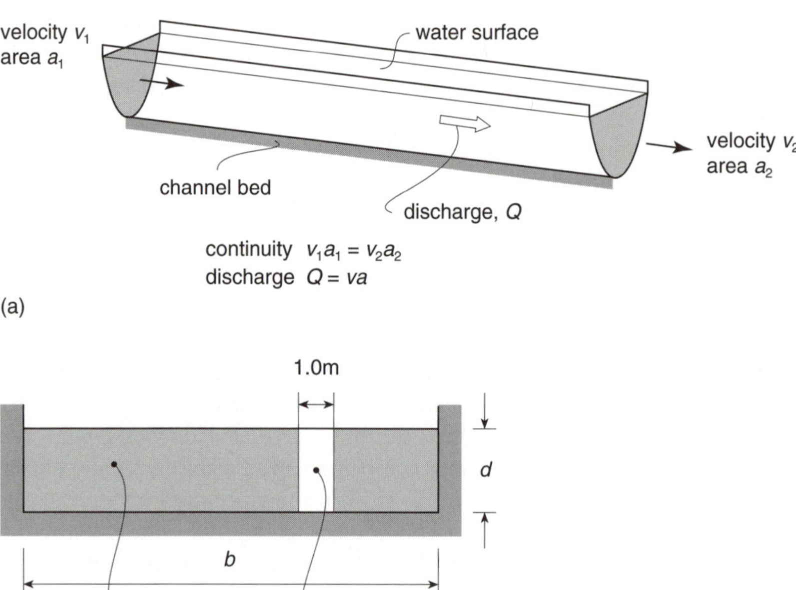


**Figure 5.2** Continuity in channels

where

$$a = bd$$

To calculate $q$ assume

$$b = 1.0\text{m}$$

Therefore

$$a = 1.0 \times d = d$$

and so

$$q = vd$$

When the channel width ($b$) is known, say 7m, and it carries a known discharge ($Q$), of say 10m$^3$/s, then the flow per metre width is calculated as follows:

$$q = \frac{Q}{b} = \frac{10}{7} = 1.43\text{m}^3/\text{s/m width of channel}$$

The discharge and continuity equations for channels are often written in terms of discharge per metre width as follows:

$$q = vd$$

$$v_1 d_1 = v_2 d_2$$

### 5.4.2 Energy

The idea of total energy being the same at different points in a system is also useful for channel flow. So when water flows between two points 1 and 2 in a channel, the total energy at 1 will be the same as the total energy at 2. As in the case of pipe flow this is only true when there is no energy loss. For some channel problems this is a reasonable assumption to make but for others an additional energy loss term is needed.

The energy equation for channel flow is a little different to the equation for pipe flow (Figure 5.3). For pipe flow the pressure energy is $p/\rho g$. For channel flow it is replaced by the depth of water $d$. Remember that $p/\rho g$ is a pressure head in metres and for channels this is the same as the pressure on the channel bed resulting from the depth of water $d$. The potential energy $z$ is measured from some datum point to the bed of the channel. The velocity energy $v^2/2g$ remains the same. Note that all the terms are measured in metres and so they can all be added together to determine the total energy in a channel. Writing the total energy equation for an

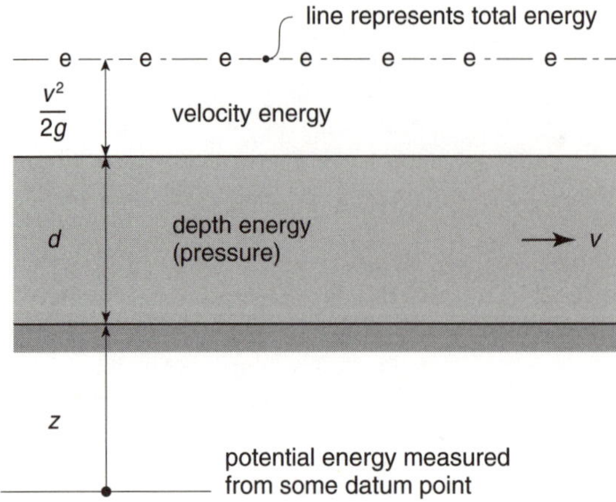


**Figure 5.3 Energy in channels**

open channel:

$$\text{total energy} = d + \frac{v^2}{2g} + z$$

Sometimes the velocity $v$ is written in terms of the discharge per metre width $q$ and depth $d$. This is done using the discharge equation:

$$q = vd$$

Rearranging this for velocity:

$$v = \frac{q}{d}$$

so the velocity energy becomes:

$$\frac{v^2}{2g} = \frac{q^2}{2gd^2}$$

Substituting this in the energy equation:

$$\text{total energy} = d + \frac{q^2}{2gd^2} + z$$

Total energy can be represented in a diagram by the **total energy line** e—e—e (Figure 5.3). This provides a visual indication of the total energy available and how it is changing. Notice that the line only slopes downwards in the direction of the

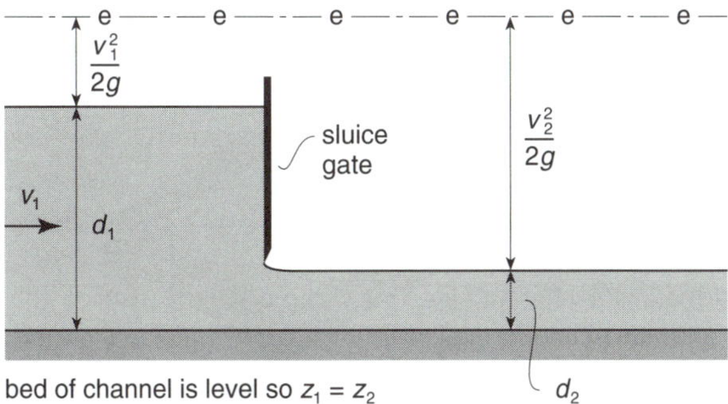


(a)

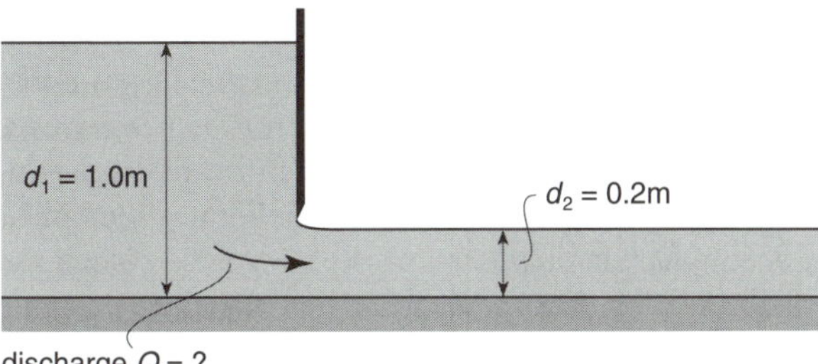


(b)

(c) Sluice gates controlling discharge into irrigation canal, Iraq

**Figure 5.4 Using energy and continuity**

flow to show the gradual loss of energy from friction. The water surface is the channel equivalent of the hydraulic gradient for pipes.

### 5.4.3 Using energy and continuity

Determining the discharge under a sluice gate is one example of the use of the continuity and energy equations in an open channel (Figure 5.4a). The sluice gate is a common structure for controlling flows in channels and it can also be used to measure flow if the water depths upstream and downstream of the gate are measured. The approach is very similar to the venturi problem in pipe flow but in this case a gate is used to change the energy conditions in the channel. Notice how the energy line has been drawn to indicate the level of total energy. Firstly it shows there is no energy loss as water flows under the gate. This is reasonable because the flow is converging under the gate and this tends to suppress turbulence, which means little or no energy loss. Secondly it shows that there is a significant change in the components of the total energy across the gate even though the total is the same. Upstream the flow is slow and deep whereas downstream the flow is very shallow and fast. The discharge is the same on both sides of the gate but it is clear that the two flows are quite different. In fact they behave quite differently too, but more about this later in section 5.7.

The example in the box illustrates how to calculate the discharge under a sluice gate when the upstream and downstream water depths are known.

## Example: Calculating discharge under a sluice gate

A sluice gate is used to control and measure the discharge in an open channel (Figure 5.4b). When the upstream and downstream water depths are 1.0m and 0.2m respectively, calculate the discharge in the channel.

When the flow is contracting, as it does under a sluice gate, turbulence is suppressed and the flow transition occurs smoothly. Very little energy is lost and so the energy equation can be applied as follows:

total energy at point 1 = total energy at point 2

$$d_1 + \frac{v_1^2}{2g} + z_1 = d_2 + \frac{v_2^2}{2g} + z_1$$

As the channel is horizontal

$$z_1 = z_2$$

and so

$$d_1 + \frac{v_1^2}{2g} = d_2 + \frac{v_2^2}{2g}$$

Bringing the $d$ terms and $v$ terms together and putting in the values for depth:

$$1.0 - 0.2 = \frac{v_2^2}{2g} - \frac{v_1^2}{2g}$$

Both velocities $v_1$ and $v_2$ are unknown and so the continuity equation is needed to solve the problem:

$$v_1 d_1 = v_2 d_2$$

Putting in the depths

$$v_1 \times 1.0 = v_2 \times 0.2$$

and so

$$v_1 = 0.2 v_2$$

Substituting for $v_1$ in the energy equation:

$$0.8 = \frac{v_2^2}{2g} - 0.04 \times \frac{v_2^2}{2g}$$

Rearranging this to find $v_2$:

$$v_2^2 = \frac{0.8 \times 2 \times 9.81}{1 - 0.04} = 16.35$$

$$v_2 = 4.04\text{m/s}$$

To calculate the discharge:

$$q = v_2 d_2 = 4.04 \times 0.2 = 0.81\text{m}^3\text{/s/m width of channel}$$

### 5.4.4 Taking account of energy losses

Energy loss occurs in channels due to friction. In short lengths of channel such as in the sluice gate example this is very small and so it is not taken into account in any calculations. But energy loss in long channels must be taken into account in the energy equation to avoid serious errors (Figure 5.5). Writing the energy equation for two points in a channel:

$$\text{total energy at 1 (TE}_1) = \text{total energy at 2 (TE}_2) + h_f$$

$$d_1 + \frac{v_1^2}{2g} + z_1 = d_2 + \frac{v_2^2}{2g} + z_2 + h_f$$

where $h_f$ is energy loss due to friction (m).

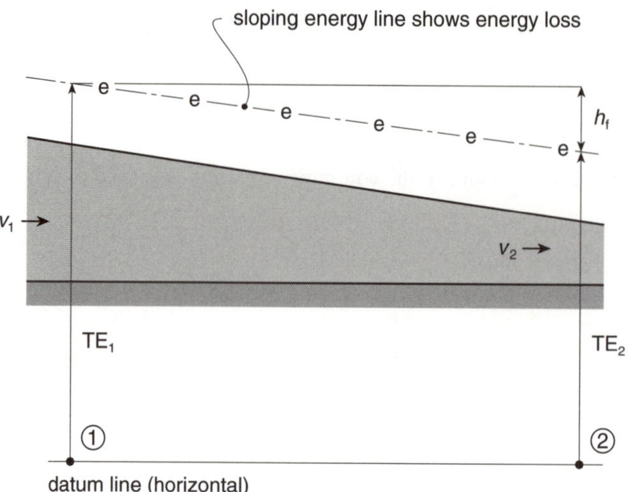


**Figure 5.5 Energy losses in channels**

This equation is very similar to that for pipe flow and in that case the Darcy–Weisbach formula was used to calculate the energy loss term $h_f$. This was the link between energy losses and pipe size. Similar formulae have been developed to calculate $h_f$ for open channels and these link energy loss to both the size and the shape of channels needed to carry a given discharge.

## 5.5 Uniform flow

All the energy loss formulae for open channels are based on **uniform flow.** This is a special condition that only occurs when water flows down a long, straight, gently sloping channel (Figure 5.6a). The flow is pulled down the slope by the force of gravity but there is friction from the bed and sides of the channel slowing it down. When the friction force is larger than the gravity force it slows down the flow. When the friction force is smaller than the gravity force the flow moves faster down the slope. But the friction force is not constant, it depends on velocity and so as the velocity increases so does the friction force. At some point the two forces become equal. Here the forces are in balance and as the flow continues down the channel the depth and velocity remain constant (Figure 5.6b). This flow condition is called **uniform flow** and the water depth is called the **normal depth.**

Unfortunately, in most channels this balance of forces rarely occurs and so the depth and velocity are usually changing gradually even though the discharge is constant. Even in long channels where uniform flow has a chance of occurring there is usually some variation in channel shape or slope or a hydraulic structure which changes the depth and the velocity (Figure 5.6c). So most channels have **non-uniform flow.** It is also called **gradually varied flow** because the changes take place gradually along the channel.

So if non-uniform flow is the most common and uniform flow rarely occurs, why are all the formulae based on uniform flow? Why not accept that non-uniform

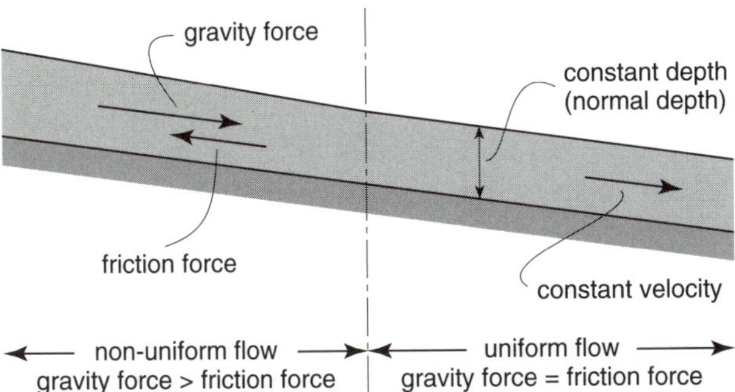


(a) Uniform flow occurs in a long, gently sloping channel

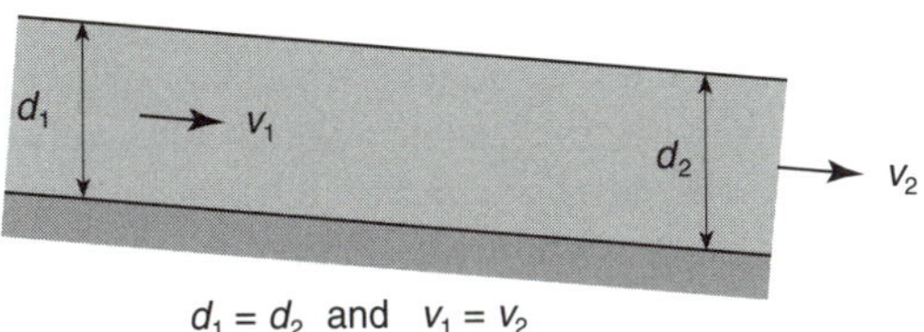


(b) Uniform flow

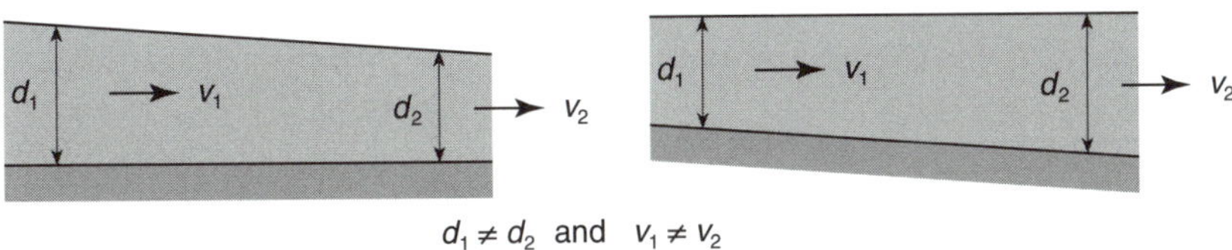


(c) Non-uniform flow

**Figure 5.6 Uniform and non-uniform flow**

flow is the norm and develop formulae for this condition? The answer is quite simple. Uniform flow is much easier to deal with from a calculation point of view and engineers are always looking for ways of simplifying problems but without losing accuracy. There are methods for designing channels for non-uniform flow but they are much more cumbersome to use and usually they produce the same shape and size of channel as uniform flow methods. So it has become accepted practice to assume that channel flow is uniform for all practical purposes. For all gently sloping channels on floodplains (i.e. 99% of all channels including rivers, canals and drainage ditches) this assumption is a good one. Only in steep sloping channels in the mountains does it cause problems.

Remember too that great accuracy may not be necessary when designing channels and dimensions do not need to be calculated to the nearest millimetre for construction purposes. The nearest 0.05m is accurate enough for concrete channels and probably 0.1m for earth channels. From a practical construction point of view it will be difficult to find a hydraulic excavator operator who can (or who would want to) trim channel shapes to an accuracy greater than this.

### 5.5.1 Channel shapes

For pipe flow the issue of shape does not arise. Pipes are all circular in section and so their hydraulic shape is determined by one dimension – the pipe diameter – and so both shape and size are taken into account in the Darcy–Weisbach formula. But channels come in a variety of shapes, the more common ones being rectangular, trapezoidal or semi-circular (see Figure 5.1). They also come in different sizes with different depths and widths. So any formula for channels must take into account both shape and size.

To demonstrate the importance of shape consider two rectangular channels each with the same area of flow but one is narrow and deep and the other is shallow and wide (Figure 5.7a). Both channels have the same flow area of $10m^2$ and so they might be expected to carry the same discharge. But this is not the case. Friction controls the velocity in channels and when the friction changes the velocity will also change. The channel boundary in contact with the water (called the **wetted perimeter**) is the main source of friction. In the narrow channel the length of the boundary in contact with the water is 9m whereas in the wide channel it is 12m. So the wide channel produces more friction than the narrow one and as a result the velocity (and hence the discharge) in the wide channel will be less than in the narrow one. So channels with the same flow area have different carrying capacities depending on their shape.

Understanding this can be very useful when deciding on the general shape of channels. Suppose a channel is to be constructed in natural soil and there are worries about erosion of the bed and sides because of a high water velocity. By making the channel wide and shallow the water will be slowed down by the increased friction so avoiding the problem (Figure 5.7b). Many natural river channels have a shallow, wide profile as they have adapted over many years to the erosion of the natural soils in which they flow.

For lined channels (e.g. concrete) the main issue is one of cost and not erosion. Lined canals are very expensive and so it is important to minimise the amount of lining needed. This is done by using a channel shape that has a small wetted perimeter (Figure 5.7c). The friction will be low which means the velocity will be high but this is not a problem as the lining will resist erosion. Minimum wetted perimeters for selected channel shapes are shown in Table 5.1.

**Table 5.1 Minimum wetted perimeters for different channel shapes**

| *Channel shape* | *Wetted perimeter** | *Hydraulic radius** |
|---|---|---|
| Rectangle | $4D$ | $0.5D$ |
| Trapezoid (half a hexagon) | $3.463D$ | $0.5D$ |
| Semi-circle | $\pi D$ | $0.5D$ |

**D* is the depth of flow.

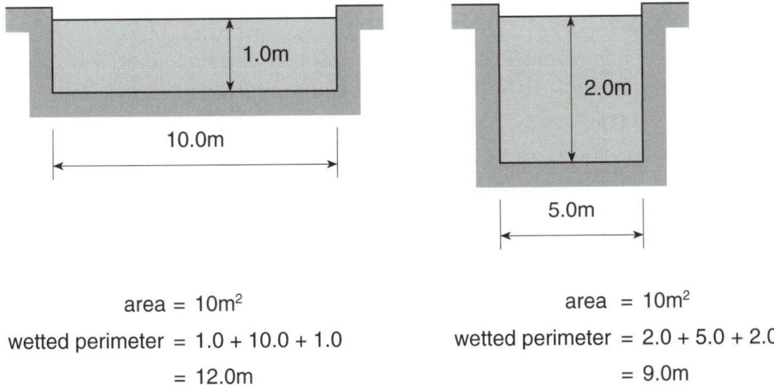


(a) Importance of shape

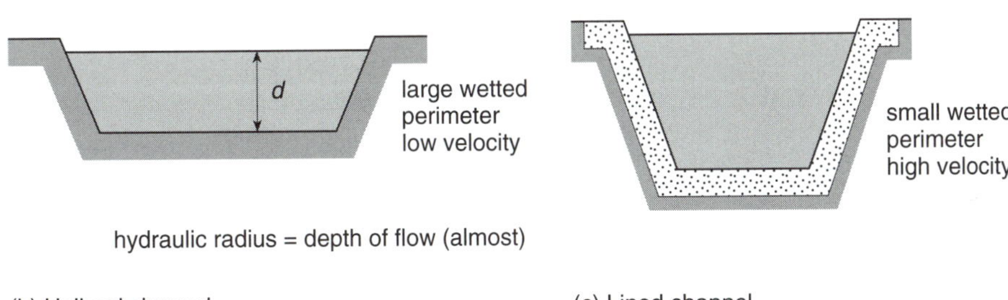


(b) Unlined channel

(c) Lined channel

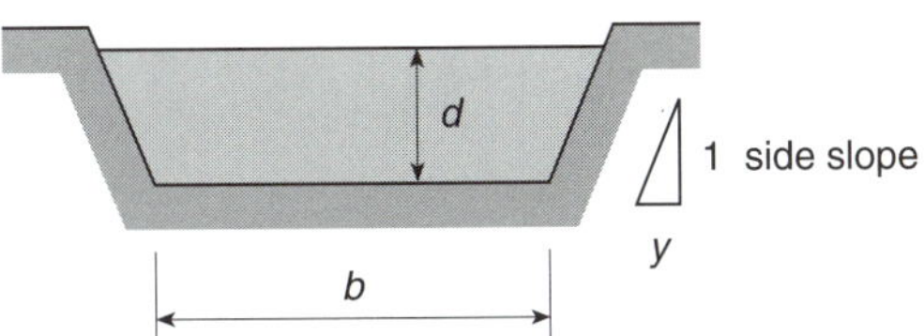


(d) Trapezoidal channel section

**Figure 5.7 Channel shapes**

### 5.5.2 Factors affecting flow

Channel flow is influenced not just by the channel shape and size but also by slope and roughness.

#### 5.5.2.1 *Area and wetted perimeter*

The cross-sectional area of a channel ($a$) defines the flow area and the wetted perimeter ($p$) defines the boundary between the water and the channel. This boundary in contact with the water is the source of frictional resistance to the flow of water. The greater the wetted perimeter, the greater is the frictional resistance of the channel.

The area and wetted perimeter for rectangular and circular channels are easily calculated but trapezoidal channels are a bit more difficult. Unfortunately they are the most common and so given below are formulae for area and wetted perimeter (Figure 5.7d):

$$\text{area of waterway } (a) = (b + yd)d$$

$$\text{wetted perimeter } (p) = b + 2d\sqrt{(1 + y^2)}$$

where $b$ is bed width (m), $d$ is depth of flow (m) and $y$ is side slope.

#### 5.5.2.2 *Hydraulic radius*

As the wetted perimeter can vary considerably for the same area, some measure of the hydraulic shape of a channel is needed. This is called the **hydraulic radius** and it is determined from the area and the wetted perimeter as follows:

$$\text{hydraulic radius (m)} = \frac{\text{area (m}^2\text{)}}{\text{wetted perimeter (m)}}$$

In the two channels in Figure 5.7a, the hydraulic radius would be 0.83m and 1.11m respectively and this shows numerically just how hydraulically different are the two channels.

#### 5.5.2.3 *Slope*

Water only flows downhill in channels and the steepness of the slope affects the velocity and hence the discharge. As the slope gets steeper the velocity increases and so does the discharge (remember $Q = va$).

Slope is measured as a gradient rather than an angle in degrees. So a channel slope is expressed as 1 in 1000, i.e. 1.0m drop in 1000m of channel length (Figure 5.8).

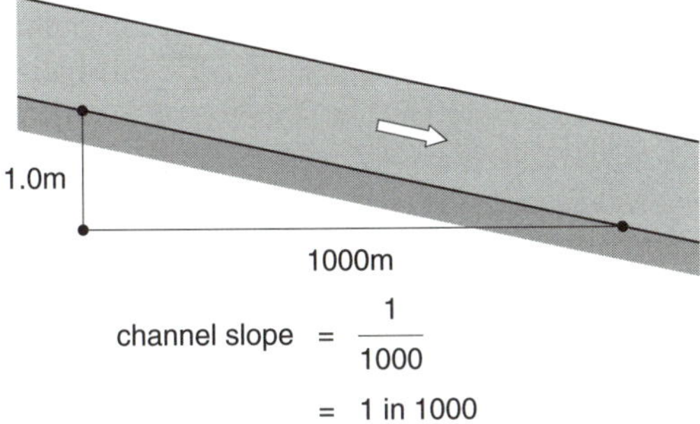


**Figure 5.8** Channel slope

Slopes need not be very steep for water to flow. Many of the irrigation canals in the Nile Valley in Egypt have slopes of only 1 in 10 000. This is the same as 1.0m in 10km or 100mm per kilometre. This is a very gentle slope and you would not be able to detect it by just looking at the landscape, but it is sufficient to make water flow as the evidence of the Nile shows.

A question that sometimes arises about channel slopes is: Does it refer to the water surface, the channel bed or the energy line? For uniform flow the question is irrelevant because the depth and velocity remain the same along the entire channel and so the water surface and the bed are parallel and have the same slope. For non-uniform flow it is the slope of the energy line that is important and is the driving force for the flow. Even when the bed is flat, water will still flow provided there is an energy gradient.

#### 5.5.2.4 Roughness

The **roughness** of the bed and sides of a channel also contribute to friction. The rougher they are, the slower will be the water velocity. Channels tend to have much rougher surfaces than pipes. They may be relatively smooth when lined with concrete but they can be very rough when excavated in the natural soil or infested with weeds. Roughness is taken into account in channel design formulae and this is demonstrated in the next section.

### 5.5.3 Channel design formulae

There are two commonly used formulae that link energy loss in channels to their size, shape, slope and roughness: the **Chezy** formula and the **Manning** formula. Both are widely used and were developed on the assumption that the flow is uniform.

#### 5.5.3.1 Chezy formula

This formulae was developed by Antoine Chezy, a French engineer who, in 1768, was asked to design a canal for the Paris water supply. The Chezy formula, as it is now known, is usually written as follows:

$$v = C\sqrt{RS}$$

where $v$ is velocity (m/s), $R$ is hydraulic radius (m), $S$ is channel slope (m/m) and $C$ is the Chezy coefficient describing channel roughness.

This may not look much like a formula for friction loss in a channel but it is derived from the energy equation allowing for energy loss in the same way as was done for pipe flow. For those interested in its origins a derivation is shown in the box. The formula shown above is the more familiar way of presenting the Chezy formula in hydraulic textbooks.

Once the velocity has been calculated the discharge can be determined using the discharge equation:

$$Q = va$$

## Derivation: Chezy formula

To see how Chezy developed his formula look first at the energy equation describing the changes that take place between two points in a long channel (Figure 5.6b) but taking into account energy loss in the channel $h_f$:

$$d_1 + \frac{v_1^2}{2g} + z_1 = d_2 + \frac{v_2^2}{2g} + z_2 + h_f$$

Chezy suggested that the energy loss $h_f$ could be determined by

$$h_f = \frac{Lv^2}{C^2R}$$

where $L$ is the length of channel over which the energy loss occurs (m), $v$ is velocity (m/s), $R$ is hydraulic radius (m) and $C$ is Chezy coefficient describing roughness.

Notice how similar this equation is to the Darcy–Weisbach equation. Friction depends on the length and the square of the velocity. The Chezy coefficient $C$ describes the friction in the channel and is similar to $\lambda$ in the Darcy–Weisbach formula. Like $\lambda$ it does not have a constant value. $C$ depends on the Reynolds number and also on the dimensions of the channel.

Putting this into the energy equation:

$$d_1 + \frac{v_1^2}{2g} + z_1 = d_2 + \frac{v_2^2}{2g} + z_2 + \frac{Lv^2}{C^2R}$$

Now the definition of uniform flow is that the depths and velocities remain the same along the whole length of a channel and so

$$d_1 = d_2$$

and

$$v_1 = v_2$$

This reduces the energy equation to

$$\frac{Lv^2}{C^2R} = z_1 - z_2$$

Now divide both sides of the equation by $L$:

$$\frac{v^2}{C^2R} = \frac{z_1 - z_2}{L}$$

But $(z_1 - z_2)/L$ is the slope $S$ of the channel bed. It is also the slope of the water surface. Remember that the two are parallel for uniform flow. Hence

$$\frac{z_1 - z_2}{L} = S$$

and so

$$\frac{v^2}{C^2R} = S$$

Rearranging this to calculate the velocity:

$$v = C\sqrt{RS}$$

This is the familiar form of the Chezy equation that is quoted in hydraulics textbooks.

#### 5.5.3.2 *Manning formula*

The Manning formula is an alternative to Chezy and is one of the most commonly used formulae for designing channels. This was developed by Robert Manning (1816–1897), an Irish civil engineer. It is an empirical formula developed from many observations made on natural channels:

$$v = \frac{R^{2/3}S^{1/2}}{n}$$

where $v$ is velocity (m/s), $R$ is hydraulic radius (m), $S$ is channel bed slope (m/m) and $n$ is Manning's roughness coefficient. Manning's $n$ values depend on the surface roughness of a channel. Typical values are listed in Table 5.2.

**Table 5.2 Values of Manning's *n***

| *Channel type* | *Manning's n values* |
|---|---|
| Concrete-lined canals | 0.012–0.017 |
| Rough masonry | 0.017–0.030 |
| Roughly dug earth canals | 0.025–0.033 |
| Smooth earth canals | 0.017–0.025 |
| Natural river in gravel | 0.040–0.070 |

The value of Manning's $n$ is not just determined by the material from which the channel is made but it is also affected by vegetation growth. This can make it difficult to determine with any accuracy. The $n$ value can also change over time as weeds grow and it can also change with changes in flow. At low discharges weeds and grasses will be upright and so cause great roughness but at higher discharges they may be flattened by the flow and so the channel becomes much smoother. There is an excellent book – *Open Channel Hydraulics* by Ven Te Chow (1981) – that has a series of pictures of channels with different weed growths and suggested $n$ values. These pictures can be compared with existing channels to get some indication of $n$. But how is Manning's $n$ selected for a natural, winding channel with varying flow areas, with trees and grasses along its banks (perhaps also including the odd bicycle or supermarket trolley) and flowing under bridges and over weirs? Clearly, in this situation, choosing $n$ is more of an art than a science. It may well be that several values are needed to describe the roughness along different sections of the river.

### 5.5.4 Using Manning's formula

Manning's formula is not the easiest of formulae to work with. It is quite straightforward to use when calculating discharge for a given shape and size of channel but it is not so easy to use the other way round, i.e. to calculate channel dimensions for a given discharge. Unfortunately this is by far the most common use of Manning. One approach is to use a trial-and-error technique to obtain the channel dimensions. This means guessing suitable values for depth and width and then putting them into the formula to see if they meet the discharge requirements. If they do not then the values are changed until the right dimensions are found. Usually there can be a lot of trials and a lot of errors. Modern computer spreadsheets can speed up this painful process.

Another approach is the method developed by H.W. King – see *Handbook of Hydraulics for the Solution of Hydrostatic and Fluid Flow Problems* by King and Brater (1996). This is a very simple and useful method and is ideally suited to designing trapezoidal channels, which are the most common. He modified Manning's formula to look like this:

$$Q = \frac{1}{n} jkd^{8/3} S^{1/2}$$

**Table 5.3 Values of *j* and *k* for Manning's formula**

| | *Ratios of bed width (b) to water depth (d)* | | | | | |
|---|---|---|---|---|---|---|
| | *Values of j* | | | *Values of k* | | |
| *Side slope* | $b = d$ | $b = 2d$ | $b = 3d$ | $b = d$ | $b = 2d$ | $b = 3d$ |
| Vertical | 1 | 2 | 3 | 0.48 | 0.63 | 0.71 |
| 1 in 1 | 2 | 3 | 4 | 0.64 | 0.73 | 0.77 |
| 1 in 1.5 | 2.5 | 3.5 | 4.5 | 0.66 | 0.73 | 0.77 |
| 1 in 2 | 3 | 4 | 5 | 0.66 | 0.72 | 0.76 |
| 1 in 3 | 4 | 5 | 6 | 0.67 | 0.71 | 0.74 |

where $d$ is depth of flow (m), $S$ is channel slope and $j$ and $k$ are constants. The values of $j$ and $k$ depend on the ratio of the bed width to depth and the channel side slope. This is the slope of the side embankments and not the longitudinal slope $S$ of a channel. King and Brater's book has a very comprehensive range of $j$ and $k$ values. A selection is shown in Table 5.3.

To use the method, values of the ratio of channel bed width to depth and side slope are first chosen. Values of $j$ and $k$ are then obtained from Table 5.3 and put into the formula, from which a value of depth can be calculated. As the bed width to depth ratio is known, the bed width can now be calculated. If the resulting channel shape or its dimensions appear to be unsuitable for any reason (e.g. the velocity may be too high) then another ratio of bed width to depth ratio can be chosen and the calculation repeated. As well as providing $j$ and $k$ values, King and Brater also supply values of the power function 8/3 so that it is easy to calculate the depth of flow.

Examples of the use of Manning's formula are shown in the boxes.

## Example: Calculating discharge using Manning's formula

A rectangular concrete-lined channel of width 2.5m and depth 0.5m has a slope of 1 in 2000. If the Manning's $n$ value is 0.015 calculate the discharge (Figure 5.9a).

The first step is to calculate the velocity but before this can be done the area, wetted perimeter and hydraulic radius must be determined:

$$\text{area } (a) = \text{depth} \times \text{width} = 0.5 \times 2.5 = 1.25\text{m}^2$$

$$\text{wetted perimeter } (p) = 0.5 + 2.5 + 0.5 = 3.5\text{m}$$

$$\text{hydraulic radius } (R) = \frac{a}{p} = \frac{1.25}{3.5} = 0.36\text{m}$$

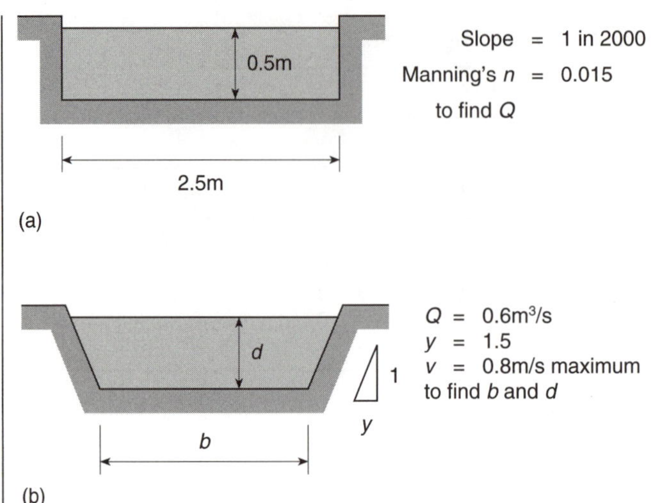


**Figure 5.9** Calculating discharge and channel dimensions

To calculate velocity:

$$v = \frac{0.36^{2/3} \times (1/2000)^{1/2}}{0.015} = 0.75\text{m/s}$$

Now calculate discharge:

$$Q = va = 1.25 \times 0.75 = 0.94\text{m}^3/\text{s}$$

Try calculating the discharge using the Chezy equation with a C value of 70.

## Example: Calculating depth of flow and bed width using King's method

Calculate a suitable bed width and depth of flow for an unlined trapezoidal channel to carry a discharge of $0.6\text{m}^3/\text{s}$ on a land slope of 1 in 1000 (Figure 5.9b). The soil is a clay loam and so the side slope will be stable at 1.5:1 and the maximum permissible velocity is 0.8m/s (see Table 5.4).

The first step is to select a suitable value for Manning's $n$ ($n = 0.025$ for natural soil) and then select a bed width to depth ratio (try $b = d$). Now obtain values for $j$ and $k$ from Table 5.3: $j = 2.5$ and $k = 0.66$. Calculate $d$ using the Manning formula:

$$Q = \frac{1}{n} jkd^{8/3} S^{1/2}$$

$$0.6 = \frac{1}{0.025} \times 2.5 \times 0.66 \times d^{8/3} \times 0.001^{1/2}$$

Rearranging this for *d*:

$$d^{8/3} = 0.286$$

$$d = 0.63\text{m}$$

As the ratio of bed width to depth is known *b* can now be calculated. In this case

$$b = d$$

and so

$$b = 0.63\text{m}$$

All the channel dimensions are now known but do they comply with the velocity limit? Check the velocity using the discharge equation:

$$Q = av$$

For a trapezoidal channel

$$\begin{aligned} a &= (b + yd)d \\ &= (0.63 + 1.5 \times 0.63)0.63 \\ &= 0.993\text{m}^2 \end{aligned}$$

Substitute this and the value for discharge into the discharge equation:

$$0.6 = 0.993 \times v$$

to calculate velocity

$$v = 0.6\text{m/s}$$

This is less than the maximum permissible velocity of 0.8m/s and so these channel dimensions are acceptable.

Note that there are many different channel dimensions that could be chosen to meet the design criteria. This is just one answer. Choosing another *b*:*d* ratio would produce different dimensions but they would be acceptable provided they met the criteria. Increasing the *b*:*d* ratio would reduce the velocity whereas decreasing the *b*:*d* ratio would increase the velocity. The latter would not be an option in this example as the velocity is close to the maximum permissible already.

A freeboard would normally be added to this to ensure that the channel is not overtopped.

### 5.5.5 Practical design

In engineering practice the usual design problem is to determine the size, shape and slope of a channel to carry a given discharge. There are many ways to approach this problem but here are some guidelines.

Whenever possible the channel slope should follow the natural land slope. This is done for cost as it helps to reduce the amount of soil excavation and embankment construction needed. But when the land slope is steep, high water velocities may occur and cause erosion in unlined channels. The most effective way to avoid erosion is to limit the velocity. Maximum non-scouring velocities for different soil types are shown in Table 5.4. Channels can also be lined for protection. Slope can also be reduced to lower the velocity to an acceptable level by using drop structures to take the flow down the slope in a series of steps – like a staircase (see section 7.10).

It is important to understand that there is no single correct answer to the size and shape of a channel, but a range of possibilities. If three people were each asked to design a trapezoidal channel for a given discharge, it is likely that they would come up with three different answers – and all could be acceptable. It is the designer's job to select the most appropriate one. Usually the selection is made simpler because of the limited range of values that are practicable. For example, land slope will limit the choice of slope and the materials of construction will limit the velocity. But even within these boundaries there are still many possibilities.

One of the problems of channel design is that of choosing suitable values of depth and bed width. King's method gets around this problem by asking the designer to select a ratio between them rather than the values themselves. Another way to simplify the problem is to assume that the hydraulic radius $R$ is equal to the depth of the water $d$. This is a reasonable assumption to make when the channel is shallow and wide. Referring to the example in Figure 5.7a the hydraulic radius was 0.83m in the wider channel when the depth was 1.0m. This is close enough for channel design purposes. The depth can then be calculated using the Manning formula and the bed width determined using the area and discharge.

The depth and width of a channel also influence velocity. For lined channels, which are expensive, it is important to keep the wetted perimeter ($p$) as small as possible as this keeps the cost down. This results in channels that are narrow and deep (Figure 5.7c). For unlined channels the velocity must be kept well within the limits set in Table 5.4. Making channels wide and shallow increases the wetted perimeter and channel resistance and this slows down the flow (Figure 5.7b). Look at any stream or river flowing in natural soil. Unless it is constrained by rocks or special training works it will naturally flow wide and shallow. So new channels which are to be constructed in similar material should also follow this trend.

**Table 5.4 Maximum permissible velocities**

| *Material* | *Maximum velocity (m/s)* |
|---|---|
| Silty sand | 0.30 |
| Sandy loam | 0.50 |
| Silt loam | 0.60 |
| Clay loam | 0.80 |
| Stiff clay | 1.10 |

## 5.6 Gradually varied flow

There are two kinds of non-uniform flow. The first is **gradually varied flow**. This has already been described and occurs when there are gradual changes taking place in the depth and velocity due to an imbalance of the force of gravity trying to make the flow go faster down a slope and the channel friction slowing it down. The gradual changes in depth take place over long distances and the water surface follows a gradual curve.

Engineers recognise 12 different surface water curves depending on the different gradually varied flow conditions that can occur in channels but the most common is the **backwater curve**. This occurs when a channel is dammed (Figure 5.10). For example, a river flowing at a normal depth of 1.0m down a gradient of 1m in 5km is dammed so that the water level rises to a depth of 5.0m. For a level water surface behind the dam its influence extends 20km upstream. But because the river is flowing there is a backwater curve which extends the influence of the dam up to 30km. This effect can be important for river engineers who wish to ensure that a river's embankments are high enough to contain flows and for landowners along a river whose land may be flooded by the dam construction. The backwater curve can be predicted using the basic tools of hydraulics but they go beyond the scope of this book. One problem is that they depend largely for their accuracy on predicting the value of Manning's *n*, which can be very difficult in natural channels.

## 5.7 Rapidly varied flow

The second type of non-uniform flow is **rapidly varied flow**. As its name implies, sudden changes in depth and velocity occur and this is the result of sudden changes in either the shape or size of channels. The change usually takes place over a few metres, unlike gradually varied flow where changes take place slowly over many kilometres. Hydraulic structures are often the cause of rapidly varied flow and the sluice gate in section 5.4.3 is a good example of this. In this case the gate changed the flow suddenly from a deep, slow flow upstream to a fast, shallow flow downstream. Building a weir or widening (or deepening) a channel will also cause sudden changes to occur. But unfortunately, all flows do not behave in the same

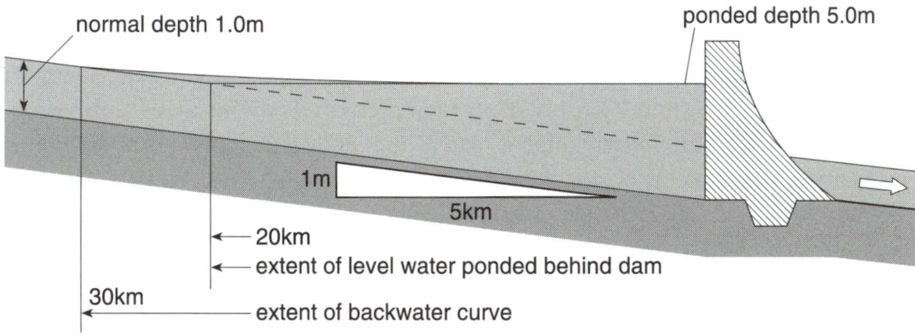


**Figure 5.10 Backwater curve**

way. For example, a weir in a channel will have quite a different effect on the deep, slow flow than on the shallow, fast flow. So a further classification of channel flow is needed, this time in terms of how flow behaves when channel size or shape is changed suddenly.

The two contrasting types of flow described above are now well recognised by engineers. The more scientific name for deep, slow flow is **sub-critical flow** and for shallow, fast flow is **super-critical flow**. This implies that there is some **critical point** when the flow changes from one to the other and that this point defines the difference between the two flow types. This is indeed the case. At the critical point the velocity becomes the **critical velocity** and the depth becomes the **critical depth**. The critical point is not just important to classify the two flow types. It plays an important role in the measurement of discharges in channels. This is discussed later in section 7.5.

## 5.7.1 Flow behaviour

Just how do sub-critical and super-critical flows behave when there are sudden changes in the channel?

### *5.7.1.1 Sub-critical flow*

This is by far the most common flow type and is associated with all natural and gently flowing rivers and canals. The effect of a sluice gate on this kind of flow has already been described. The effect of a weir is very similar (Figure 5.11a). A weir is like a step up on the bed of a channel. Such a step causes the water level to drop and the velocity to increase. The step up reduces the flow area in a channel but the water does not slow down because of this. Its velocity increases (remember the way flow behaves in constrictions – section 3.7.1). This increases the kinetic energy, but as there is no change in the total energy this is at the expense of the depth (pressure) energy. So the depth is reduced causing a drop in the water level. Weirs are a common sight on rivers and most people will have seen this sudden but smooth drop in water level over a weir. A similar, though not so dramatic, drop in water level occurs when water flows under a bridge. The water level drops because the reduced width of the river increases its velocity.

Interestingly, the converse is also true. When a channel is made larger by increasing its width or depth, the water level rises. This is not so easy to believe. But it follows from the energy equation and it actually happens in practice (Figure 5.11b). This was highlighted by a problem facing engineers who were troubled by flooding from a river flowing through a town and under the town bridge (Figure 5.11c). During stormy weather, the river level rises and reaches the underside of the bridge. The extra friction from the bridge slows the flow and so the water level upstream of the bridge rises even further and floods the town. The problem was how to increase the carrying capacity of the river through the town, and particularly under the bridge, to avoid the flooding. The engineers decided that the most obvious solution was to make the channel larger, but the flooding got worse, not better. Clearly the engineers did not understand the hydraulic tools of

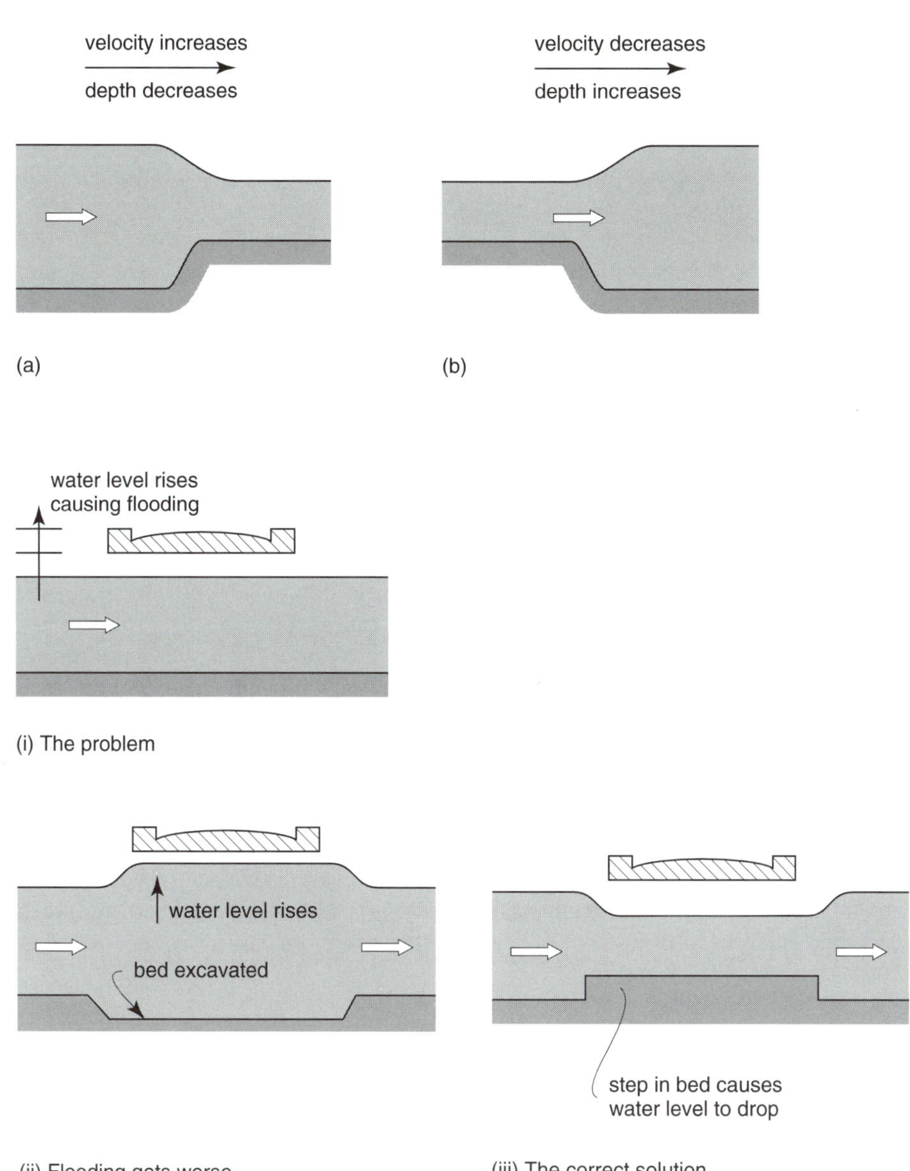


**Figure 5.11** Rapidly varied flow – sub-critical

continuity and energy. The increase in channel depth reduced the velocity and hence the kinetic energy. As the total energy remained the same, the depth energy increased causing the river level to rise and not fall as expected. They eventually opted for the correct solution, which was to reduce the flow area under the bridge by constructing a step on the bed of the river. This increased the velocity energy and reduced the depth of flow. So even when the river was in flood, the flow was able to pass safely under the bridge.

Canoeists will be well aware of the way in which rapid changes in water surface levels are a direct result of changes on the river bed. Beware those parts of a river where the current looks swifter. It may be tempting to steer your canoe into the faster-moving water but it is a sign of shallow water and there may be rocks just below the surface which can damage a canoe. The slower-moving water may not be so attractive but at least it will be deep and safe.

### 5.7.1.2 *Super-critical flow*

This type of flow behaves in completely the opposite way to sub-critical flow. A step up on the bed of a channel in super-critical flow causes the water depth to rise as it passes over it and a channel that is excavated deeper causes the water depth to drop (Figure 5.12). Super-critical flow is very difficult to deal with in practice. Not only does the faster-moving water cause severe erosion in unprotected channels, it is also difficult to control with hydraulic structures. Trying to guide a super-critical flow around a bend in a channel, for example, is like trying to drive a car at high speed around a sharp road bend. It has a tendency to overshoot and to leave the channel. Fortunately super-critical flows rarely occur and are confined to steep rocky streams and just downstream of sluice gates and dam spillways where water can reach speeds of 20m/s and more. When they do occur engineers have developed ways of quickly turning them back into sub-critical flows so they can be dealt with more easily (see section 5.7.6).

### 5.7.1.3 *General rules*

So another way of classifying channel flow is in terms of how a flow behaves when the size or shape of a channel is changed suddenly: *For sub-critical flow the water*

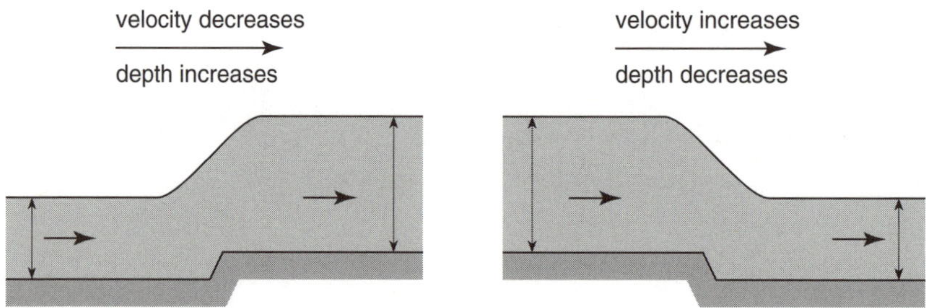


**Figure 5.12 Rapidly varied flow – super-critical**

*depth decreases when a channel flow area is reduced either by raising its bed or reducing its width – conversely, the depth increases when the flow area is increased. For super-critical flow the water depth increases when the flow area is reduced and decreases when it is increased.*

### 5.7.1.4 Spotting the difference

In the sluice gate example both sub-critical and super-critical flow occur in the same channel, at the same discharge and with the same total energy. In this situation there is a clear visual difference between them. But if the two flows occurred in separate straight channels it would be more difficult to tell them apart just by looking. However, if some obstruction is put into the two flows such as a bridge pier or a sharp bend the difference between them would be immediately obvious.

A more scientific way of distinguishing between the two flows is to establish the point of change from sub-critical to super-critical flow – the **critical point**. There are several very practical ways of doing this but before describing these it might be helpful to look first at another critical point that is similar to, but perhaps more familiar than, channel flow.

### 5.7.1.5 An airflow analogy

Everyone is now very familiar with aeroplanes and many will have travelled on one. The way air flows around an aeroplane in flight is, in fact, very similar to water flow. They are both fluids and so a look at air flow may help in understanding some of the complexities of water flow, and in particular the critical point.

Most people will have noticed that jumbo jets and Concorde have very different shapes (Figure 5.13). This is because the two aeroplanes are designed to travel at very different speeds. Jumbo jets are relatively slow and travel at only 800km/h whereas Concorde travels at much higher speeds of 2000km/h and more. But the change in aircraft shape is not a gradual one; a sudden change is needed when aeroplanes fly over 1200km/h. This is the speed at which sound waves travel through still air. Sound waves move through air in much the same way as waves travel across a water surface and although they cannot be seen, they can be heard. When someone fires a gun 1km away it takes 3s before you hear the bang. This is the time it takes for sound waves to travel through the air from the gun to your ear at a velocity of 1200km/h. Notice how you see the gun flash immediately. This is because light waves travel much faster than sound waves at a velocity of 300 000km/s. This is the reason why lightning in a storm is seen long before the thunder is heard when the storm is several kilometres away.

When an aeroplane is flying the noise from its engines travels outwards in all directions in the form of sound waves. When it is travelling below the speed of sound, the sound travels faster than the aeroplane and so an observer hears the aeroplane coming before it reaches him (Figure 5.13a). This is known as sub-sonic flight and aeroplanes that fly below the speed of sound have large rounded shapes like the jumbo jets. When an aeroplane is flying faster than the speed of sound, the sound travels slower than the aeroplane and is left far behind. An observer will see the aeroplane approaching before hearing it (Figure 5.13b). This is known as super-sonic flight and aeroplanes travelling at such speeds have slim, dart-like shapes. When the observer does eventually hear it, there is usually a very loud bang. This is the result of a pressure wave, known as the sonic boom, which comes from all the sound waves being bunched up together behind the aeroplane.

So there are two types of airflow, sub-sonic and super-sonic, and there is also a clear point at which the flow changes from one to the other – the speed of sound in still air.

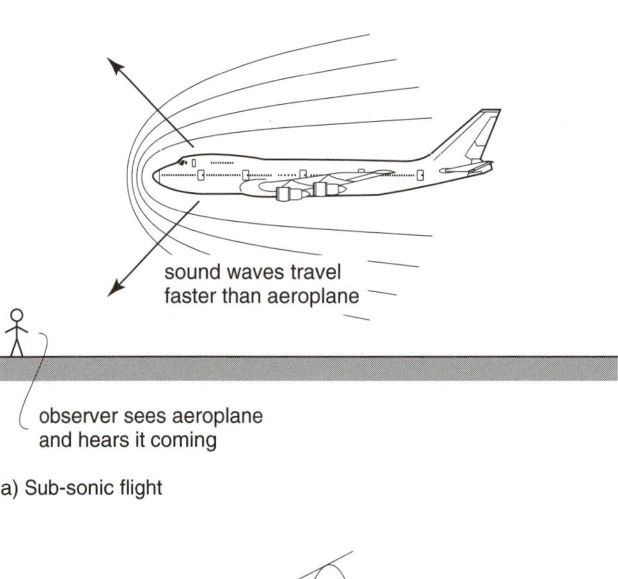
sound waves travel
faster than aeroplane
observer sees aeroplane
and hears it coming

(a) Sub-sonic flight

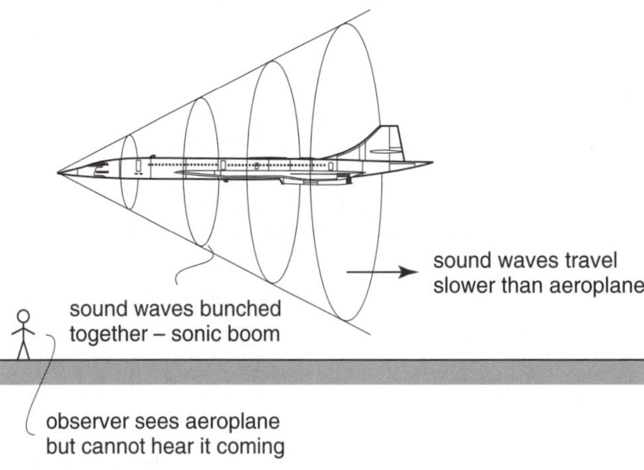
sound waves travel
slower than aeroplane
sound waves bunched
together – sonic boom
observer sees aeroplane
but cannot hear it coming

(b) Super-sonic flight

**Figure 5.13 Airflow analogy**

### *5.7.1.6 Back to water*

The purpose of this lengthy explanation of aeroplanes in flight is to demonstrate the close similarity between air flow and water flow. Sub-critical and super-critical flow are very similar to sub-sonic and super-sonic flight respectively. The majority of aeroplanes travel at sub-sonic speeds and there are very few design problems. In contrast, very few aeroplanes travel at super-sonic speeds and their design problems are much greater and more expensive to solve. The same is true for water. Most flows are sub-critical and are easily dealt with. But in a few special cases the flow is super-critical and this is much more difficult to deal with.

The change from sub- to super-sonic occurs when the aeroplane reaches the speed of sound waves in still air. But this is where water is a little different. The change does not occur at the speed of sound in water, although sound does travel through water very effectively. It occurs when the flow reaches the *same velocity as waves on the water surface*. To avoid confusion between wave velocity and water velocity, wave velocity is often referred to as **wave celerity** (see section 6.2).

Waves occur on the surface of water when it is disturbed. When a stone is thrown into a still pond of water, waves travel out across the surface towards the bank (Figure 5.14a). Although there seems to be a definite movement towards the bank, it is only the waves that are moving outwards and not the water. The water only moves up and down as the waves pass. If a duck was floating on the pond it would only bob up and down with the wave motion and would not be washed up on the bank! But the wave celerity is not a fixed value like the speed of sound. It depends on the depth of water and it can be calculated using the equation (see section 6.4):

$$c = \sqrt{gd}$$

where $c$ is wave celerity (m/s), $g$ is gravity constant (9.81m/s$^2$) and $d$ is depth of water (m).

So wave celerity sets the boundary between sub-critical and super-critical flow for a given flow. When the flow velocity is less than the wave velocity, the flow is sub-critical. When it is greater, the flow is super-critical.

As water waves are easily seen they provide a good visual way of determining the type of flow. When there is a disturbance in a stream, waves move out in all directions from the point of disturbance but the pattern is distorted by the velocity of the water $v$ (Figure 5.14b). Some waves move upstream but struggle against the flow and so appear to move more slowly than on the still pond. Others move downstream and are assisted by the flow and so they move faster. Because waves can still move upstream of the disturbance it means that the stream velocity $v$ is less than the wave celerity $c$ and so the flow must be sub-critical. When the stream velocity $v$ is increased and becomes greater than the wave celerity $c$, then waves can no longer travel upstream against the flow. They are all swept downstream and form a vee pattern. This means the flow must be super-critical (Figure 5.14b).

When the stream velocity $v$ is equal to the wave celerity $c$ then the flow is at the change-over point – the **critical point**. At this point the depth of the flow is the critical depth and the velocity is the critical velocity.

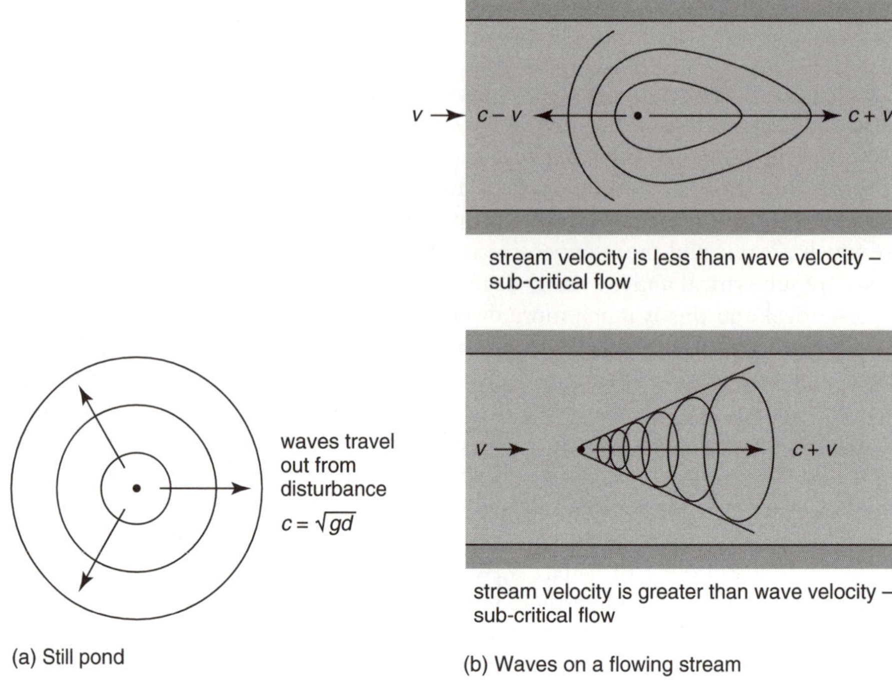


**Figure 5.14 Using waves to determine flow type**

Notice the similarity between the sound waves around an aeroplane and the water wave patterns around the disturbance in a stream. There is even an equivalent of the sonic boom in water although it is much less noisy. This is the hydraulic jump which is described in more detail in section 5.7.6.

### 5.7.2 Froude number

Another way of determining whether a flow is sub- or super-critical is to use the Froude number. Returning to the airflow analogy for a moment, aircraft designers use the **Mach number** to describe sub- and super-sonic flight. This is a dimensionless number and is calculated as follows:

$$\text{Mach number} = \frac{\text{velocity of aircraft}}{\text{velocity of sound in still air}}$$

A Mach number less than 1 indicates sub-sonic flight and a Mach number greater than 1 indicates super-sonic flight. It follows that a Mach number of 1 means that the aircraft is travelling at the speed of sound.

A dimensionless number similar to the Mach number was developed by William Froude (1810–1879) to describe sub- and super-critical flow in channels and is now referred to as the **Froude number** ($F$). It is the ratio of the stream velocity to the wave celerity and is calculated as follows:

$$\text{Froude number } (F) = \frac{\text{stream velocity (m/s)}}{\text{wave celerity (m/s)}}$$

Note that Froude number has no dimensions. Now wave celerity is

$$c = \sqrt{gd}$$

and so

$$F = \frac{v}{\sqrt{gd}}$$

A Froude number less than 1 indicates sub-critical flow and a Froude number greater than 1 indicates super-critical flow. It follows that a Froude number of 1 means that the channel is flowing at critical depth and velocity. So calculating the Froude number is another way of determining when the flow is sub- or super-critical.

### 5.7.3 Specific energy

It should be possible to quantify the changes in depth and velocity resulting from sudden changes in a channel by making use of the energy and continuity equations. Remember that a similar problem occurred in pipes when a venturi meter was inserted to measure discharge (see section 4.9). The equations of energy and continuity were used to work out the pressure and velocity changes as a result of the sudden changes in the size of the pipe (Figure 5.15a). The solution was straightforward because the area of flow was fixed by the pipe diameter and so only the velocity needed to be calculated. But for a channel the flow area is not fixed because it is open to the atmosphere and so it can flow at many different depths (Figure 5.15b). So both the flow area and the velocity are unknown. If the energy and continuity equations are applied to this problem the result is a cubic equation which means there are three possible answers for the downstream depth and velocity. One answer is negative and this can be dismissed immediately as impracticable. The two remaining answers are both possibilities, but which one is the right one?

To help solve this problem Boris Bakhmeteff (1880–1951) introduced a very helpful concept which he called **specific energy** ($E$). Simply stated: *Specific energy is the energy in a channel measured from the bed of a channel.* Writing this as an equation:

$$E = d + \frac{q^2}{2gd^2}$$

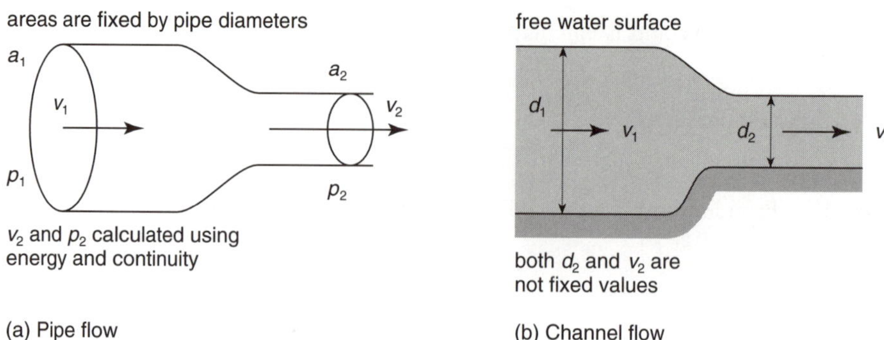


**Figure 5.15 Predicting changes in depth and velocity in a channel is not straightforward**

It is important at this point to draw a clear distinction between total energy and specific energy because they are quite different (Figure 5.16a). Total energy (TE) is measured from some fixed datum and its value can only reduce as energy is lost through friction. When there is a change in the bed level of a channel (e.g. when water flows over a weir) there are also changes in the energy components but no change in the total energy. Specific energy (SE), in contrast, is measured from the bed of a channel and so when the bed level changes the specific energy also changes. It also means that specific energy can rise as well as fall depending on what is happening in the channel. When the flow is on top of the weir the specific energy falls and when it comes off the weir it rises again.

The difference between total and specific energy is highlighted by uniform flow (Figure 5.16b). Total energy falls gradually as energy is lost through friction. But specific energy remains constant along the channel because there are no changes in depth and velocity.

The physical significance of specific energy beyond its simple definition is not so obvious and many engineers still struggle with it. However, it is a very easy and very practical concept to use. Rather than be too concerned about its significance, it is better to think of it as a simple mechanism for solving a problem. It is like a key for opening a lock. It is not necessary to know how a lock works in order to use it. You just put the key in and turn it. In the same way, specific energy unlocks the problem of quantifying the effects that sudden changes in a channel have on depth and velocity and also helps to determine which of the two possible answers is the right one. It also unlocks the problem of how to measure discharges in channels (see section 7.5).

The best way to show how this works is with an example. A channel is carrying a given discharge per metre width $q$. From the specific energy equation it is possible to calculate a range of values for specific energy by putting in different values of $d$. When the results of the calculations are plotted on a graph (Figure 5.17a) the result is the **specific energy diagram**. There are two limbs to the specific energy diagram and this shows the two possible solutions for depth for any given value of $E$. These are called the **alternate depths** and are the sub- and super-critical depths described earlier. The upper limb of the curve describes sub-critical flow and

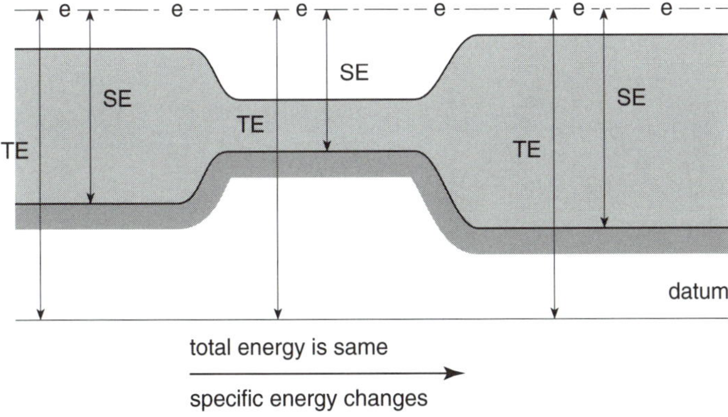


(a) Change in bed level

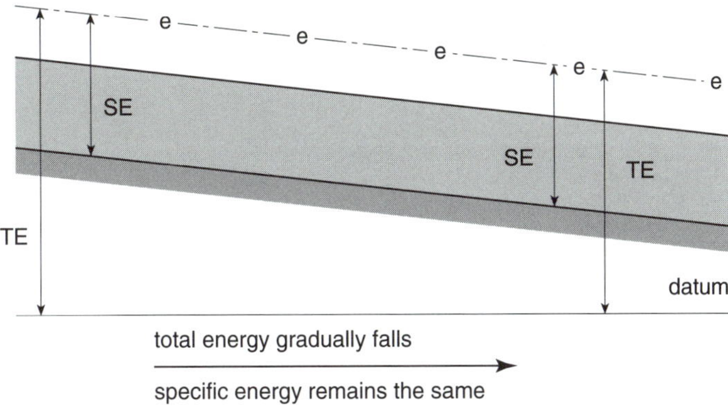


(b) Uniform flow

**Figure 5.16** Specific energy

the lower limb describes super-critical flow. The change-over between the two types of flow occurs at the point C on the graph and this is the **critical point**. It is the only place on the graph where there is only one depth of flow for a given value of $E$ and not two.

So the specific energy diagram defines sub-critical and super-critical flow by defining the critical depth. It also confirms the earlier descriptions of the effects on depth and velocity of sudden changes in a channel. Take any point $E_1$ on the sub-critical part of the curve and look what happens when the value of $E$ changes as a result of raising or lowering the channel bed (Figure 5.17b). A step up on the bed reduces $E$ and the graph shows that $d$ decreases also (remember $E$ is measured from the bed of the channel). A step down on the bed increases $E$ and the graph shows that $d$ increases. A similar example can be applied to the super-critical part of the diagram to show the effects of changing $E$ on the depth of flow.

So the depth and velocity change, but by how much? This is where the specific energy diagram becomes very useful for quantifying these changes. To see how this

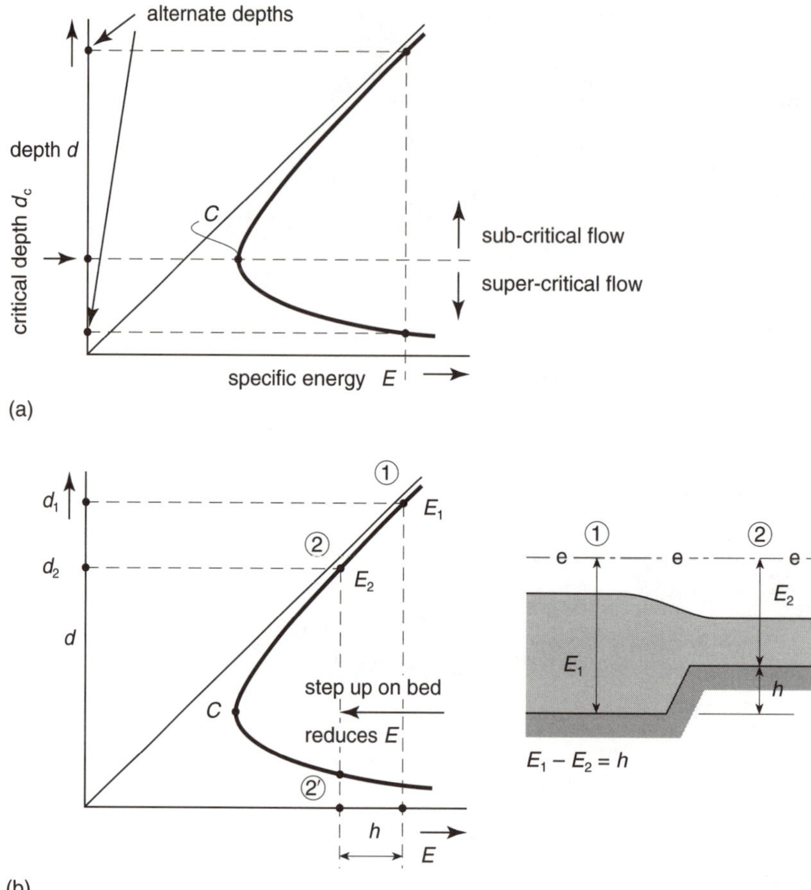


**Figure 5.17 Specific energy diagram**

is done consider what happens when there is a step up of height $h$ on the bed of a channel from point 1 to point 2 (Figure 5.17b). This reduces the specific energy $E$ by an amount $h$. So

$$E_1 - E_2 = h$$

and

$$E_2 = E_1 - h$$

So $E_2$ on the curve can be found by subtracting $h$ from the value of $E_1$ and this represents the condition on the step from which it is possible to determine the depth $d_2$ and velocity $v_2$. The same logic can also be applied to super-critical flow. An example in the box shows how this is done in practice for both sub-critical and super-critical flows.

## Example: Calculating the effect on depth of changing the channel bed level

A channel with a discharge per metre width of $0.5\text{m}^3/\text{s}$ is to be changed either by constructing a 0.3m step up on the bed of the channel or by excavating the channel bed deeper by 0.3m. Calculate the effects of these changes on the water level in both sub-critical and super-critical flow assuming the specific energy in the channel is $E_1 = 1.0\text{m}$.

The first step is to calculate specific energy for a range of depths for a discharge of $0.5\text{m}^3/\text{s}$ and to plot the results on a graph (Table 5.5 lists the results of the calculation and Figure 5.18 shows the results as a graph).

From the graph the alternative depths for $E_1 = 1\text{m}$ are $d_1 = 0.99\text{m}$ (sub-critical) and 0.12m (super-critical).

### For sub-critical flow

- Effect on water level with a 0.3m high step up on the bed of the channel

Specific energy in the channel is

$$E_1 = 1.0\text{m}$$

and

$$d_1 = 0.99\text{m}$$

Next calculate the specific energy on the step which is 0.3m higher than the channel bed:

$$E_2 = E_1 - 0.3 = 0.7\text{m}$$

**Table 5.5 Calculating specific energy**

| *Depth of flow (m)* | *Specific energy* (m)* |
|---|---|
| 0.1 | 1.374 |
| 0.12 | 1.005 |
| 0.15 | 0.716 |
| 0.2 | 0.519 |
| 0.25 | 0.454 |
| 0.3 | 0.442 |
| 0.35 | 0.454 |
| 0.4 | 0.480 |
| 0.5 | 0.551 |
| 0.6 | 0.635 |
| 0.7 | 0.726 |
| 0.8 | 0.820 |
| 0.9 | 0.916 |
| 1 | 1.013 |
| 1.2 | 1.209 |
| 1.4 | 1.407 |
| 1.6 | 1.605 |

* Specific energy for a range of depths for a channel carrying a discharge $q$ of $0.5\text{m}^3/\text{s/m}$

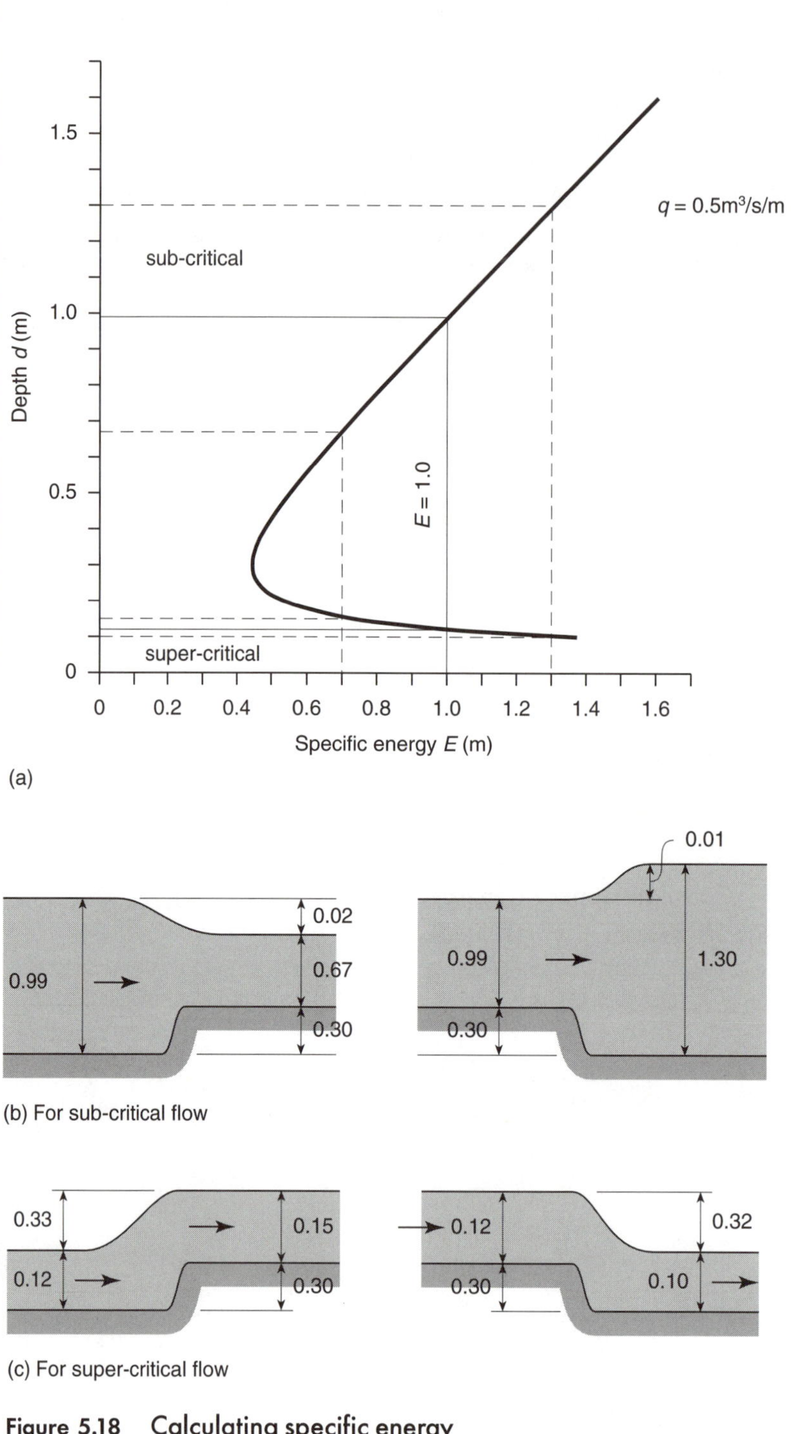


**Figure 5.18 Calculating specific energy**

Now locate $E_2$ on the graph and read off the value for $d_2$:

$$d_2 = 0.67\text{m}$$

Now depth $d_2$ is measured from the step and so the water level is now 0.97m above the original channel bed. This means that the water level has dropped 0.02m as a result of raising the channel bed.

- Effect on water level with a 0.3m high step down on the bed of the channel

Specific energy in the channel is

$$E_1 = 1.0\text{m}$$

and

$$d_1 = 0.99\text{m}$$

Next calculate the specific energy where the channel has been excavated by 0.3m:

$$E_2 = E_1 + 0.3 = 1.3\text{m}$$

Now locate $E_2$ on the graph and read off the value for $d_2$:

$$d_2 = 1.30\text{m}$$

Now depth $d_2$ is measured from the step down and so the water level is now 1.30m above the channel bed. This means that the water level rises by 0.01m as a result of the step down in the channel bed.

#### For super-critical flow

- Effect on water level with a 0.3m high step up on the bed of the channel

Specific energy in the channel is

$$E_1 = 1.0\text{m}$$

and

$$d_1 = 0.12\text{m}$$

Next calculate the specific energy on the step which is 0.3m higher than the channel bed:

$$E_2 = E_1 - 0.3 = 0.7\text{m}$$

Now locate $E_2$ on the graph and read off the value for $d_2$:

$$d_2 = 0.15\text{m}$$

Now depth $d_2$ is measured from the top of the raised bed and so the water level is now 0.45m above the original channel bed. This means that the water level rises 0.33m as a result of raising the channel bed.

- Effect on water level with a 0.3m high step down on the bed of the channel

Specific energy in the channel is

$$E_1 = 1.0\text{m}$$

and

$$d_1 = 0.12\text{m}$$

Next calculate the specific energy where the channel be has been excavated by 0.3m:

$$E_2 = E_1 + 0.3 = 1.3\text{m}$$

Now locate $E_2$ on the graph and read off the value for $d_2$:

$$d_2 = 0.10\text{m}$$

Now depth $d_2$ is measured from the step down and so the water level is now 0.20m below the original channel bed. This means that the water level drops 0.32m as a result of the step down in the channel bed.

One question is raised by Figure 5.17b: Why does the flow stay sub-critical when it moves from point 1 to point 2? Why does it not go to the point 2′ which has the same value of specific energy and so become super-critical? The answer comes from the specific energy diagram. Remember the diagram is for a given value of discharge. It is not possible suddenly to 'leap' across the diagram from 2 to 2′ as this would mean a change in discharge. The only way to get from 2 to 2′ is down the specific energy curve and through the critical point C and this can only be done by increasing the value of $h$ (i.e. raising the step even further) so that $E_2$ gets smaller until it reaches the critical point. At this point the flow can go super-critical. As $h$ in this case is not high enough to create critical conditions, the flow moves from point 1 to point 2 and stays sub-critical.

The same argument can be applied to changes in super-critical flow also. The flow can only go sub-critical by going around the specific energy curve and through the critical depth.

To summarise some points about specific energy:

- Specific energy is used to quantify the changes in depth and velocity in a channel as a result of sudden changes in the size and shape of a channel. It also helps to determine which of the two possible answers for depth and velocity is the right one.
- Specific energy is different from total energy. It can increase as well as decrease. It depends on what happens to the bed of the channel. In contrast,

total energy can only decrease as energy is lost through friction or sudden changes in flow.

- The specific energy diagram in Figure 5.17 is for one value of discharge. When the discharge changes a new diagram is needed. So for any channel there will be a whole family of specific energy diagrams representing a range of discharges.
- Specific energy is the principle on which many channel flow measuring devices such as weirs and flumes are based. They depend on changing the specific energy enough to make the flow go critical. At this point there is only one value of depth for one value of specific energy and from this it is possible to develop a formula for discharge (see section 7.5). Such devices are sometimes referred to as **critical depth structures.**
- For uniform flow the value of specific energy remains constant along the entire channel. This is because the depth and velocity are the same. In contrast, total energy gradually reduces as energy is lost along the channel.

#### 5.7.3.1 *Which flow type will occur?*

This question can be answered by calculating the normal depth of flow, using a formula such as Manning's and then comparing it with the critical depth. When the depth is greater than the critical depth the flow will be sub-critical and when it is less it will be super-critical.

### 5.7.4 Critical depth

The critical depth $d_c$ can be determined directly from the specific energy diagram but it can be difficult to locate its exact position because of the rounded shape of the curve close to the critical point. To overcome this problem it can be calculated using a formula derived from the specific energy equation:

$$d_c = \sqrt[3]{\frac{q^2}{g}}$$

This formula shows that the critical depth is determined only by the discharge per metre width $q$. It has nothing to do with the slope or the normal depth. For the mathematically minded a proof of this is given in the box.

**Derivation: Critical depth equation**

Derive a formula for the critical depth and its location on the specific energy diagram (Figure 5.17). Using the specific energy equation

$$E = d + \frac{q^2}{2gd^2}$$

At the critical point the specific energy $E$ is at its lowest value and so the gradient of the curve $\mathrm{d}E/\mathrm{d}d$ is equal to zero. The equation for the gradient can be found using calculus and differentiating the above equation for the curve:

$$\frac{\mathrm{d}E}{\mathrm{d}d} = 1 - \frac{q^2}{gd^3} = 0$$

Depth $d$ now becomes the critical depth $d_c$ and so

$$\frac{q^2}{gd_c^3} = 1$$

Rearranging this for $d_c$

$$d_c^3 = \frac{q^2}{g}$$

$$d_c = \sqrt[3]{\frac{q^2}{g}}$$

So the critical depth $d_c$ depends only on the discharge per metre width $q$.

To calculate the specific energy at the critical point first write down the specific energy equation for critical conditions:

$$E_c = d_c + \frac{q^2}{2gd_c^2}$$

To find another way of writing the kinetic energy term use the above equation:

$$\frac{q^2}{gd_c^3} = 1$$

Dividing both sides by 2 and multiplying by $d_c$:

$$\frac{q^2}{2gd_c^2} = \frac{d_c}{2}$$

Now put this into the specific energy equation:

$$E_c = d_c + \frac{d_c}{2} = \frac{3d_c}{2}$$

So for any given discharge the critical depth can be calculated and also the specific energy at the critical point. These two values locate exactly the critical point on the specific energy diagram.

Note also from the above analysis that when

$$\frac{q^2}{gd_c^3} = 1$$

$$v_c^2 = gd_c$$

and so

$$v_c = \sqrt{gd_c}$$

This is the equation for the celerity of surface water waves and it shows that at the critical point the water velocity $v_c$ equals the wave celerity $\sqrt{gd_c}$.

## Example: Calculating critical depth

Using the previous example of a channel with a discharge per metre width of $0.5\text{m}^3/\text{s}$ (Figure 5.18a), calculate the critical depth and the step up in the bed level required to ensure that the flow will reach the critical depth. Assume the initial specific energy $E_1 = 1.0\text{m}$.

First determine the critical depth:

$$d_c = \sqrt[3]{\frac{q^2}{g}}$$

$$d_c = \sqrt[3]{\frac{0.5^2}{9.81}} = 0.29\text{m}$$

Now calculate the specific energy on the step up:

$$E_2 = d_2 + \frac{q^2}{2gd_2^2}$$

When this is critical flow then

$$d_2 = d_c$$

and so

$$E_2 = 0.29 + \frac{0.5^2}{2 \times 9.81 \times 0.29^2} = 0.44\text{m}$$

But

$$E_1 - E_2 = h$$

i.e. the change in specific energy is a direct result of the height $h$ of the step up. So

$$h = 1.0 - 0.44 = 0.56\text{m}$$

The bed level of the channel must be raised by 0.56m to ensure that the flow goes critical.

### 5.7.5 Critical flow

Although critical flow is important, it is a flow condition best avoided in uniform flow. There is no problem when flow goes quickly through the critical point on its way from sub- to super-critical or from super- to sub-critical, but there are problems when the normal flow depth is near to the critical depth. This is a very unstable condition as the flow tends to oscillate from sub- to super-critical and back to sub-critical again, resulting in surface waves that can travel for many kilometres eroding and damaging channel banks. The explanation for the instability is in the shape of the specific energy diagram close to the critical point (Figure 5.17a). Small changes in specific energy $E$, possibly as a result of small channel irregularities, can cause large changes in depth as the flow oscillates between sub- and super-critical flow. As the flow **hunts** back and forth it sets up waves. So although critical flow is very useful in some respects it can cause serious problems in others.

### 5.7.6 Flow transitions

Changes in a channel that result in changes in flow from sub-critical to super-critical and vice versa are referred to as **transitions**. The following are examples of some common transitions.

#### *5.7.6.1 Sub- to super-critical flow*

When flow goes from sub- to super-critical it does so smoothly. In Figure 5.19a the channel gradient is increased which changes the flow from sub- to super-critical. The water surface curves rapidly but smoothly as the flow goes through the critical point. There is no energy loss as the flow is contracting. Notice how the critical depth is shown as c—c—c so that the two types of flow are clearly distinguishable. Remember, the critical depth is the same in both sections of the channel because it depends only the discharge and not on slope.

Another example of this type of transition is the sluice gate (Figure 5.19b). In this case a gate is used to force the change in flow. Again the transition occurs smoothly with no energy loss.

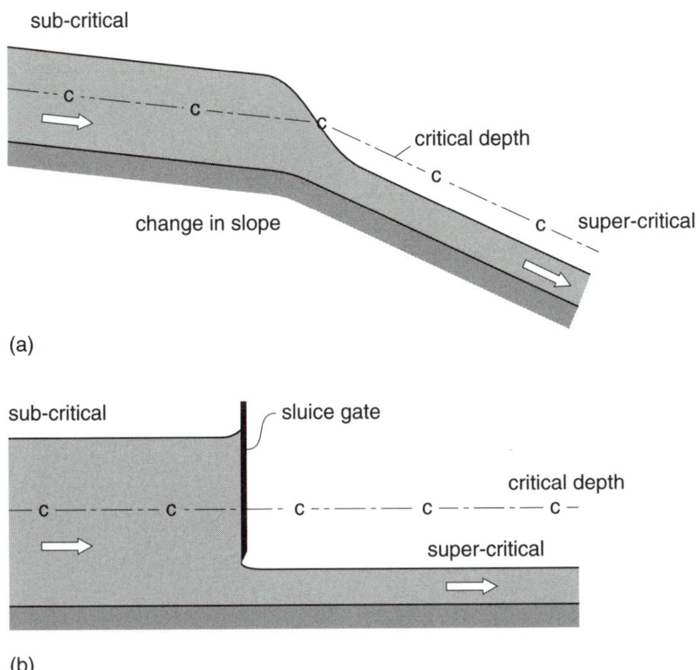


**Figure 5.19** Flow transitions – sub- to super-critical

#### 5.7.6.2 *Super- to sub-critical flow (hydraulic jump)*

The change from super- to sub-critical is not so smooth. In fact a vigorous turbulent mixing action occurs as the flow jumps abruptly from super- to sub-critical flow (Figure 5.20). It is aptly called a **hydraulic jump** and as the flow expands there is a significant loss of energy due to the turbulence.

Hydraulic jumps are very useful for many purposes:

- They get rid of unwanted energy, such as at the base of dam spillways.
- They are useful places for mixing chemicals in water. The vigorous turbulence ensures that any added chemical is thoroughly dispersed throughout the flow.
- They convert super-critical flow downstream of hydraulic structures into sub-critical flow and so avoid erosion damage in unprotected channels.

Hydraulic jumps are usually described by their strength and the Froude number of the super-critical flow. A **strong jump** is the most desirable. It is very vigorous, has a high Froude number, well above 1, and the turbulent mixing is confined to a short length of channel. A **weak jump**, on the other hand, is not so violent. It has a low Froude number, approaching 1, which means the depth of flow is close to the critical depth. This kind of jump is not confined and appears as waves which can travel downstream for many kilometres. This is undesirable because the waves can do a great deal of damage to channel banks.

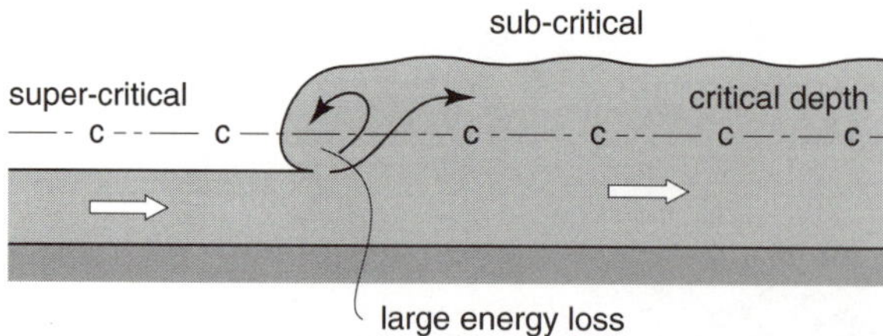


(a) Strong hydraulic jump

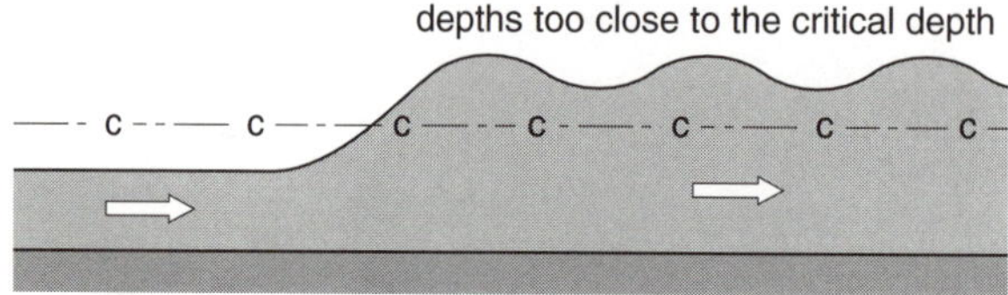


(b) Weak hydraulic jump

**Figure 5.20 Flow transitions – super- to sub-critical**

### 5.7.6.3 *Creating a hydraulic jump*

There are two conditions required to form a hydraulic jump:

- The flow upstream of the jump must be super-critical, i.e. the Froude number must be greater than 1.
- The downstream flow must be sub-critical and deep enough for the jump to form.

Once there is super-critical flow in a channel it is the downstream depth of flow that determines if a jump will occur. To create a jump the downstream depth must be just right. If the depth is too shallow a jump will not form and the super-critical flow will continue down the channel (Figure 5.21a). Conversely, if the flow is too deep the jump will move upsteam and if it reaches a sluice gate it may drown out (see section 7.2.1 for drowned flow).

When the upstream depth and velocity are known it is possible to calculate the downstream depth and velocity that will create a jump by using the momentum equation. The energy equation cannot be used at this stage because of the large and unknown energy loss at a jump.

The formula derived from the momentum equation which links the two depths of flow $d_1$ and $d_2$ is as follows (Figure 5.21b):

$$\frac{d_2}{d_1} = \frac{1}{2}\left(\sqrt{1 + 8F_1^2} - 1\right)$$

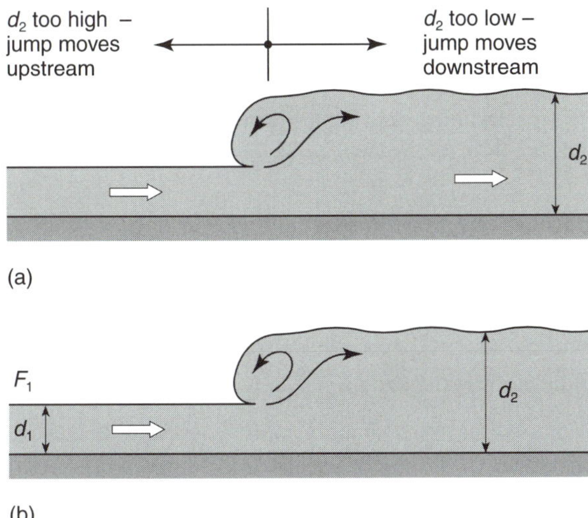


**Figure 5.21 Forming a hydraulic jump**

where $d_1$ is upstream depth, $d_2$ is downstream depth and $F_1$ is upstream Froude number.

Most hydraulic jump problems involve calculating the downstream depth $d_2$ at which a jump will occur. But determining a value for $d_2$ is fine in theory, but in practice the formation of a jump is very sensitive to the downstream depth. This means that when the downstream depth is a little more or less than the calculated value, the jump does not stabilise at the selected location but moves up and down the channel **hunting** for the right depth of flow. In practice it is very difficult to control water depths with great accuracy and so some method is needed to remove the sensitivity of the jump to downstream water level and so stabilise it. This is the job of a **stilling basin** which is a concrete apron located downstream of a weir or sluice gate. Its job is to ensure that a hydraulic jump forms in the basin even though the downstream water level may vary considerably. This is discussed further in section 7.10.

### *5.7.6.4 Calculating energy losses*

Once the downstream depth and velocity have been calculated using the momentum equation, the loss of energy at a jump can be determined using the total energy equation as follows:

total energy upstream = total energy downstream + energy loss at jump

$$d_1 + \frac{v_1^2}{2g} + z_1 = d_2 + \frac{v_2^2}{2g} + z_2 + \text{losses}$$

## Example: Calculating the downstream depth to form a hydraulic jump

A hydraulic jump is to be formed in a channel carrying a discharge of $0.8\text{m}^3/\text{s}$ per m width of channel with a depth of flow of 0.25m. Calculate the depth required downstream to create the jump.

The downstream depth can be calculated using the formula:

$$\frac{d_2}{d_1} = \frac{1}{2}\left(\sqrt{1 + 8F_1^2} - 1\right)$$

First calculate the velocity using the discharge equation:

$$q = v_1 d_1$$

$$v_1 = \frac{0.8}{0.25} = 3.2\text{m/s}$$

Then the upstream Froude number:

$$F_1 = \frac{v_1}{\sqrt{gd_1}} = \frac{3.2}{\sqrt{9.81 \times 0.25}} = 2.04$$

Substitute the values into the above formula:

$$\frac{d_2}{0.25} = \frac{1}{2}\left(\sqrt{1 + 8 \times 2.04^2} - 1\right)$$

$$d_2 = 0.25 \times 2.43 = 0.61\text{m}$$

To summarise all the various types of flow that can occur in channels:

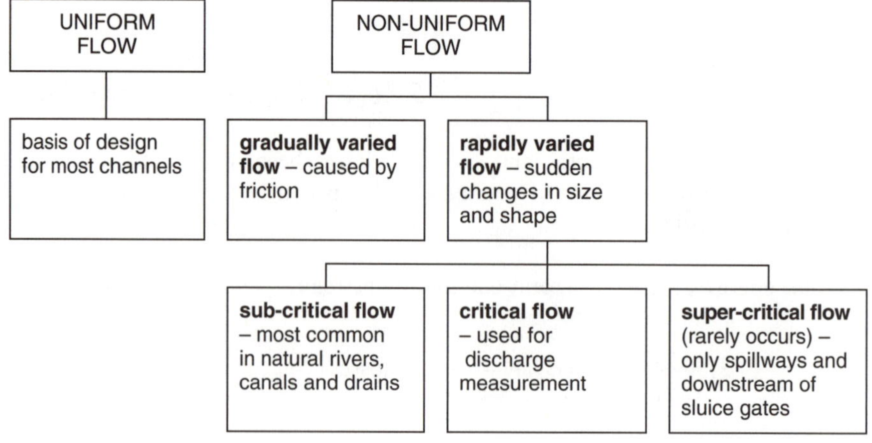

## 5.8 Secondary flows

One interesting aspect of channel flow (which all anglers know about) is **secondary flows**. These are small but important currents that occur in flowing water and explain many important phenomena.

In real channels the velocity is usually much higher in the middle than at the sides and bed. Figure 5.22a shows the velocity profile in a typical channel and in cross-section, where **isotachs** (lines of equal velocity) have been drawn. The changes in velocity across the channel cause small changes in pressure (remember the energy equation) and these are responsible for setting up cross-currents which flow from the sides of the channel to the centre. As the water does not pile up in the middle of a channel there must be an equivalent flow from the centre to the edge. These circulating cross-flows are called **secondary flows**. In very wide channels several currents can be set up in this way. So water does not just flow straight down a channel, it flows along a spiral path.

### 5.8.1 Channel bends

An important secondary flow occurs at channel bends (Figure 5.22b). This is created by a combination of the difference in velocity between the surface and the bed and the centrifugal forces as the water moves around the bend. A secondary current is set up which moves across the bed from the outside of the bend to the inside and across the surface from the inside to the outside. The secondary flow can erode loose material on the outside of a bend and carry it across a river bed and deposit it on the inside of the bend. This is contrary to the common belief that sediment on the bed of the river is thrown to the outside of a bend by the strong centrifugal forces.

One consequence of this in natural erodible river channels is the process known as **meandering**. Very few rivers are straight. They tend to form a snake-like pattern of curves which are called **meanders**. The outsides of bends are progressively scoured and the insides silt up causing the river cross-section to change shape (Figure 5.22c). The continual erosion gradually alters the course of the river. Sometimes the meanders become so acute that parts of the river are eventually cut off and form what are called **ox-bow lakes**.

Note that it is not a good idea to go swimming on the outside bend of a river. The downward current can be very strong and pull the unwary swimmer down into the mud on the river bed!

### 5.8.2 Siting river off-takes

A common engineering problem is to select a site for abstracting water from a river for domestic use or irrigation. This may be a pump or some gated structure. The best location is on the outside of a river bend so that it will be free from siltation

(Figure 5.23). If located on the inside of a bend it would be continually silting up as a result of the actions of the secondary flows. The outside of a bend may need to be protected with stone pitching to stop any further erosion which might destroy the off-take.

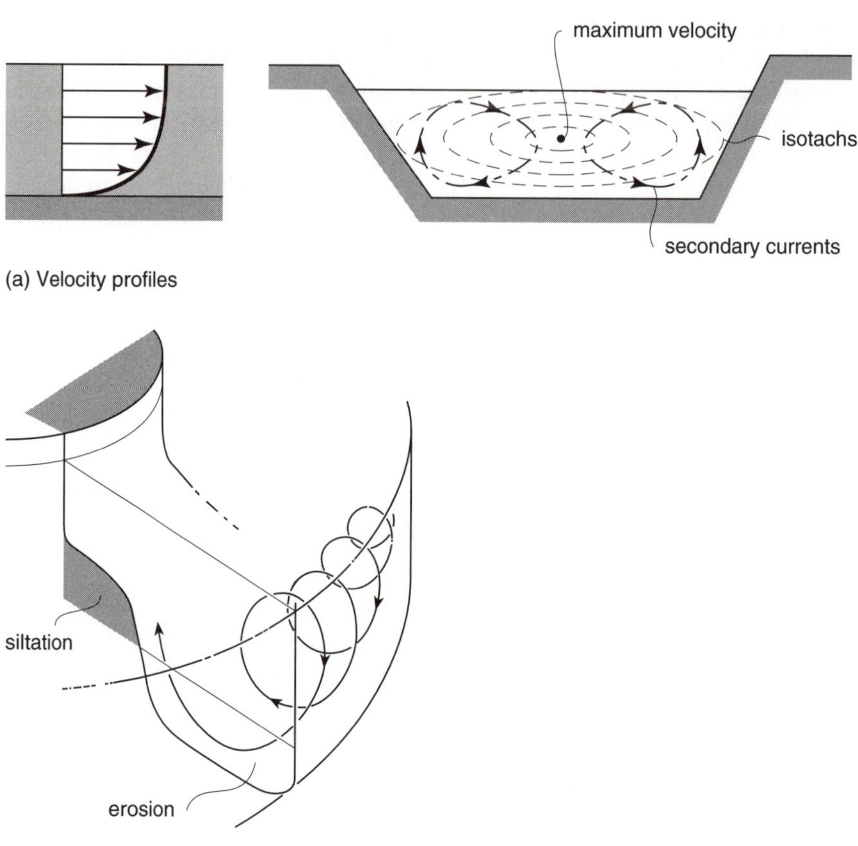


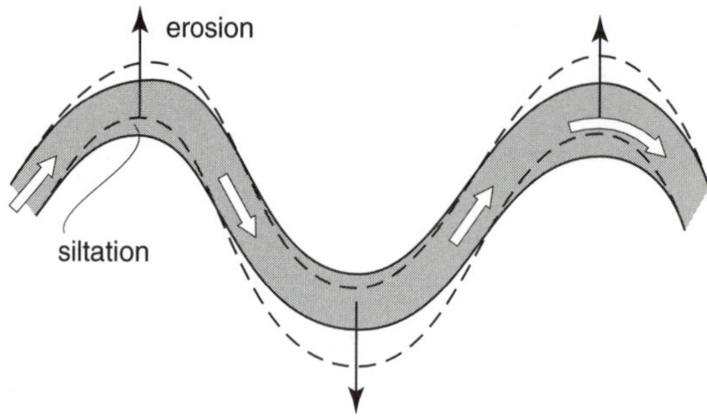


**Figure 5.22** Secondary flows in channels

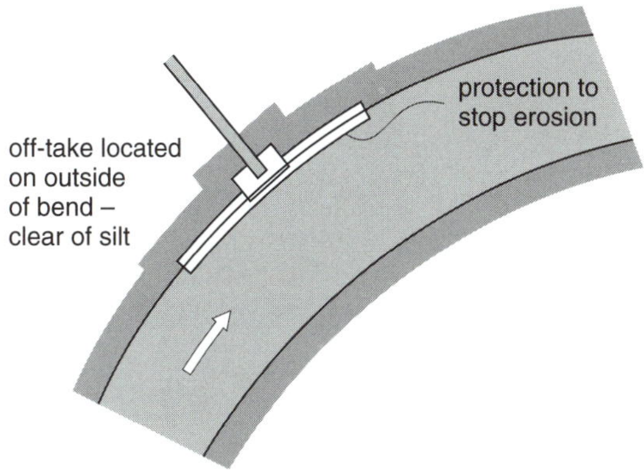


**Figure 5.23** Siting river off-takes

## 5.8.3 Bridge piers

Scouring around bridge piers can be a serious problem. This is the result of a secondary flow set up by the stagnation pressure on the nose of a pier (Figure 5.24). The rise in water level as the flow is stopped causes a secondary downward current towards the bed. This is pushed around the pier by the main flow into a spiral current, which can cause severe scouring both in front and around the sides of piers. Heavy stone protection can reduce the problem but a study of the secondary flows has shown that the construction of low walls upstream can also help by upsetting the pattern of the destructive secondary currents.

## 5.8.4 Vortices at sluice gates

Vortices can develop upstream of sluice gates and may be so strong that they extend from the water surface right underneath the gate drawing air down into its core (Figure 5.25). They can become so severe that they reduce the flow through the

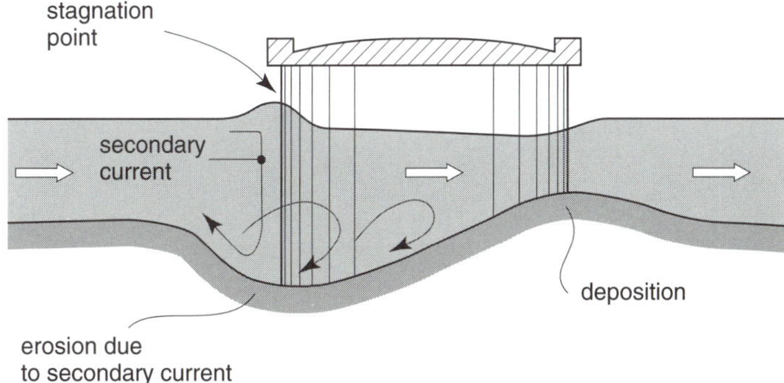


**Figure 5.24** Flow around bridge piers

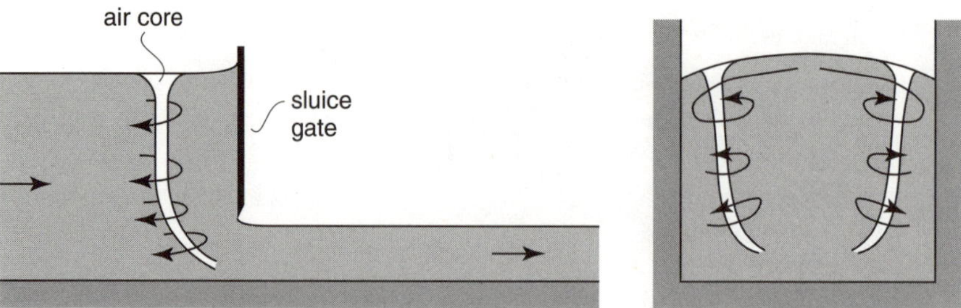


**Figure 5.25** Vortices at sluice gates

gate. They look like small tornadoes and are the result of secondary currents. They form in the following way: When the surface flow reaches a sluice gate the water stops, i.e. it stagnates. But the flow in the middle of the stream is moving faster than near the sides and so the rise in water level due to the stagnation is higher in the middle than at the sides. This causes a secondary flow from the middle of the stream to the sides and sets up two circulating vortices.

## 5.8.5 Tea cups

An interesting secondary flow occurs when stirring a cup of tea (Figure 5.26). First make sure there is no milk in the tea to obscure the view, then notice how the tea leaves at the bottom of the cup move in towards the centre when the tea is stirred.

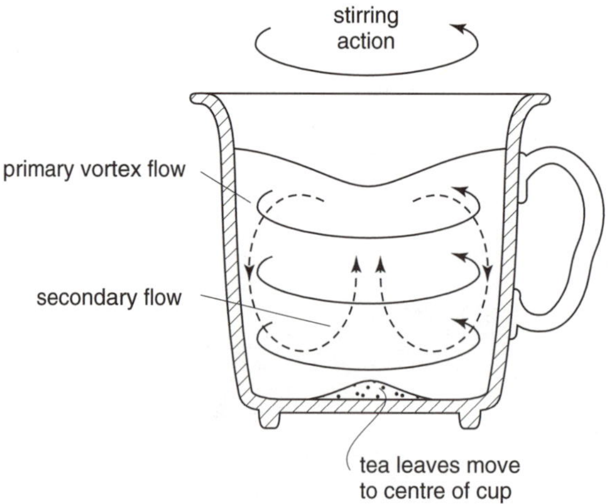


**Figure 5.26** Stirring the tea (redrawn with permission of Macmillan Press Ltd from Fox, J. (1997) *An Introduction to Engineering Fluid Mechanics*)

The stirring action sets up a vortex which is similar to the flow round a bend in a river. The water surface drops in the centre of the flow causing a pressure difference which results in a downward current on the outside of the cup, across the bottom and up the middle. Any tea leaves lying on the bottom of the cup are swept along a spiral path towards the centre of the cup.

## 5.9 Sediment transport

Sediment movement in channels is usually referred to as **sediment transport** and it is not a subject normally covered in texts on basic hydraulics. But a study of channels would not be complete without mentioning it. Most channels are either naturally occurring or excavated in the natural soil and so are prone to scouring and silting. Very few have the luxury of a lining to protect them against erosion. Natural rivers often carry silt and sand washed from their catchments, and some even carry large boulders in their upper reaches. Man-made canals not only have to resist erosion but need to avoid becoming blocked with silt and sand. Indeed the sediment is often described as the sediment load, indicating the burden that channels must carry.

Channels carrying sediment are designed in a different way to those carrying clear water. Normally Manning or Chezy formulae are used for clear water but they are not well suited to sediment-laden water. There is no simple accepted theory that provides a thorough understanding of sediment movement on which to base channel design. When engineers meet a problem for which there is no acceptable theory they do not wait for the scientists to find one. They try to find a way round the problem and develop alternative design methods. This is what happened in India and Pakistan at the turn of the century when British engineers were faced with designing and operating large canals which carried both water and silt from the Indus and Ganges rivers for the irrigation of vast tracts of land. They observed and measured the hydraulic parameters of existing canals that seemed to have worked well under similar conditions over a long period of time. From these data they developed equations which linked together sediment, velocity, hydraulic radius, slope and width and used them to design new canals. They came to be known as the **regime equations**. The word 'regime' described the conditions in the canals where, over a period of time, they neither silted nor scoured and all the silt that entered the canals at the head of the systems was transported through to the fields. In fact an added benefit of this was that the silt brought with it natural fertilisers for the farmers. But this is not claimed to be a perfect solution. Often the canals silted up during heavy floods and often they would scour when canal velocities where excessive. But on balance over a period of time (which may be several years) the canals did not change much and were said to be **in regime**. In spite of all the research over the past century, engineers still use these equations because they are still the best available today.

The lack of progress in our understanding of sediment transport comes from the nature of the problem. In other aspects of hydraulics there is a reasonably clear path to solving a problem. In channels one single force dominates channel design – the gravity force. All other factors such as viscosity can be safely ignored without it causing much error. But in sediment transport there are several factors which control what happens and no single one dominates. Gravity influences both water and sediment, but viscosity and density also appear to be important. This makes any fundamental analysis of the problem complex.

At the heart of the sediment transport problem is how to determine when sediment begins to move – the **threshold of movement**. Some investigators, particularly engineers, have tried to link this with average stream velocity because the latter is simple to measure and it is obviously linked to the erosive power of a channel. But research has shown that it is not as simple as this. Look at the particles of sand on the bed of a channel (Figure 5.27). Is it the average velocity that is important or the local velocity and turbulence close to the sand grains? Some grains are more exposed than others. Do they move first? Does grain size and density matter? Do the rounded grains move more easily than the angular ones? Is there a Bernoulli (energy change) lifting effect when flow moves around exposed grains which will encourage them to move? How important is the apparent loss in weight of sand grains when they are submerged in water? There are no clear answers to these questions but what is clear is that many factors influence the threshold of movement and this has made it a very difficult subject to study from an analytical point of view.

There is, however, some good news which has come from experimental work. It is in fact very easy to observe the threshold of movement and to say when it has been reached. Imagine a channel with a sandy bed with water flowing over it. When the flow is increased the sand will at some point begin to move. But the interesting point is that this begins quite suddenly and not gradually as might be expected. When the threshold is reached, the whole channel bed comes alive suddenly as all the sand begins to move at the same time. So if several observers, watching the channel, are asked to say when they think the threshold has been reached, they will have no problem in agreeing the point at which it occurs. What they will not be able to say for certain is what caused it.

Because of this clear observation of the threshold, much of the progress has been made by scientists using experimental methods. A. Shields in 1936 successfully established the conditions for the threshold of movement on an experimental basis for a wide range of sediments and these are the data that are still used today for designing channels to avoid erosion. It provides a much sounder basis for design than simply using some limiting velocity.

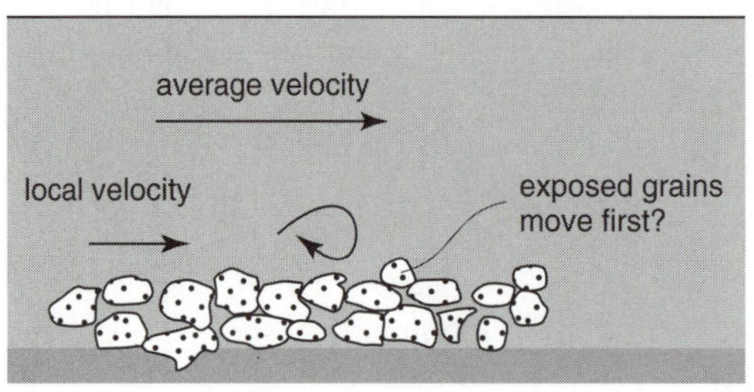


(a)

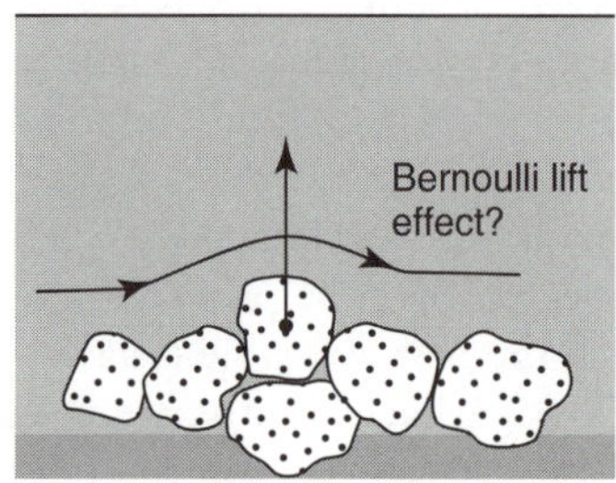


(b)

**Figure 5.27 Threshold of movement**

Working out the amount of sediment being transported once it begins to move is fraught with difficulties. The reason for this is that once movement begins the amount of sediment on the move is very sensitive to small changes in the factors that caused the movement in the first place. This means that small changes in what could be called the erosive power of a channel can result in very large changes in sediment transport. Even if it were possible to calculate such changes, which some experimenters have tried to do, it is even more difficult to verify this by measuring sediment transport in the laboratory and almost impossible to measure it with any accuracy in the field. For these reasons it seems unlikely that there will be any significant improvements in the predictions of sediment transport and that engineers will have to rely on the regime equations for some time to come.

## 5.10 Some examples to test your understanding

1. An open channel of rectangular section has a bed width of 2.0m. If the channel carries a discharge of 1.0m$^3$/s calculate the depth of flow when the Manning's roughness coefficient is 0.015 and the bed slope is 1 in 1000. Calculate the Froude number in the channel and the critical depth.
2. A rectangular channel of bed width 2.5m carries a discharge of 1.75m$^3$/s. Calculate the normal depth of flow when the Chezy coefficient is 60 and the slope is 1 in 2000. Calculate the critical depth and say whether the flow is sub-critical or super-critical.
3. A trapezoidal channel is to be designed and constructed in a sandy loam with a longitudinal slope of 1 in 5000 to carry a discharge of 2.3m$^3$/s. Calculate suitable dimensions for the depth and bed width assuming Manning's $n$ is 0.022 and the side slope is 1 in 2.
4. A trapezoidal channel carrying a discharge of 0.75m$^3$/s is to be lined with concrete to avoid seepage problems. Calculate the channel dimensions that will minimise the amount of concrete when Manning's $n$ for concrete is 0.015 and the channel slope is 1 in 1250.
5. A hydraulic jump occurs in a rectangular channel 2.3m wide when the discharge is 2.5m$^3$/s. If the upstream depth is 0.25m calculate the Froude number, the depth of flow downstream of the jump and the energy loss in the jump.

# Chapter 6

# Waves

## 6.1 Introduction

Waves are very familiar to everyone, particularly those which toss about at sea during windy, stormy weather and those which roll in rhythmically on the beach. The tides too are waves but they are not so obvious as they slowly build up and subside twice a day and move many millions of tonnes of water across the oceans. But waves are not just confined to the sea. Earlier, in Chapter 5, waves were described on a still pond and on a flowing stream when a stone was thrown into the water to help determine critical flow conditions. Surge waves can sometimes be seen in rivers when control gates are suddenly closed and during high tides when tidal bores travel upstream from the mouths of rivers. Floods flowing down rivers too are another kind of wave which can be several hundreds of kilometres long.

Generally waves in rivers depend on gravity for their shape and size in much the same way that channels themselves depend on the force of gravity down the land slope for their energy. Sea waves are different as they depend on the circulation of the atmosphere and the resulting winds for their energy. Although it is possible for winds to create waves on lakes, they are not usually as large as those which can be generated by strong winds blowing over vast stretches of the oceans. These are the waves which play a large part in shaping our shorelines.

Sea waves tend to affect only the water surface and their movement is different from the movement of the water in which they are travelling. Watching a single wave, it seems to travel a great distance but the water hardly moves at all. Just look at any seagull floating on the water surface to appreciate this. When a wave passes it only bobs up and down. Leonardo da Vinci (1452–1519) compared water waves with the waves that can be seen when the wind blows across a field of corn. The wave pattern seems to travel across the entire field and yet individual stalks only sway back and forth. Another example is that of a rope which is held at one end and shaken. A wave pattern travels along the rope but the rope only moves up and down. So if the water (or the corn or rope) is not being transported then what is? The answer is energy. It is energy which is being transported across the water and through the corn and along the rope.

Our understanding of water waves and how they are generated is far from complete. This is because is it difficult to observe waves at sea and also because all the mathematical formulae are based on ideal fluids and the sea does not always fit in with the ideal.

## 6.2 Describing waves

There is established terminology to describe waves. Wave **height** $H$ is the dimension from the crest of a wave (peak) to the wave trough (Figure 6.1a). The height of a wave is twice its **amplitude** and the wave **length** $L$ is the distance between two successive wave peaks.

As well as having dimensions in space, waves also have dimensions in time. So when waves move past an observer the time interval between successive peaks is called the wave **period** $T$ and the number of peaks that pass an observer each second is the **frequency** $f$.

The velocity of waves is called the **celerity** $c$ and this word is used to distinguish clearly the wave velocity from that of the water. If the water is also moving then the wave velocity is increased or decreased depending on whether the wave is moving with or against the flow. Although water waves have been likened to wave motion along a rope, water is a little different. While a rope is free to rise

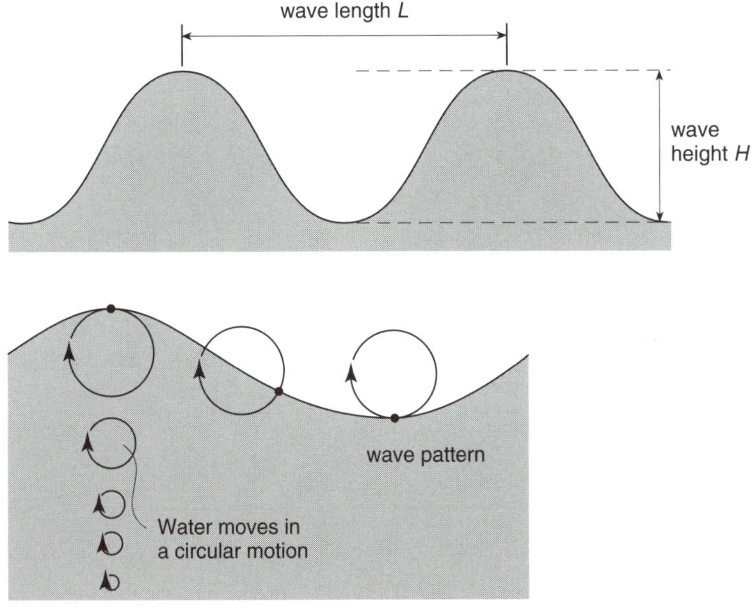


**Figure 6.1 Wave dimensions and movement**

and fall leaving gaps around it, this is not possible with water and so as the water rises when a wave passes, water nearby flows into the space. This gives rise to a circular motion which extends some distance below the water surface but with diminishing effect (Figure 6.1b). At a depth of half the wave length the effects of surface waves are negligible. A submarine submerged at 150m would be able to avoid all the severe waves that are produced by a storm at sea.

## 6.3 Waves at sea

Sea waves come in many different sizes (Figure 6.2). The babies in the family are the **capillary waves**, which are generated by wind and are only a few millimetres in length. Their shape and size is influenced by surface tension. This is a very small force and so, for waves longer than this, the Earth's gravity takes over control and these are often referred to as **gravity waves**. These also are generated by the wind. The longest waves such as the tsunamis are caused by earthquakes (see section 6.6.3) and storm surges, but the longest of all, the tides, are controlled by the movement of the Sun and Moon.

The general formula for sea wave celerity is as follows:

$$c = \sqrt{\frac{gL}{2\pi}\tanh\left(\frac{2\pi d}{L}\right)}$$

where $g$ is gravity constant ($9.81\text{m/s}^2$), $L$ is wave length (m) and $d$ is water depth (m). The term 'tanh' is a mathematical function known as the *hyperbolic tangent* and values can be obtained from mathematical tables in the same way as other function such as sin and tan.

In deep water (defined as water deeper than half the wave length), as is the case of sea waves, the depth of the water has no effect on wave speed and so

<table>
<tr><td rowspan="3">WAVE TYPE</td><td rowspan="3">capillary waves</td><td colspan="4">gravity waves</td></tr>
<tr><td rowspan="2">wind waves</td><td colspan="2">long-period waves</td><td rowspan="2">tide waves</td></tr>
<tr><td>seiches and storm surges</td><td>tsunamis</td></tr>
<tr><td>CAUSE</td><td colspan="2">wind</td><td>wind, storms and other wind waves</td><td>storms and earth-quakes</td><td>Sun and Moon</td></tr>
<tr><td>SIZE</td><td colspan="5">increasing</td></tr>
</table>

Figure 6.2 Types of sea waves

the formula simplifies to:

$$c = \sqrt{\frac{gL}{2\pi}}$$

This formula shows that the celerity of sea waves depends only on wave length and so waves of different length travel at different speeds. So in a storm in mid-Atlantic when waves of many different lengths are created, the longer waves tend to overtake the shorter waves as they move away from the storm area. Waves can travel many hundreds of kilometres and when they reach the shores of Europe they are well sorted out with the longer waves arriving first followed by the shorter waves. The rhythmic waves arriving on a beach in this way are often referred to as **swell**. By timing the waves and noting the change in their frequency, it is possible to work out how far the waves have travelled since they were formed. In other words, it is possible to link waves to the particular weather events at sea that created them, perhaps several days before.

It was this kind of detailed study of waves and the weather patterns that form them that helped scientists to predict wave heights on the beaches of France during the very successful D-Day landings during the Second World War. A scientist, H.U. Sverdrup, developed a technique for predicting wave heights from weather patterns at sea. They also studied the celerity of waves travelling out from their source. From this they were able to predict the wave heights on the Normandy beaches resulting from bad weather conditions out in the Atlantic occurring several days earlier. This information was crucial for those landing on the beaches because the landing craft being used could only land safely at certain limited wave heights. Knowing the way in which the sea can change suddenly in the English Channel it would have been a great risk to have gone ahead with such a major operation without some prior knowledge of what the sea was going to be like.

Similar analyses are used regularly today to predict sea conditions when tankers are refuelling ships at sea or ships are taking supplies to oil platforms. Predicting the wave heights that can be expected ensures successful and safe operations.

## 6.4 Waves in rivers and open channels

Waves that affect only the surface can occur in channels and are usually the result of some disturbance – like the waves that characterise super- and sub-critical flow. But in this case water is shallow and so the celerity of waves of this kind is related to the depth of the water. The general formula is modified accordingly. When depth $d$ is significant:

$$\tanh\left(\frac{2\pi d}{L}\right) = \frac{2\pi d}{L}$$

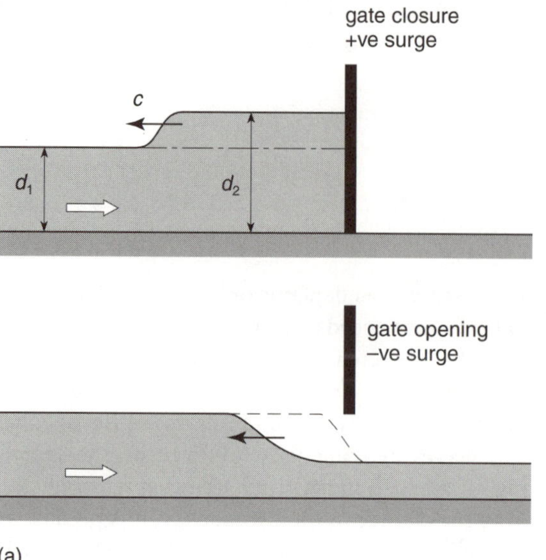


(a)

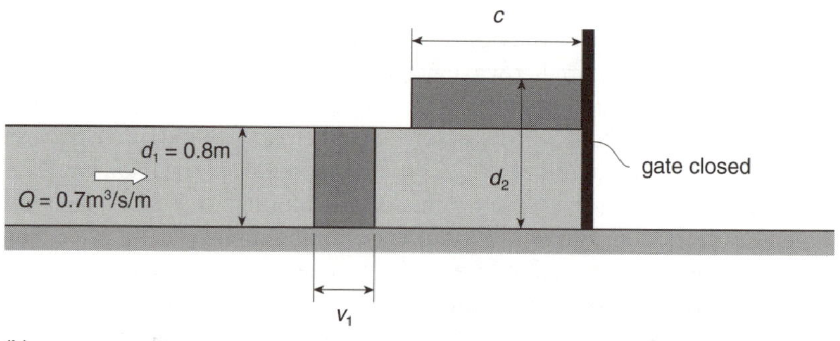


(b)

(c) Tidal bore on R. Severn, UK

**Figure 6.3 Surges in channels**

and so

$$c = \sqrt{gd}$$

where $c$ is wave celerity (m/s), $d$ is depth of the water (m) and $g$ is the gravity constant (9.81m/s$^2$). This formula was developed by Joseph Lagrange (1736–1813) and was further verified by John Scott Russel (1808–1882) who spent a great deal of time observing and measuring the speed of bow waves created on canals by horse-drawn barges.

But channels tend to be associated more with waves that have a significant effect on the whole flow and not just on the surface. Such waves include surges (or bores) which are sometimes seen moving upstream on tidal rivers or along channels after the closure of hydraulic gates. The hydraulic jump is sometimes described as a **standing wave.** It is similar to a surge but it stays in one place.

### 6.4.1 Surges

Surges are sometimes called **solitary waves,** i.e. there is only one wave. They occur when there is a sudden change in flow such as when a gate is closed or opened (Figure 6.3a). The sudden closure of a gate produces a positive surge whereas a sudden opening produces a negative surge.

The strength of a surge depends on the change in the flow. When the change is very small the surge is undular (i.e. like a surface wave). When the change is large a much stronger surge develops. If it is a positive surge then it will have a vigorous rolling action and may have the appearance of a moving hydraulic jump. A negative surge is much weaker and usually produces weak surface waves.

The celerity of a surge in a rectangular channel can be calculated using the formula:

$$c = \sqrt{\frac{gd_2(d_1 + d_2)}{2d_1}} - v_1$$

where $d_1$ is upstream depth (m), $d_2$ is downstream depth (m) and $v_1$ is upstream velocity (m/s). This formula can be derived from the momentum equation, but this is not shown in this text. When the wave celerity is zero, i.e. $c = 0$, the formula, if rearranged, is the same as that for the hydraulic jump (see section 5.7.6). So one way of looking at a hydraulic jump is as a stationary (standing) wave or surge.

#### Example: Calculating the celerity and height of a surge wave

Calculate the height and celerity of a surge wave resulting from the closure of a sluice gate on a canal when the discharge is 0.7m$^3$/s per m width of channel and the normal depth of flow is 0.8m.

The formula for calculating the celerity is derived from the momentum equation:

$$c = \sqrt{\frac{gd_2(d_1 + d_2)}{2d_1}} - v_1$$

There are two unknown values, wave celerity $c$ and the depth near the gate just after the sudden closure $d_2$. So another equation is needed before a solution can be found.

This is the continuity equation but applied to surge (Figure 6.3b). This is done by calculating the volume of water coming down the channel in one second and equating this to the volume of water in the surge (the two volumes are shown shaded). So

$$v_1 d_1 = c(d_2 - d_1)$$

$$c = \frac{v_1 d_1}{d_2 - d_1}$$

Now

$$d_1 = 0.8\text{m}$$

and

$$v_1 = \frac{q}{d_1} = \frac{0.7}{0.8} = 0.88\text{m/s}$$

Putting these values into the continuity equation:

$$c = \frac{0.88 \times 0.8}{d_2 - 0.8}$$

Putting this equal to the wave celerity in the momentum equation:

$$\frac{0.88 \times 0.8}{d_2 - 0.8} = \sqrt{\frac{gd_2(0.8 + d_2)}{2 \times 0.8}} - 0.88$$

Solving this equation by trial and error, i.e. by putting in different values of $d_2$ until one fits the equation:

$$d_2 = 1.14\text{m}$$

and so

$$c = \frac{0.88 \times 0.8}{1.14 - 0.8}$$

$$c = 2.07\text{m/s}$$

When a surge wave is not very high, i.e. the depth $d_2$ is not significantly greater than the original depth in the channel $d_1$, then the wave celerity equation can be simplified by assuming that $d_1 = d_2$. So

$$c = \sqrt{gd_1} - v_1$$

When the water velocity $v_1 = 0$ the celerity becomes

$$c = \sqrt{gd}$$

This is identical to the formula for calculating the celerity of gravity waves on a still pond (see section 5.7.1).

### 6.4.2 Bores in tidal rivers

Some rivers regularly experience surges because they flow into the sea where there is a high tidal range and where wide estuaries converge into a narrow river channel. They are called **bores** or **eagres**. The rivers Severn and Trent in the UK are famous for their bores. They can be best observed during the spring tides when the tidal range is greatest and when river flows are at their lowest. The Severn bore (Figure 6.3c) starts in the estuary as high tide approaches and moves upstream reaching celerities of 5m/s with a height of 1.5m.

## 6.5 Flood waves

Flood waves that pass down rivers are the result of rain storms on river catchments and can be many hundreds of kilometres long. The approach to dealing with these waves is quite different to those of the much smaller waves already described. Rather than dealing with a whole wave along the entire length of a river, engineers deal with what happens to the discharge and water levels at particular sites over a period of time. A site may have been chosen because it is prone to flooding and there is a need to know what the effects of flooding will be, or it may be a convenient site for accurately measuring the discharge and water levels. Such observations lead to a graph of the discharge and the water level which is called a **hydrograph** (Figure 6.4). This can be very useful. For example, the area under the curve represents the volume of water that has passed the site during the flood. If the normal flow was also known it is possible to determine how much water was brought down by the flood.

If another site is chosen further downstream and another hydrograph drawn it will be different from the first. Generally it will be flatter and longer showing that the peak discharge is less and the duration of the flood is longer. But the total amount of water passing this site will be the same as passed the first site (remember continuity).

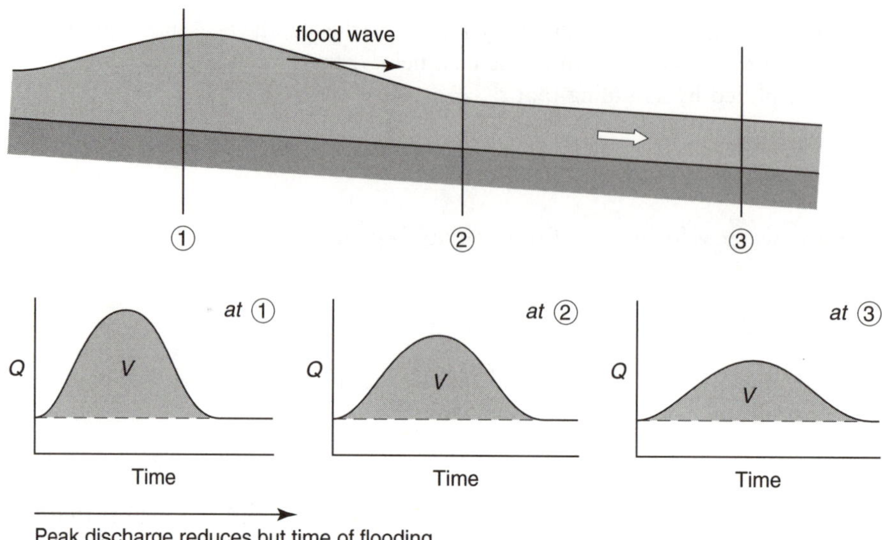


**Figure 6.4 Flood waves**

Gathering information on floods in this way provides valuable knowledge for river engineers who will be able to predict the effects of different rain storms on river catchments and so design and construct engineering works which will help to alleviate flooding.

## 6.6 Some special waves

### 6.6.1 Density currents

When two fluids of different densities flow together they do not mix easily. The slow movement of sea water up estuaries during a rising tide under the out-flowing fresh water from a river is an example of this. Similarly, the flow of sediment-laden river water along the bed of a reservoir does not disperse into the main body of water (Figure 6.5a). Such flows, which occur when there are small differences in density, are called **density currents**. Another example is hot and cold water which do not mix easily because they have slightly different densities. Most people will have experienced this in their bath when left to run, one side is hot and the other cold. Stirring the water is necessary to get an even temperature. Power stations sometimes have this same problem. They use a lot of cooling water and if the intake is close to the outlet there can be a problem of sucking hot water back into the station before it has had a chance to cool down through turbulent mixing with cooler water.

Waves can also occur at the interface between two fluids of different densities and these can be quite intriguing. Oceanographers call these **internal waves** because the waves do not affect the water surface at all. Such waves seem to move in slow

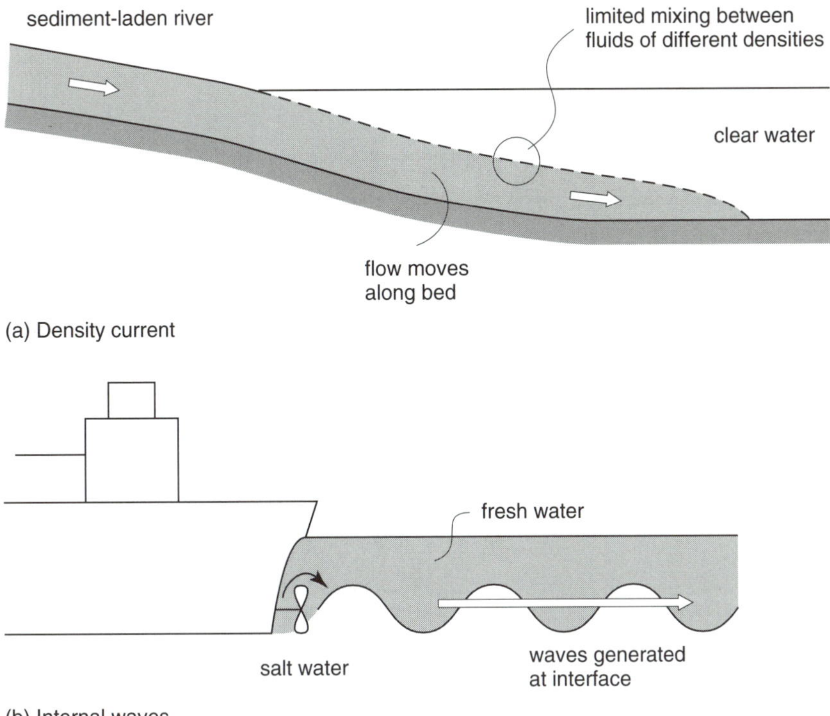


**Figure 6.5 Density currents**

motion as if the force of gravity, which is controlling them, has been significantly reduced. This can be explained by the apparent loss in weight of the less dense fluid as it lies on top of the denser lower fluid. The wave celerity equation still works but the value of $g$ is much reduced by this buoyancy effect. When $g$ is reduced the celerity is also reduced which means the waves move very slowly.

One internal wave system which caused some consternation occurred in the North Atlantic when a scientist was observing icebergs. The weather had been mild and the ice had been melting so that there was about one metre of fresh water lying on top of the salt sea water (Figure 6.5b). Because of the slight density difference the two did not mix easily. When the observation ship's engines were started, to the surprise of the crew the ship did not move, although the propellers were turning. The reason was that the ship's propellers just happened to be located at the interface between the fresh and salt water and all the energy was being dissipated as wave energy along the interface. The sea surface was quite calm but just below, the waves where moving up and down at the interface and absorbing all the ship's energy.

### 6.6.2 Waves in harbours

Harbours are normally designed to keep out waves so that an area of calm water is created for ships to shelter from the sea for servicing and for loading cargo. This is

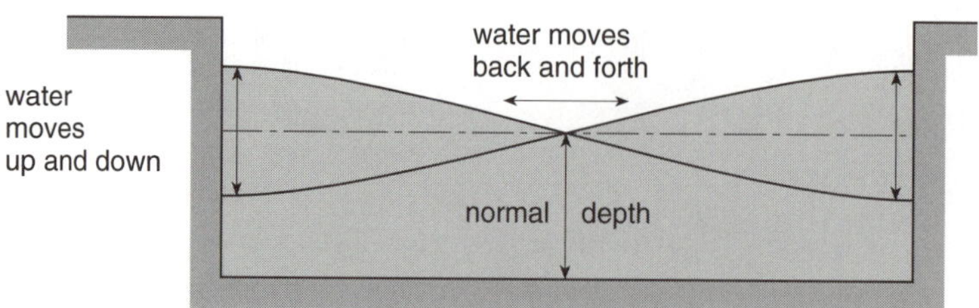


(a) Harbour seiche

(b) In the bath

**Figure 6.6 Waves in harbours**

done by having a narrow entrance. Most harbours do this successfully but there are cases when narrowing the harbour entrance has had the opposite effect – known as the **harbour paradox**. The narrow entrance has the effect of tuning certain incoming wave frequencies so, rather than stopping the waves, the harbour amplifies them. So the waves in the harbour become worse than those outside. This is known as **harbour seiche** (Figure 6.6a). When this happens the waves reflect back and forth as there is very little in harbours to absorb the wave energy. It is very much like sliding up and down in the bath tub at home. The sliding action makes the water in the bath slosh back and forth (Figure 6.6b). The bath tub has solid almost vertical sides which are very good at reflecting the waves but not so good at absorbing the wave energy. The waves can continue for some time until they finally settle down as the small amount of friction from the bath and your body take their toll. Harbours are very similar. They have lots of solid concrete surfaces and so waves tend to bounce back and forth rather than be absorbed.

The main concern in harbours is not so much with wave celerity but with the movement of water. As waves are reflected back and forth there is a great deal of water movement from one end of the harbour to the other (remember the bath again). The water velocity at the middle of the harbour may be as much as 0.5m/s as water flows from one side to the other following the wave. This can create lots of problems. A ship moored at the midpoint could move by as much as 15m back and forth following the movement of the wave. It is clearly undesirable to have a large ship moving about so much on its moorings when it is being loaded or unloaded. In harbours prone to this problem it is better to moor ships near the edge of the harbour where the water only moves up and down. From experience of harbour operation the most dangerous waves are those with a period of about two minutes. Such waves have been known to resonate in harbours, which means that the frequency of the waves and the characteristics of the harbour, ships and their mooring systems combine to amplify the waves, which makes the situation very much worse. All these factors are now taken into account when designing new harbour works or in repairing existing ones. Harbour designers wisely opt for model testing prior to construction to avoid these problems.

### 6.6.3 Tsunami wave

An infamous long wave at sea is the **tsunami**. This is Japanese for a long wave caused by earthquakes under the ocean. They occur most often in the Pacific Ocean and they travel at very high celerity with devastating consequences when they reach land. In the open ocean the wave may be only 0.5m high but the wave celerity can be around 200m/s when the ocean is say 5000m deep. This might appear to be a surface wave but because of its great length its celerity is controlled by the depth of the ocean (remember the wave celerity equation $c = \sqrt{gd}$). Even so there is not much water displacement as it passes over the open ocean. A ship meeting this wave would hardly notice its passing. However, when the wave suddenly runs into much shallower water, say 100m deep, the wave slows down to 30m/s but as the energy in the wave is still the same the wave height increases substantially. This speed of 30m/s is still quite fast and with the height increasing further as it runs up the beach it can do a great deal of damage to shore installations. The more destructive tsunami waves are those which are funnelled into a narrow space when the width of a beach or harbour is restricted in some way. This has the effect of funnelling the energy of the wave into the harbour with destructive consequences.

## 6.7 Tidal power

Waves can be very useful for generating power. The most promising approach is to hold incoming and outgoing tides behind a dam (also called a barrage) and use the head to drive turbines for electricity generation. A power station using this idea was built on the estuary of the Raunce in Brittany, France, in 1966 and there are plans to build a large barrage in the Severn estuary on the west coast of Britain. Although it has been estimated that this station could provide up to 6% of Britain's power needs the scheme is hotly debated because it would affect the pattern of the tides and sediment movements in the estuary and many ecologically sensitive wetland sites could be adversely affected.

Tidal barrages are an economic possibility when the tidal range exceeds 5m but taking energy out of the tides may cause problems. In estuaries that naturally absorb tidal energy through friction and reflect very little energy back out to sea there is the chance that a power station could take out the energy from the tides without serious effect. But in cases where there is very little friction and all the tidal energy is reflected back out to sea there may be dangers in extracting tidal energy. The effects of the energy not being reflected back again cannot be predicted.

Some studies were once undertaken to establish the feasibility of constructing tidal power stations across the Irish Sea between Ireland and Wales and Ireland and Scotland. An unlikely but hydraulically similar model for the Irish Sea was Salisbury Plain in the south of England where the winds across the plain produced similar Reynolds numbers to the flow of water in the Irish Sea. The study concluded that the Irish Sea was more reflective than energy-absorbing and so there were great doubts about the prospects for power generation.

Chapter 7

# Hydraulic structures for channels

## 7.1 Introduction

Hydraulic structures in channels have three main functions:

- Measuring and controlling discharge
- Controlling water levels
- Dissipating unwanted energy

The measurement and control of discharge in channels is perhaps one of the more obvious uses of hydraulic structures (Figure 7.1). Large irrigation networks, for example, require structures at each canal junction to measure and control discharge so that there is a fair and equitable distribution of water. It is not enough just to construct a canal junction and hope that the flow will divide itself properly between the two. Natural rivers too need regular flow measurement, so that engineers can make sure there is an adequate supply to meet the growing demands for domestic and industrial uses. It is important to ensure that minimum base flows are maintained in dry summer periods to protect fish stocks and environmentally sensitive wetlands. Flood flows are also measured so that adequate precautions can be taken to avoid flooding, particularly in urban areas where damage can be very costly.

The need to control water levels in channels may not be so obvious. On irrigation schemes water level control is just as important as discharge control. The canals are built up higher than the surrounding ground level so there is enough energy for water to flow by gravity through pipes from the channels into the farms (Figure 7.2a). The water level (known as the **command**) must be carefully controlled if each farm is to receive the right discharge. But all too often the water level drops because of low flows or seepage losses. This reduces the discharge through the pipes, making it difficult for farmers to irrigate properly. To avoid this problem, hydraulic structures are built across the canals to raise the water levels

(a) Discharge regulator in a canal system in France

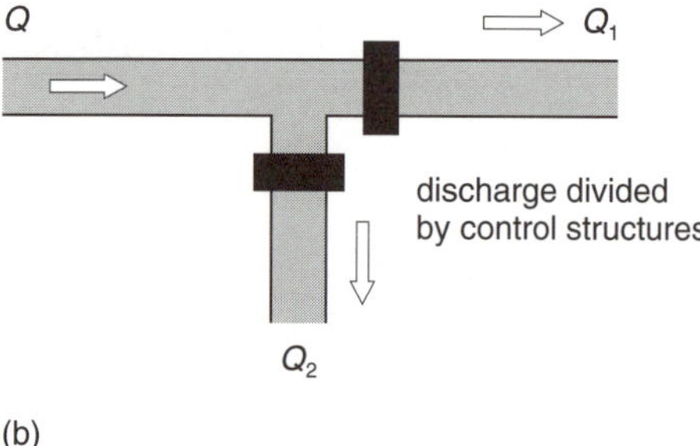


(b)

**Figure 7.1 Measuring and controlling discharge**

back to their command levels. Such structures are called **cross-regulators** (Figure 7.2b).

Another example of the need for water level control might be on a river close to a natural wetland site that is valued for its bird population or its special plants (Figure 7.2c). Water might enter the site either by the flooding from the river as it overtops its banks or through seepage from its bed and sides. Either way the wetland is very dependent on the water level in the river as well as its flow to avoid it drying out and causing irreparable damage to flora and fauna. Fluctuations in water level can be avoided by building a structure across the river to hold the water at the desired level throughout the year even though the discharge may vary significantly.

Hydraulic structures are also very useful for getting rid of unwanted energy. When water flows down dam spillways it can reach speeds of 60km/h and more and is capable of doing a lot of damage. Hydraulic structures are used to stop such high-speed flows and dissipate the kinetic energy by creating hydraulic jumps.

Some hydraulic structures only carry out one of the functions described above whilst others perform all three functions at the same time. So a hydraulic structure

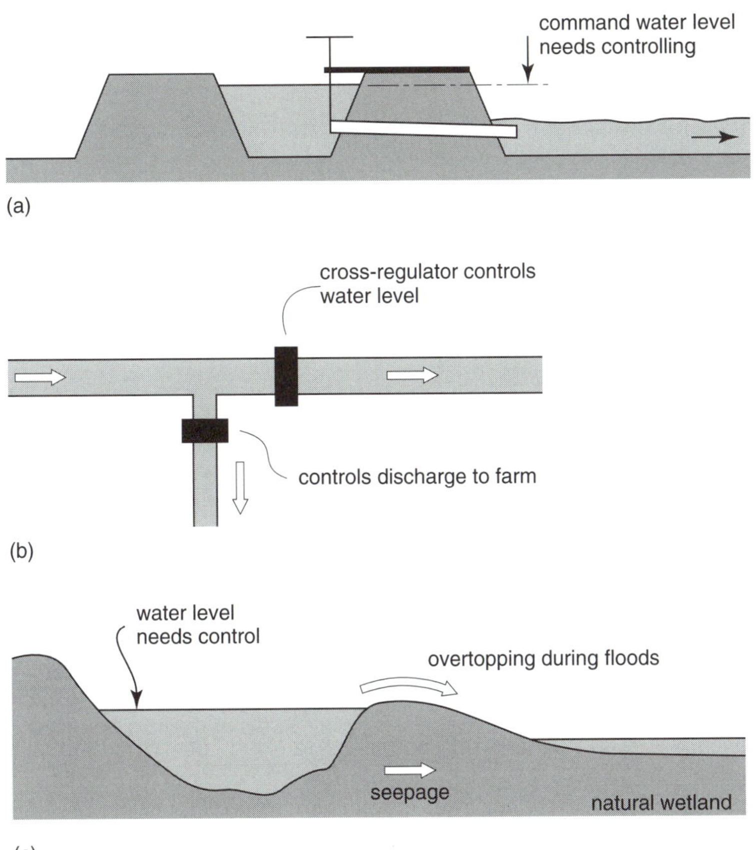


**Figure 7.2** Controlling water levels

may be used for discharge measurement, and at the same time it may be performing a water level control function and dissipating unwanted energy.

From the point of view of measuring discharge and controlling water levels, there are only two types of structure. Some structures allow water to flow through them and these are called **orifice structures**. Others allow water to flow over them and these are called **weirs** or **flumes**. Hydraulically, they behave in quite different ways and so each has certain applications for which it is best suited. The energy dissipating function can be attached to both of these structure types.

## 7.2 Orifice structures

The principles of orifice flow were described earlier in Chapter 3. In practice orifice structures have fixed or moveable gates rather than just a simple opening. The sluice gate described in section 5.4.3 is a good example of this type of structure. The flow under the gate is very similar to orifice flow but not quite the same (Figure 7.3a). Firstly, the flow contracts only on its upper surface as it goes under the gate and, secondly, there is additional friction from the bed of the channel. So to find a formula for discharge for this structure the orifice formula is a good starting point but it needs modifying.

The formula for discharge from an orifice is:

$$Q = a\sqrt{2gh}$$

Modifying this for a sluice gate:

$$Q = C_d a\sqrt{2gd_1}$$

where $Q$ is discharge ($m^3/s$), $a$ is area of gate opening ($m^2$), $C_d$ is a coefficient of discharge and $d_1$ is the water depth upstream of the orifice (m).

This looks to be a simple formula. It is an attempt to relate the discharge to the area of the gate opening $a$ and the upstream water depth $d_1$ because both are easy to measure. However, the relationship is not so simple and as a result $C_d$ is not a simple coefficient of discharge as defined earlier in Chapter 3. It takes account of the contraction of the flow under the gate but in addition it allows for the energy losses and the effects of the size of gate opening and the head on the gate. So $C_d$ is not a simple constant number like the coefficient of contraction $C_c$. Usually the manufacturer of hydraulic gates will supply suitable values of $C_d$ so that the 'simple' discharge formula can be used.

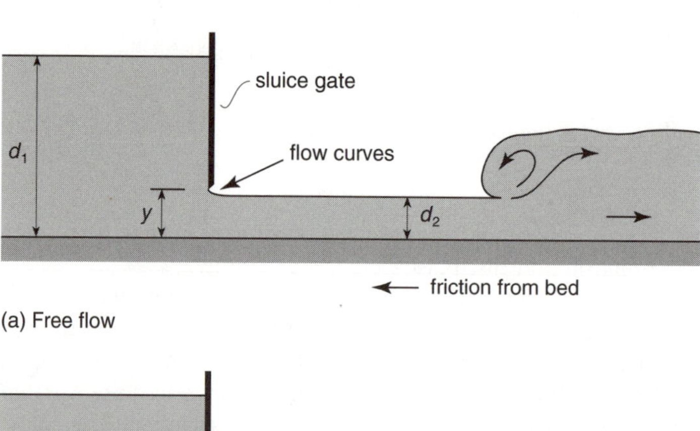


(a) Free flow

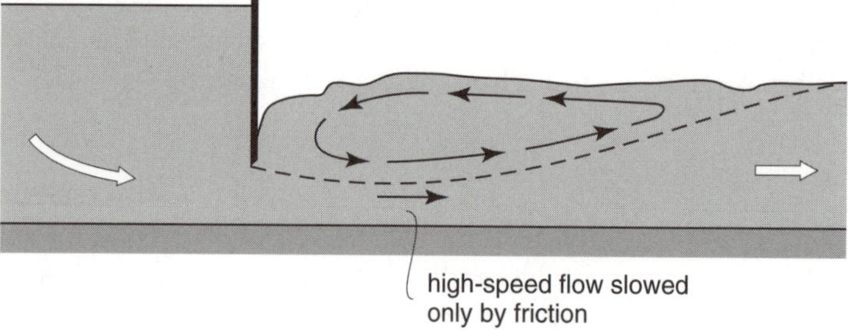


(b) Drowned flow

**Figure 7.3 Orifice structures**

### 7.2.1 Free and drowned flow

The sluice gate example in Figure 7.3a shows the flow freely passing under the gate with a hydraulic jump downstream. The downstream depth $d_2$ has no effect on the upstream depth $d_1$. This is referred to as **free flow** and the formula quoted above for calculating discharge is based on this condition.

In some circumstances the jump can move upstream and drown out the gate and is referred to as **drowned flow** (Figure 7.3b). The flow downstream may look very turbulent and have the appearance of a jump but inside the flow the action is quite different. There is very little turbulent mixing taking place and the super-critical flow is shooting underneath the sub-critical flow. This high-speed jet is not stopped quickly as it would be in a jump but slows down gradually over a long distance through the forces of friction on the channel bed. This flow can do a lot of damage to an unprotected channel even though the water may appear to be quite tranquil on the surface. Under drowned conditions the formula for discharge must be modified to take account of the downstream water level, which now has a direct influence on the upstream water level.

## 7.3 Weirs and flumes

Weirs and flumes are both overflow structures with very different characteristics to orifices. Many different types of weirs have been developed to suit a wide range of operating conditions, some comprising just a thin sheet of metal across a channel (**sharp-crested weirs**), whereas others are much more substantial (**solid weirs**). Both are based on the principle of changing the energy in a channel and using the energy and continuity equations to develop a formula for discharge based on depth (pressure) measurements upstream. But solid weirs rely on an energy change that is sufficient to make the flow go through the critical point. Because of this they are sometimes called **critical-depth structures**. Sharp-crested weirs do not have this constraint – but they do have others.

Flumes are also critical-depth structures but rely on changing the energy by narrowing the channel width rather than raising the bed. Sometimes engineers combine weirs and flumes by both raising the bed and narrowing the width to achieve the desired energy change. It does not really matter which way critical flow is achieved so long as it occurs.

## 7.4 Sharp-crested weirs

Sharp-crested weirs are used to measure relatively small discharges (Figure 7.4). They comprise a thin sheet of metal such as brass or steel (sometimes wood can be used for temporary weirs) into which a specially shaped opening is cut. This must be accurately cut leaving a sharp edge with a bevel on the downstream side. When located in a channel, the thin sheet is sealed into the bed and sides so that all the water flows through the opening. By measuring the depth of water above the opening, known as the head on the weir, the discharge can be calculated using a formula derived from the energy equation. There is a unique relationship between the head on the weir and the discharge and one simple depth measurement determines the discharge.

### 7.4.1 Rectangular weirs

This weir has a rectangular opening (Figure 7.4b). Water flows through this and plunges downstream. The overflowing water is often called the **nappe**. The discharge is calculated using the formula:

$$Q = \tfrac{2}{3} C_d L \sqrt{2g} H^{1.5}$$

where $C_d$ is a coefficient of discharge, $L$ is length of weir (m) and $H$ is the head on the weir measured above the crest (m). $C_d$ allows for all the discrepancies between theory and practice.

### 7.4.2 Vee notch weirs

This weir has a triangular notch and is ideally suited for measuring small discharges (Figure 7.4c and d). If a rectangular weir was used for low flows, the head would be very small and difficult to measure accurately. Using a vee weir, the small flow is concentrated in the bottom of the vee providing a reasonable head for measurement. The discharge is calculated using the formula:

$$Q = \tfrac{8}{15} C_d \sqrt{2g} \tan(\theta/2) H^{1.5}$$

where $\theta$ is the angle of the notch.

### 7.4.3 Some practical points

There are several conditions that must be met for these weirs to work properly. These are set out in detail in British Standard BS3680 (see references for details). The following are some of the key points:

- The water must fall clear of the weir plate into the downstream channel. Notice the bevelled edge on the crest facing downstream which creates the sharp edge and helps the water to spring clear. If this did not happen the flow clings to the downstream plate and draws down the flow reducing the head on the weir (Figure 7.4e). Using the above formula with the reduced value of head would clearly not give the right discharge.
- Flow over the weir must be open to the atmosphere so that the pressure around it is always atmospheric. Sometimes the falling water draws air from

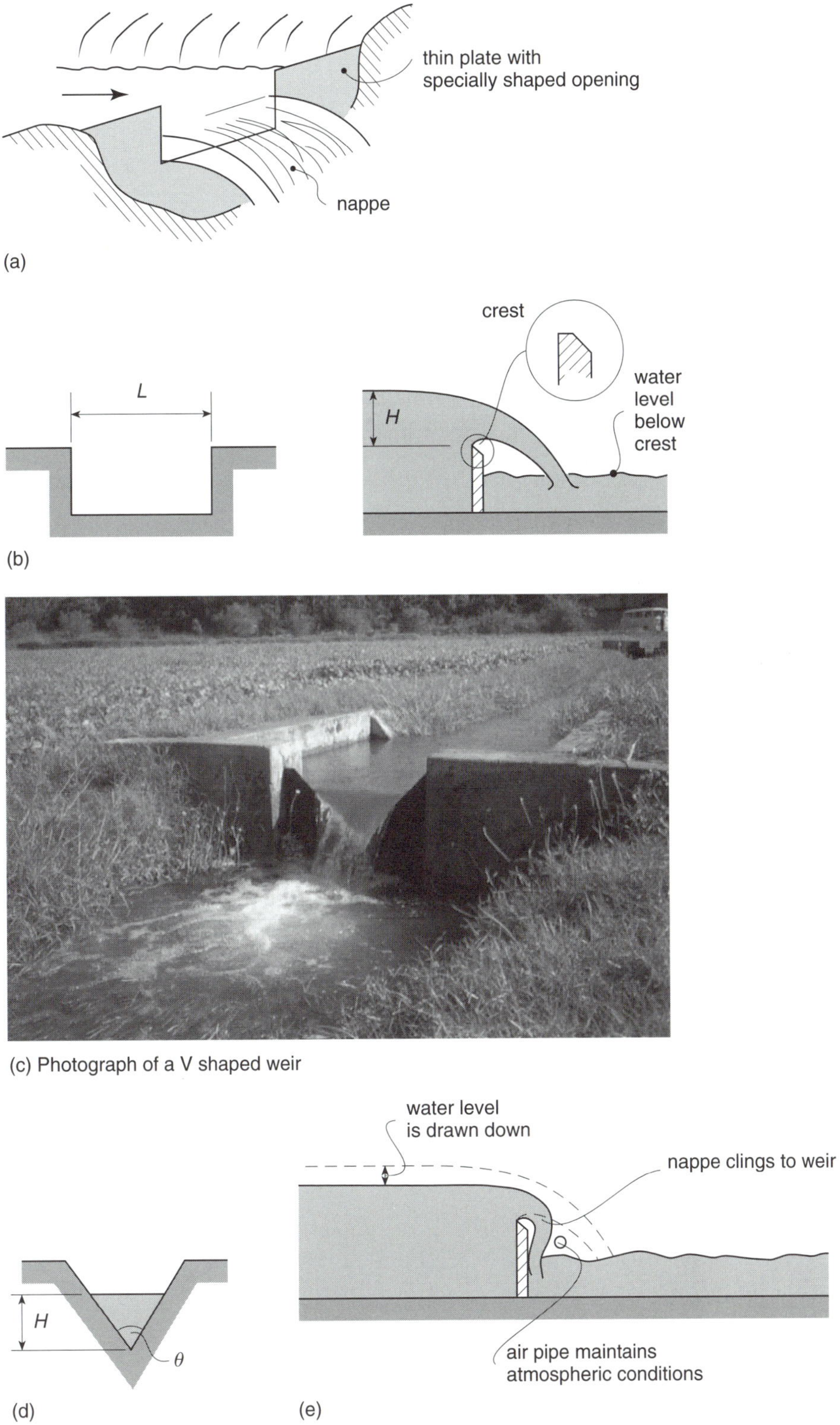

thin plate with
specially shaped opening

nappe

(a)

crest

$L$

$H$

water
level
below
crest

(b)

(c) Photograph of a V shaped weir

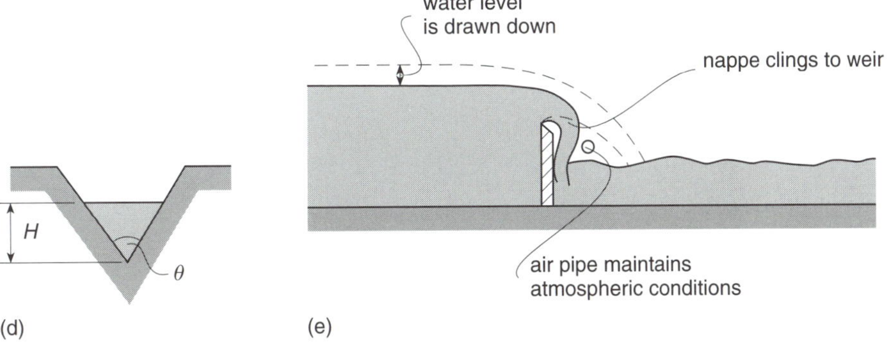


(d) (e)

**Figure 7.4** Sharp-crested weirs

underneath the weir and unless this air is replaced a vacuum may form which causes the flow to cling to the downstream face (Figure 7.4e). This draws down the upstream water level reducing the head on the weir and giving a false value of discharge when it is put into the formula. To prevent this, air must be allowed to flow freely under the nappe.

- The weir crest must always be set above the downstream water level. This is the **free flow** condition for sharp-crested weirs. If the downstream level rises beyond the crest, it starts to raise the upstream level and so the weir becomes **drowned**. Another word that is used to describe this condition is **submerged flow**. The formula no longer works when the flow is drowned and so this situation must be avoided by careful setting of the weir crest level.
- The head $H$ must be measured a few metres upstream of the weir to avoid the draw-down effect close to the weir.
- When deciding what size of weir to use it is important to make sure there is a reasonable head so that it can be measured accurately. This implies that you need to have some idea of the discharge to be measured before you can select the right weir size to measure it. If the head is only, say, 4mm then 1mm error in measuring it is a 25% error and will result in a significant error in the discharge. However, if the head is 100mm then a 1mm error in measuring the head is only a 1% error and so is not so significant.

Sharp-crested weirs can be very accurate discharge measuring devices provided they are constructed carefully and properly installed. However, they can be easily damaged, in particular the sharp crest. If this becomes rounded or dented through impact with floating debris, the flow pattern over the weir changes and this reduces its accuracy. For this reason they tend to be unsuited for long-term use in natural channels but well suited for temporary measurements in small channels, in places where they can be regularly maintained, and for accurate flow measurement in laboratories.

## 7.5 Solid weirs

These are much more robust than sharp-crested weirs and are used extensively for flow measurement and water level regulation in rivers and canals (Figure 7.5a).

### 7.5.1 Height of weir and critical flow

All solid weirs work on the principle *that the flow over the weir must go through the critical depth*. The idea of critical depth was discussed in Chapter 5 and there it was shown that it was the height of a weir that determined whether or not the flow goes critical. Once this happens a formula for discharge can be developed using the concept of specific energy and the special conditions that occur at the critical point.

The following formula links the channel discharge ($Q$) with the upstream water depth *measured above the weir crest* ($H$):

$$Q = CLH^{1.5}$$

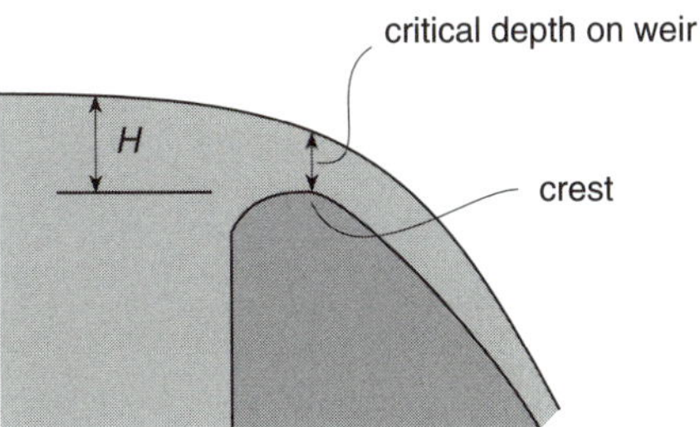


(a) Solid weir

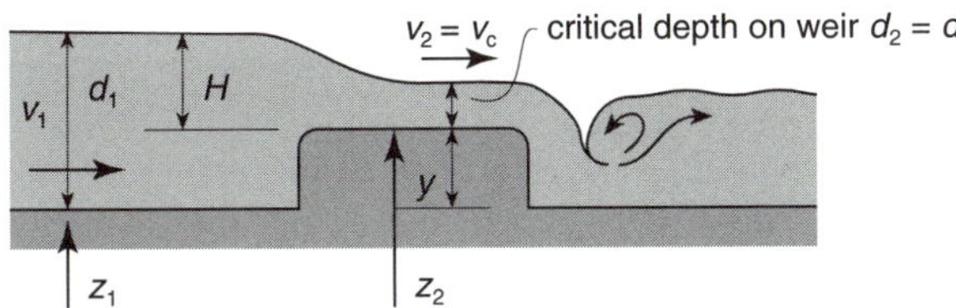


(b) broad-crested weir

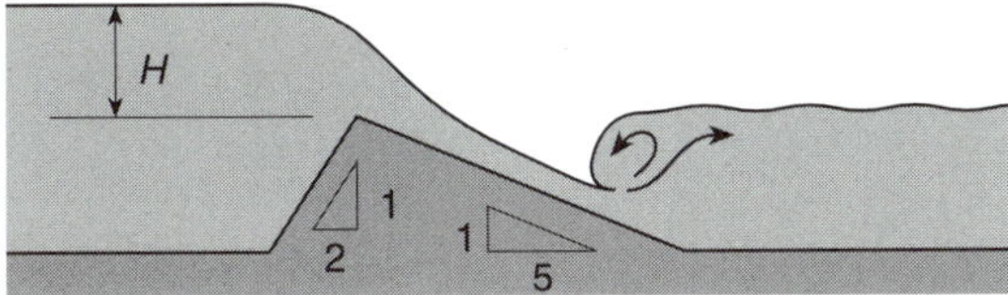


(c) Crump weir

**Figure 7.5** Solid weirs

where $C$ is weir coefficient, $L$ is length of the weir crest (m) and $H$ is head on the weir measured from the crest (m). To see how this formula is developed see the box.

As there is some draw-down close to the weir, the head is usually measured a few metres upstream where the water level is unaffected by the weir.

## Derivation: Formula for discharge over a critical flow structure

Derive a formula for discharge for a critical flow structure in an open channel. Use a broad-crested weir as an example of a critical flow structure, although the analysis would be the same for any similar structure (Figure 7.5b).

First write down the total energy equation for the flow in the channel (point 1) and the flow on the weir (point 2):

total energy at point 1 = total energy at point 2

$$d_1 + \frac{v_1^2}{2g} + z_1 = d_2 + \frac{v_2^2}{2g} + z_2$$

Now

$$z_2 - z_1 = y$$

i.e. the height of the weir is equal to the difference in the potential energy, and so

$$d_1 + \frac{v_1^2}{2g} = d_2 + \frac{v_2^2}{2g} + y$$

But at the critical depth

$$d_2 = d_c$$

and

$$v_2 = v_c$$

Substituting these into the energy equation:

$$d_1 + \frac{v_1^2}{2g} = d_c + \frac{v_c^2}{2g} + y$$

But at the critical depth

$$\frac{v_c^2}{2g} = \frac{d_c}{2}$$

(see derivation of the formula for critical depth in section 5.7.4). Putting this into the equation:

$$d_1 + \frac{v_1^2}{2g} = d_c + \frac{d_c}{2} + y$$

Rearranging this:

$$d_1 + \frac{v_1^2}{2g} - y = \frac{3}{2} d_c$$

But critical depth can be calculated from the formula:

$$d_c = \sqrt[3]{\frac{q^2}{g}}$$

(see derivation of the formula for critical depth in section 5.7.4) and put

$$d_1 + \frac{v_1^2}{2g} - y = H$$

This means that $H$ is measured from the weir crest, and so

$$H = \frac{3}{2}\sqrt[3]{\frac{q^2}{g}}$$

Rearranging this for $q$:

$$q = \left(\frac{2}{3}\right)^{3/2} g^{1/2} H^{3/2} = 1.71 H^{3/2}$$

This is the theoretical flow and an allowance now needs to be made for minor energy losses. This is usually combined with the 1.71 and introduced as a coefficient C. So

$$q = CH^{1.5}$$

For a broad-crested weir $C = 1.6$. Here $q$ is the discharge per metre width and so the full discharge $Q$ is calculated by multiplying this by the length of the weir $L$:

$$Q = CLH^{1.5}$$

Note that strictly speaking $H$ is the measurement from the weir crest to the energy line as it includes the kinetic energy term. In practice $H$ is measured from the weir crest to the water surface. The error involved in this is relatively small and can be taken into account in the value of the weir coefficient C.

As the formula is based on critical depth it is not dependent on the shape of the weir. So the same formula can be used for any critical depth weir and not just for broad-crested weirs. Only the value of C changes to take account of the different weir shapes.

#### *7.5.1.1 Determining the height of a weir*

Just how high a weir must be for the flow to go critical is determined from the specific energy diagram. The effect of constructing a weir in a channel is the same as building a step up on the bed as described in section 5.7.3. This was concerned only with looking at what happens to the depth when water flows over a step. In the case of a step up, the depth on the step decreased and the velocity increased (Figure 7.6a). At that time no thought was given to making the flow go critical. A worked example showed that for a 0.3m high step up, the depth of water was reduced from 0.99m upstream to 0.67m on the step (this is summarised in Figure 7.6b). This is still well above the critical depth of 0.29m (see calculation in section 5.7.4).

Now assume that the step up on the bed is a weir and the intention is to make the flow go critical on the weir crest. This can be achieved by raising the crest level. Raising it from 0.3m to 0.56m further reduces the depth on the weir from 0.67m to 0.29m, which is the critical depth (Figure 7.6c) – this can be worked out using the specific energy diagram in section 5.7.3. This is the minimum weir height required for critical flow. Note that although the weir height has increased by 0.26m, the

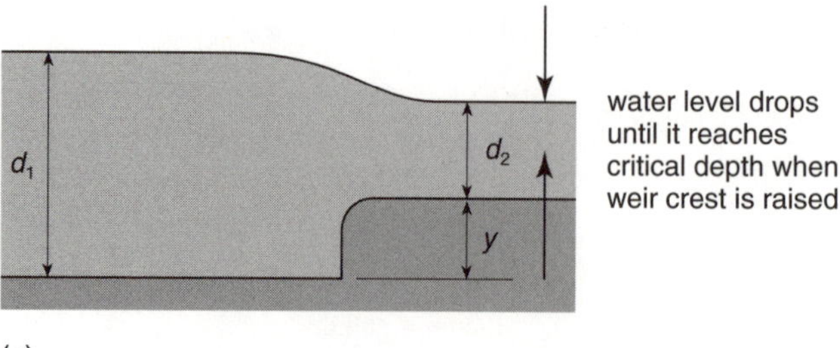


(a)

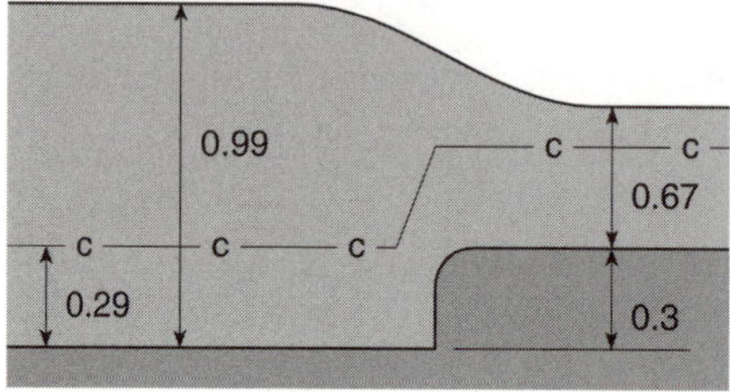


(b) Sub-critical flow on weir

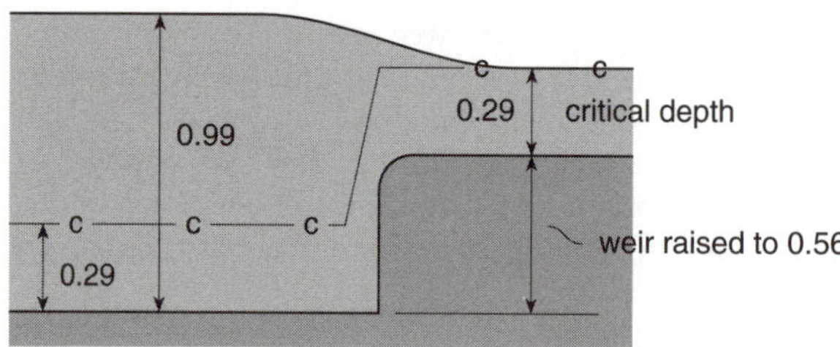


(c) Flow goes critical on weir

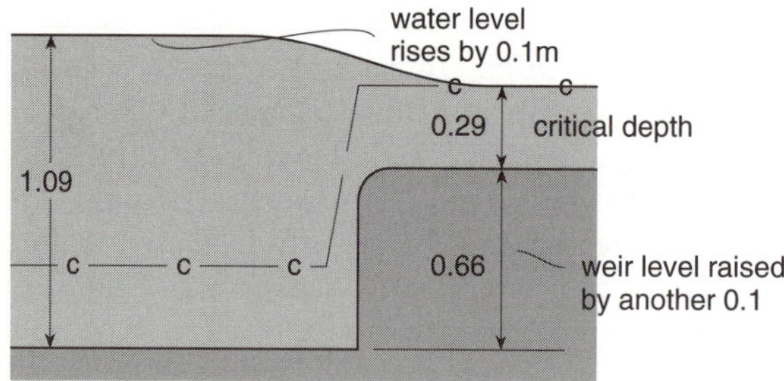


(d) Raising weir crest level affects upstream water level

**Figure 7.6 Determining the height of a weir**

upstream depth remains unchanged at 0.99m. If the weir height is increased beyond 0.56m the flow will still go critical on the crest and remain at the critical depth of 0.29m. It will not and cannot fall below this value. The difference will be in the upstream water level which will now rise. Remember there is a unique relationship between the head on a weir and the discharge. So if the weir is raised by a further 0.1m to 0.66m the upstream water level will also be raised by 0.1m to maintain the correct head on the weir (Figure 7.6d).

The operation of weirs is often misunderstood and it is believed that they cause the flow to back up and so raise water levels upstream. This only happens once critical conditions are achieved on the weir. When a weir is too low for critical flow it is the water level on the weir that drops. The upstream level is unaffected. But once critical flow is achieved, raising the weir more than is necessary will have a direct effect on the upstream water level.

#### *7.5.1.2 Being sure of critical flow*

Critical flow must occur for the discharge formula to work. But in practice it is not always possible to see critical flow and so some detective work is needed. Figure 7.7 shows the changing flow conditions as water flows over a weir. Upstream the flow is sub-critical, it then goes critical over the weir and then super-critical downstream. It changes back to sub-critical through a hydraulic jump. When this sequence of changes occurs it can be reasoned that critical flow must have occurred and so the weir is working properly. The changes are best verified in reverse from the downstream side. Remember a hydraulic jump can only form when the flow is super-critical and so if there is a hydraulic jump in the downstream channel, the flow over the weir must be super-critical. If the upstream flow is sub-critical, which can be verified by the water surface dropping as water flows over the weir, then somewhere in between the flow must have gone critical. So a hydraulic jump downstream is good evidence that critical flow has occurred.

Note that it is not important to know exactly where critical flow occurs. It is enough just to know that it has occurred for the formula to work.

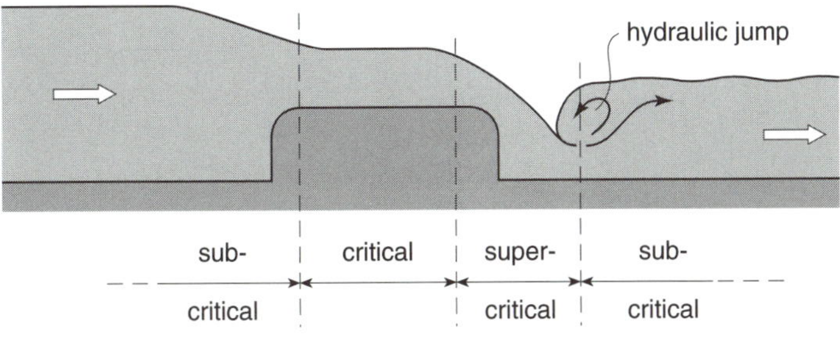


**Figure 7.7 Being sure of critical flow**

### 7.5.2 Broad-crested weirs

These are very common structures used for flow measurement. They have a broad rectangular shape with a level crest rounded at the edge (Figure 7.5b). The value of $C$ for a broad-crested weir is 1.6 and so the formula becomes:

$$Q = 1.6LH^{1.5}$$

One disadvantage of this weir is the region of dead water just upstream. Silt and debris can accumulate here and this can seriously reduce the accuracy of the weir formula. Another is the head loss between the upstream and downstream levels. Whenever a weir (or a flume) is installed in a channel there is always a loss of energy particularly if there is a hydraulic jump downstream. This is the hydraulic price to be paid for measuring the flow.

**Example: Calculating discharge using a broad-crested weir**

A broad-crested weir is used to measure discharge in a channel. If the weir is 2m long and the head on the crest is 0.35m, calculate the discharge.

The discharge over a broad-crested weir can be calculated using the formula:

$$Q = 1.6LH^{1.5}$$

Putting in values for length $L$ and head $H$:

$$Q = 1.6 \times 2 \times 0.35^{1.5} = 0.66\text{m}^3/\text{s}$$

### 7.5.3 Crump weirs

These weirs are commonly used in the UK for discharge measurement in rivers. Like the broad-crested weir it relies on critical conditions occurring for the discharge formula to work. It has a triangular shaped section (Figure 7.5c). The upstream slope is 1 in 2 and the downstream is 1 in 5. The sloping upstream face helps to reduce the dead water region that occurs with broad-crested weirs. It can also tolerate a high level of submergence. Its crest can also be constructed in a vee shape so that it can be used accurately for both small and large discharges.

### 7.5.4 Round-crested weirs

Weirs of this kind are commonly used on dam spillways (Figure 7.5a). The weir profile is carefully shaped so that it is very similar to the underside of the falling nappe of a sharp-crested weir (compare the two shapes in Figures 7.5a and 7.4b).

Many standard designs are available which have been calibrated in the laboratory using hydraulic models to obtain the $C$ values. An example is the standard weir designs produced by the US Bureau of Reclamation (USBR, 1974). By constructing a weir to the dimensions given in their publications, the discharge can be measured accurately using their $C$ values (usually between 3.0 and 4.0).

### 7.5.5 Drowned flow

Weirs that rely on critical depth are much less sensitive to being **drowned** (or **submerged**) than the sharp-crested type. This means that the downstream water level can rise above the weir crest without it affecting the performance of the structure *provided* the flow still goes critical somewhere on the weir. There are ways of using weirs even when they are completely submerged but they are far less accurate and both upstream and downstream water depths must be measured. It is better to avoid this situation if at all possible.

## 7.6 Flumes

Flumes also rely on critical flow for measuring discharges. They are sometimes called **throated flumes** because critical conditions are achieved by narrowing the width of the channel (Figure 7.8a). Downstream of the throat there is a short length of super-critical flow followed by a hydraulic jump. This returns the flow to sub-critical. The formula for discharge can be determined in the same way as for solid weirs. The result is as follows:

$$Q = 1.65bH^{1.5}$$

where $b$ is width of the flume throat (m) and $H$ is upstream depth of water (m).

The head loss through flumes is much lower than for weirs and so they are ideally suited for use in channels in very flat areas where head losses need to be kept as low as possible.

### 7.6.1 Parshall flumes

Parshall flumes are used extensively in the USA and were developed by R.L. Parshall in 1926 (Figure 7.8b). They gained popularity in many other countries because the construction details, dimensions and calibration curves relating upstream depth to discharge have been widely published. There are several different sizes available to measure flows up to $90 m^3/s$. They are relatively simple to construct from a range of materials such as wood, concrete and metal because they have no curved surfaces.

If they are made and installed as recommended they provide accurate discharge measurement.

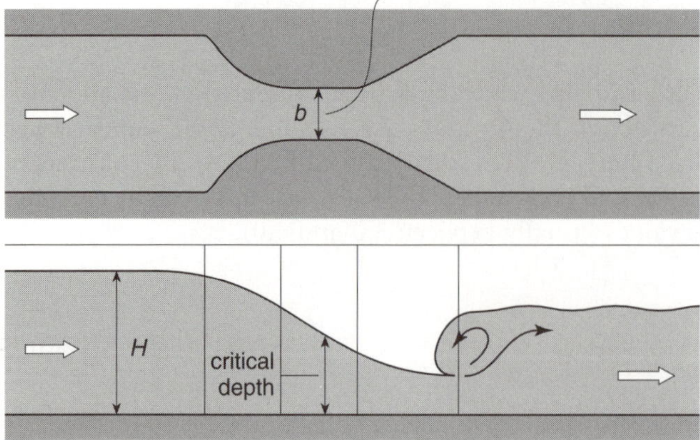


(a) Venturi flume

(b) Parshall flume

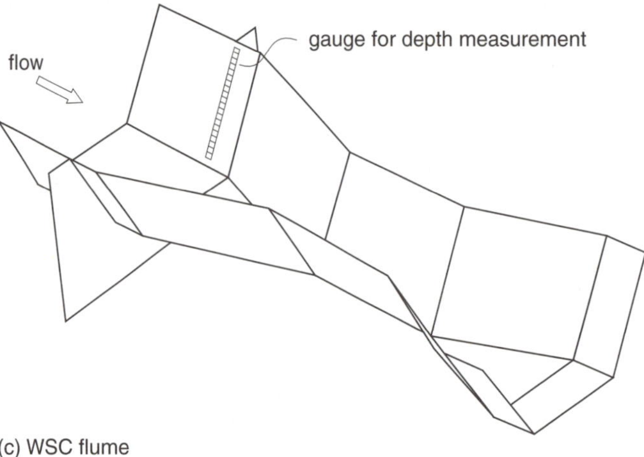


(c) WSC flume

**Figure 7.8 Flumes**

### 7.6.2 WSC flumes

This is a range of standard flumes for measuring small discharges from less than 1.0 litre/s up to 50 litre/s developed by Washington State University in the USA (Figure 7.8c). They are vee-shaped so that they can be used to measure low flows accurately and, like Parshall flumes, they can be easily made up in a workshop from metal or fibreglass. They are particularly useful as portable flumes for spot measurements in small channels and irrigation furrows.

### 7.6.3 Combination weir–flumes

Sometimes both weir and flume effects are combined to achieve critical flow. The advantages of the vee for low flows can also be added. In such cases a laboratory model test is needed to determine the $C$ value in the discharge equation.

## 7.7 Discharge measurement

Weirs, flumes and orifices can all be used for discharge measurement. But weirs and flumes are better suited to measuring discharges in rivers when there can be large variations in flow. Weirs and flumes not only require a simple head reading to measure discharge but they can also pass large flows without causing the upstream level to rise significantly and cause flooding. Orifice structures too can be used for flow measurement but both upstream and downstream water levels are usually required to determine discharge. Large variations in flow also mean that the gates will need constant attention for opening and closing.

## 7.8 Discharge control

Although orifices are rather cumbersome for discharge measurement they are very useful for discharge control. This is because the discharge through an orifice is not very sensitive to changes in upstream water level. Consider as an example an irrigation canal system where a branch canal takes water from a main canal (Figure 7.9a). The structure at the head of the branch controls the discharge to farmers downstream.

The ideal structure for this would be an orifice and the reason lies in its hydraulic characteristic curve (Figure 7.9b). This is a graph of the orifice discharge equation:

$$Q = C_d a \sqrt{2gd_1}$$

In this simple example, the orifice opening is assumed to be fixed and so discharge $Q$ changes only when the upstream depth $d_1$ changes. The point $(Q_d, d_d)$ on the graph represents the normal operating condition. Now suppose the main canal

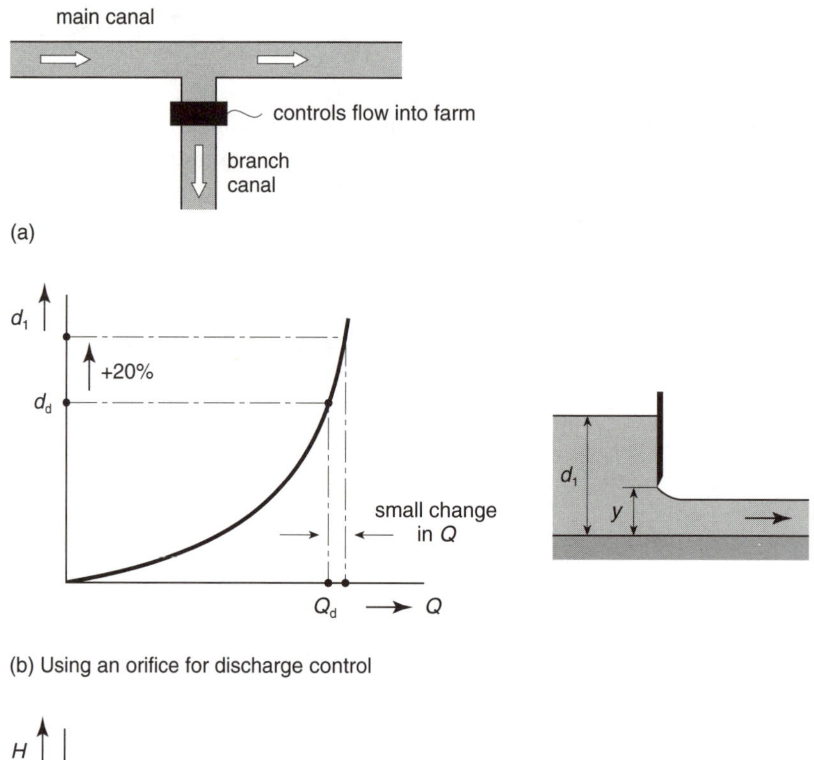


(b) Using an orifice for discharge control

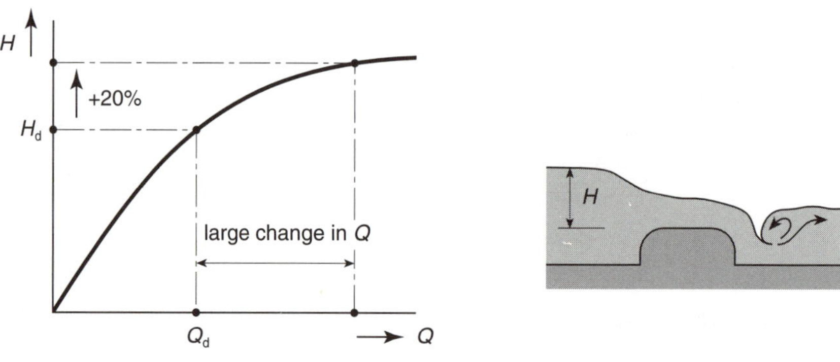


(c) Using a weir for discharge control

**Figure 7.9 Discharge control**

operating depth rises by say, 20%, because of changes in the water demand elsewhere in the system. The effect that this would have on the discharge into the branch (through the orifice) is to change it by only a small amount (5% or so). So even though there is a significant change in the main canal this is hardly noticed in the branch. This can be very useful for ensuring a reliable, constant flow to a farmer even though the main canal may be varying considerably due to changing demands.

In contrast, if a weir (or flume) is installed at the head of the branch canal, it would be very easy to use for discharge measurement but it would not be so good for controlling the flow. Look at the hydraulic characteristic curve for a weir

(Figure 7.9c). This is a graph of the weir discharge equation:

$$Q = CLH^{1.5}$$

Now $Q_d$ and $H_d$ represent the normal operating condition. If the water level in the main canal rises by 20% the resulting change in discharge into the branch canal is large (35% or more). So this type of structure is very sensitive to water level changes and would not make a very good discharge control structure.

These examples show the sensitivity of the two types of control structure. This is how they react to small changes in water level. But they refer to fixed structures. Most structures have gates (both weirs and orifices) which can be used to adjust the discharge but this adds to the burden of managing the channels. Better to use a structure that is hydraulically suited to the job to be done and which reduces the need for continual monitoring and adjustment.

## 7.9 Water level control

Orifices, weirs and flumes can all be used for water level control. But the very reason that makes an orifice a good discharge regulator makes it unsuitable for good water level control. Conversely, a weir (or flume) is well suited to water level control but not for discharge control.

Imagine that the water level in a river needs to be controlled to stabilise water levels in a nearby wetland site and it needs to be more or less the same in both winter and summer even though the river flows change from a small flow to a flood. The structure best suited for this would be a weir as it can pass a wide range of flows with only small changes in head (water level). An orifice structure would not be suitable because large changes in water level would occur as the flow changed and the structure would require a great deal of attention and adjustment.

Another water level control problem occurs in reservoirs. When a dam is built across a river to store water, a spillway is also constructed to pass severe flood flows safely into the downstream channel to avoid overtopping the dam. The ideal structure for this is a weir because large discharges can flow over it for relatively small increases in water level. The rise in water level can be calculated using the weir discharge formula and this helps to determine the height of the dam. A freeboard is also added to the anticipated maximum water level as an added safety measure. The spillway can be the most expensive part of constructing a new dam. Many small dams are built on small seasonal streams in developing countries to conserve water for domestic and agricultural use. But even a small dam will need a spillway and although the stream may look small and dry up occasionally, it can suffer from very severe floods which are difficult to determine in advance, particularly when rainfall and discharge data for the stream are not available. Building a spillway for such conditions can be prohibitively expensive and far exceed the cost of the dam and so it may be cheaper in sparsely populated areas to let the dam be washed away and then rebuild it on the rare occasions that this happens. There are of course many other factors to take into account besides dam reconstruction costs such as the effects downstream of a dam break. It is a sobering thought that even the biggest and most important dams can fail because of severe flooding. They have large spillways to protect them from very severe floods which are carefully assessed at the design stage. But it is impossible to say that they will safely carry every flood. Nature seems to have a way of testing us by sending unexpected rain storms but fortunately these events are few and far between.

One way of avoiding the expensive spillway problem is to construct a reservoir at the side of a river rather than use the river channel itself. This is called **off-stream storage**. Water is taken from the river by gravity or by pumping into a reservoir and only a modest spillway is then needed which would have the same capacity as the inlet discharge. When a flood comes down the river there is no obstruction in its path and so it flows safely past the reservoir.

## 7.10 Energy dissipators

### 7.10.1 Stilling basins

When water flows over a weir or through a flume and becomes super-critical it can do a lot of damage to the downstream channel if it is left unprotected. This is particularly true when water rushes down an overflow spillway on a dam. The water can reach very high velocities by the time it gets to the bottom. Scour can be prevented by lining the channel but this can be an expensive option.

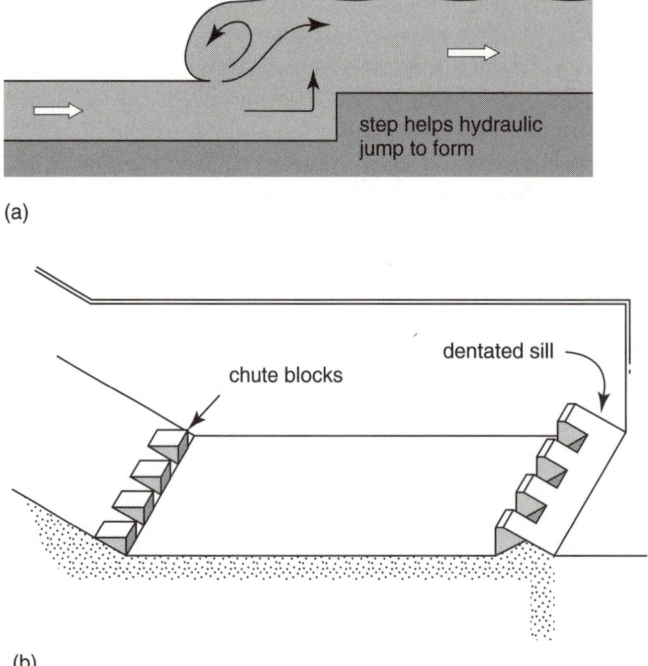


**Figure 7.10** Stilling basins

The alternative is to convert the flow to sub-critical using a hydraulic jump. The requirements for a jump are super-critical flow upstream and sub-critical flow in the downstream channel. The main problem is to create the right flow conditions in the downstream channel for a jump to occur even though the discharge may range from a small overspill flow to a large flood. Consider what happens when flow reaches the bottom of a spillway. If the tail-water is too shallow for a jump to form, the super-critical flow will shoot off downstream and no jump will form. If the water is too deep the jump will be drowned and the super-critical flow will rush underneath and still cause erosion for some distance downstream. These problems can be resolved by building **stilling basins** which create and confine hydraulic jumps even though the tail-water may not be at the ideal depth for a jump to occur naturally. There are many different designs available but perhaps the simplest is a small vertical wall placed across the channel (Figure 7.10a). Other more sophisticated designs, like the USBR stilling basin in Figure 7.10b, have been developed in laboratories using models as it is not possible to design them using formulae. The choice of stilling basin is linked to the Froude number of the upstream super-critical flow.

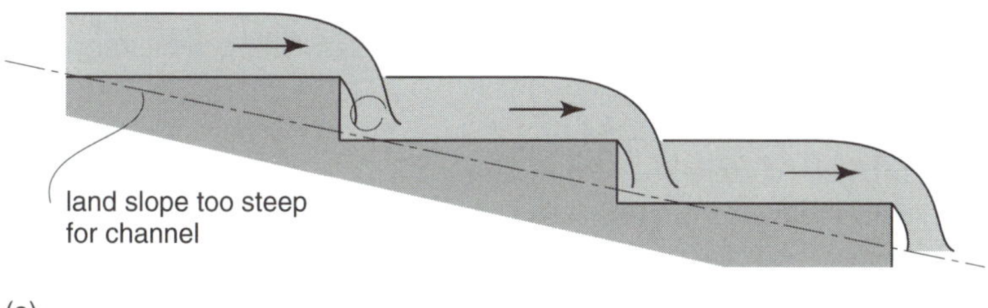


(a)

(b) Drop structure on an irrigation canal in Iraq

**Figure 7.11 Drop structures**

### 7.10.2 Drop structures

Drop structures are used to take flow down steep slopes step by step to dissipate energy and so avoid erosion (Figure 7.11). Channels on steep sloping land are prone to erosion because of the high velocities. One option to avoid this is to line channels with concrete or brick but another is to construct natural channels on a gentle gradient and to build in steps like a staircase. The water flows gently and safely along the shallow reaches of channel and then drops to the next reach through a drop structure. Often a drop is made into a weir so that it can also be used for discharge measurement. It can also be fitted with gates so that it can be used for water level and discharge control. Drop structures are usually combined with stilling basins so that unwanted energy is got rid of effectively.

## 7.11 Siphons

Siphons are hydraulic structures that have always fascinated engineers. Used long ago by the ancient Greeks and Egyptians, they began to be used seriously in civil engineering in the mid-nineteenth century as spillways on storage reservoirs. More recently, their special characteristics have been put to use in providing protection against sudden surges in hydro-power intakes and in controlling water levels in rivers and canals subjected to flooding.

Although siphons have been successfully installed in many parts of the world, there is still a general lack of guidelines for designers. This is borne out by the wide variety of siphon shapes and sizes that have been used. Invariably design is based on intuition and experience of previous siphon structures, and few engineers would attempt to install such a structure without first carrying out a model study.

The principle of siphon operation is described in section 4.7 in connection with pipe flow. In its very simplest form it is a pipe that rises above the hydraulic gradient over part of its length. The following siphon structures, although more sophisticated than a pipe, still follow this same principle.

### 7.11.1 Black-water siphons

These are the most common type of siphon and Figure 7.12 shows how one can be used as a spillway from a reservoir. It consists of an enclosed barrel which is sealed from the atmosphere by the upstream and downstream water levels. The lower part is shaped like a weir and the upper part forms the hood.

Water starts to flow through a siphon when the upstream water level rises above the crest. As the flow plunges into the downstream water it entrains and removes air from inside the barrel. As the barrel is sealed, air cannot enter from outside and so the pressure gradually falls and this increases the flow rate until the barrel is running full of water. At this stage the siphon is said to be **primed** and flow is described as **black-water flow**. This is in contrast to the flow just before priming when there is a lot of air entrained and it has a white appearance. This is termed **white-water flow**.

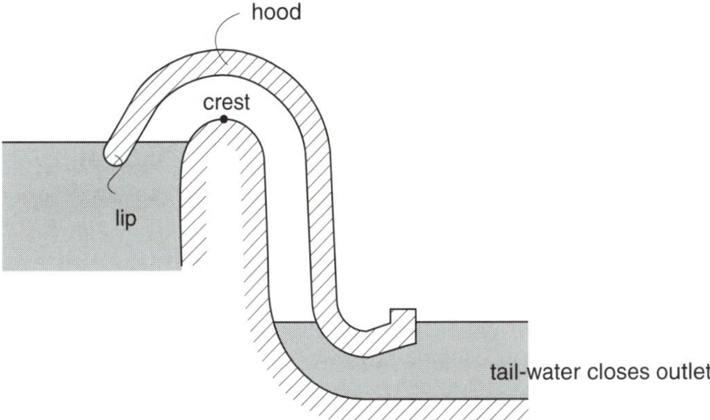


(a) Typical siphon design

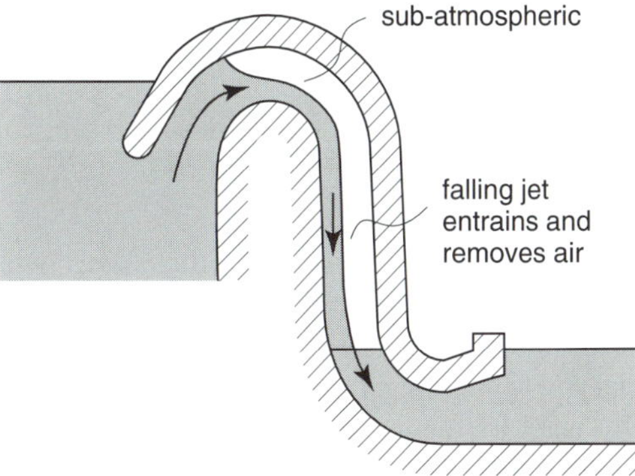


(b) Priming

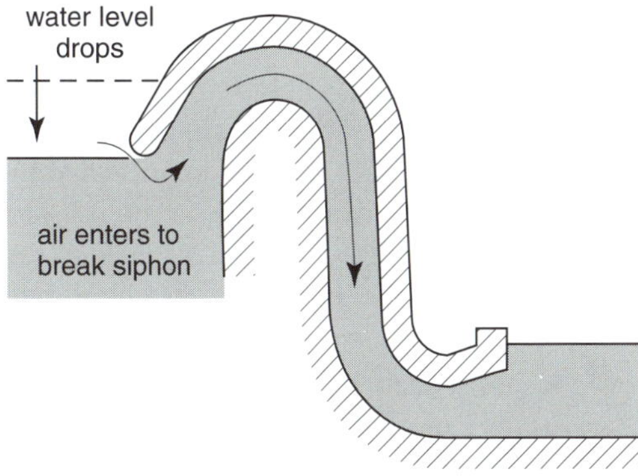


(c) Depriming

**Figure 7.12 Black-water siphon**

Priming takes place rapidly until the discharge reaches the siphon's full capacity. This is determined by the size of the barrel and the difference in energy available across the siphon. The siphon eventually starts to draw down the upstream water level and this continues even when the water level falls below the crest. Only when it is drawn down to the lip on the hood on the inlet can air enter the barrel and break the siphonic action. Flow then stops rapidly and will only begin again when the siphon is re-primed.

Black-water siphons have several advantages over conventional spillways. There are no moving parts such as gates and so they do not need constant attention from operators. They respond automatically, and rapidly, to changes in flow and water levels and so floods that come unexpectedly in the night do not cause problems. Their compactness also means that they are very useful when crest lengths for conventional weir spillways are limited. But they are not without problems. The abruptness of priming produces a sudden rush of water which can cause problems downstream. They are also prone to **hunting** when the flow towards a siphon is less than the siphon capacity. They are continually priming and de-priming and this can cause surges downstream and vibration which is not good for the structure.

## 7.11.2 Air-regulated siphons

This type of siphon is a more recent development and offers many advantages over the more common black-water siphon. It automatically adjusts its discharge to match the approach flow and at the same time maintains a constant water level on the upstream side. This is achieved by the siphon passing a mixture of air and water.

Air-regulated siphons are typically used for water level control in reservoirs and in rivers and canals. They will maintain a constant water level in a channel even though the discharge is changing. This would be an ideal structure for the wetland example discussed earlier.

Figure 7.13a shows a typical air-regulated siphon for a river. There needs to be sufficient energy available to entrain air in the barrel and take it out to prime the siphon. This one is designed to operate at very low heads of 1 to 2m (difference between the upstream and downstream water levels). The siphon is shaped in many ways like a black-water siphon and relies on the barrel being enclosed and sealed by the upstream and downstream water levels. But the main difference is the inlet to the hood or upstream lip. This is set above the crest level whereas in a black-water siphon it is set below. A step is also included in the down-leg to encourage turbulence and air entrainment.

The operation of the siphon has several distinct phases (Figure 7.13a–e):

### Phase I: Free weir flow (Figure 7.13a)

As the upstream water level starts to rise due to increased flow, water flows over the crest and plunges into the downstream pool. The structure behaves as a conventional free-flowing weir. As the water level has not yet reached the upstream lip, air that is evacuated by the flow is immediately replaced and the pressure in the barrel remains atmospheric.

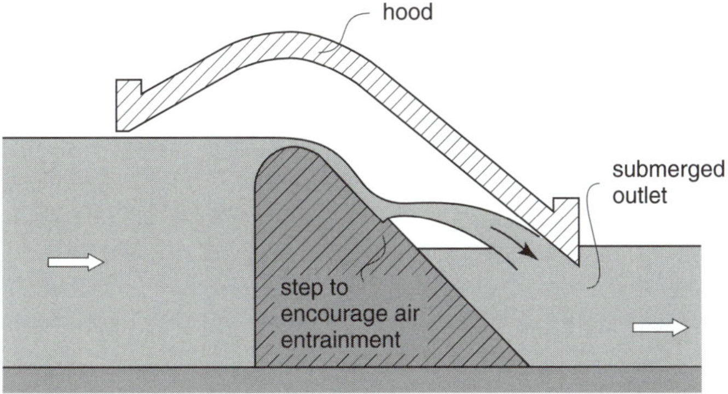


(a) Phase I

(b) Phase II begins

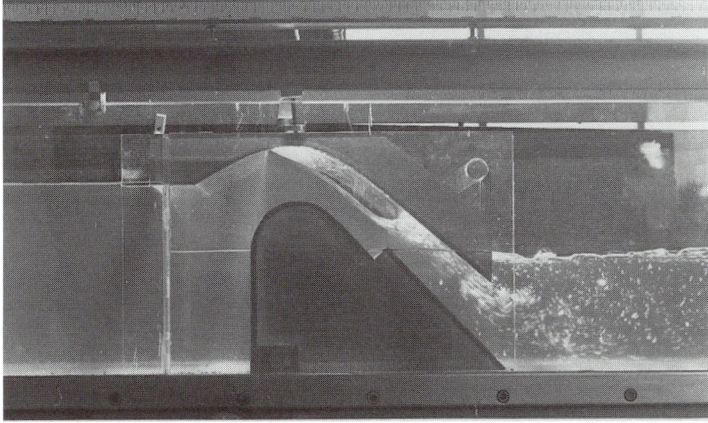

(c) Phase II

**Figure 7.13** Air-regulated siphon

(d) Phase III

(e) Phase IV

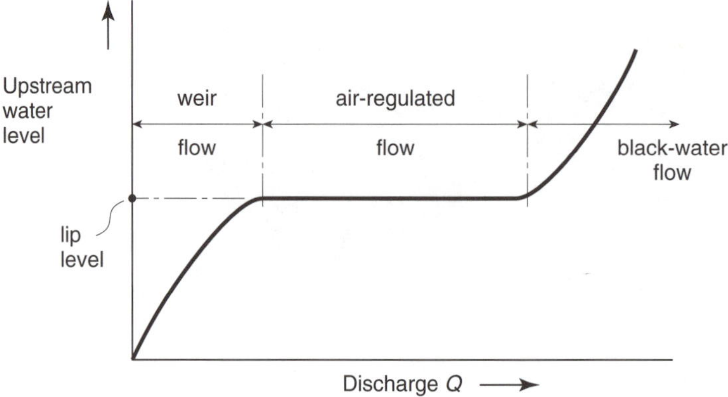


(f) Discharge characteristic

**Figure 7.13** *Continued*

### Phase II: Deflected flow (Figure 7.13b and c)

As the flow increases, the upstream water level rises further and seals the barrel. The evacuation of air continues and a partial vacuum is created. This raises the head of water over the crest and so increases the discharge through the siphon. A point is reached when the flow through the siphon exceeds the incoming flow. The water surface close to the lip is drawn down and air is sucked into the barrel to compensate for the evacuation taking place on the downstream side. This process is not cyclic but continuous. Both air and water are drawn continuously through the structure. In this manner the siphon adjusts rapidly and smoothly to the incoming flow and is said to be self-regulating. As the flow passes over the weir it is deflected by a step and springs clear of the structure. This encourages air entrainment and evacuation at low flows and is not intended to create an air seal as in the case of some black-water siphons.

### Phase III: Air-partialised flow (Figure 7.13d)

As the flow increases, the water level inside the hood rises to a point where the air pocket is completely swept out and the siphon barrel is occupied by a mixture of air and water. Changes in the discharge are now accommodated by variations in the quantity of air passing through the siphon and not by an increase in the effective head over the weir crest.

### Phase IV: Black-water flow (Figure 7.13e)

Increasing the flow beyond the air-partialised phase produces the more common black-water flow in which the barrel is completely filled with water. The discharge is now determined by the head across the siphon, i.e. the difference between the upstream and downstream water levels.

The flow changes from one phase to another quite gradually and smoothly and there is no distinct or abrupt change-over point. During phases II and III, the upstream water level remains relatively constant at a level close to that of the upstream lip. This feature makes this structure an excellent water level regulator. Only when the black-water phase is reached does an increase in discharge cause a significant rise in the upstream water level (Figure 7.13f).

## 7.12 Culverts

Culverts are very useful structures for taking water under roads and railways. They are circular or rectangular in shape and their size is chosen so that they are large enough to carry a given discharge, usually with minimum energy loss (Figure 7.14). They are important structures and can be as much as 15% of the cost of building a new road.

Although they are very simple in appearance culverts can be quite complex hydraulically depending on how and where they are used. Sometimes they flow part

**Figure 7.14 A concrete box culvert – type III flow**

full, like an open channel, and at other times they can flow full, like a pipe. Six different flow conditions are recognised depending on the size and shape of a culvert, its length and its position in relation to the upstream and downstream water levels (Figure 7.15).

The simplest condition occurs when a culvert is set well below both the upstream and downstream water levels and it runs full of water (type I). It behaves like a pipe and the difference between the water levels is the energy available which determines the discharge. This full pipe flow can still occur even when the downstream water level falls below the culvert soffit (this is the roof of the culvert) (type II). The culvert is now behaving like an orifice and the flow is controlled by the downstream water level and the size of the culvert. In both cases the discharge is controlled by what is happening downstream. When the water level falls the discharge increases and when it rises the discharge decreases. If the flow in the channel does not change then any change in the downstream water level will have a corresponding effect on the upstream water level.

The four remaining flow conditions are for open channel flow. Three occur when both the upstream and downstream water levels are below the culvert soffit (type III, IV and V). The difference between III and IV is the slope of the culvert. Type III produces sub-critical flow and so the discharge is controlled by the downstream water level. When the downstream level rises the discharge reduces or the upstream level rises to accommodate the same flow. In IV, the flow is still sub-critical but the downstream water level is low and so the flow goes through the critical depth at the outlet. This means that the flow is controlled by the upstream water level. Because the flow has gone through the critical depth any changes downstream do not affect the flow in the culvert or upstream. Condition V produces super-critical flow and so the culvert is again controlled by the upstream level. A rise in the downstream level will have no effect until it starts to drown the culvert.

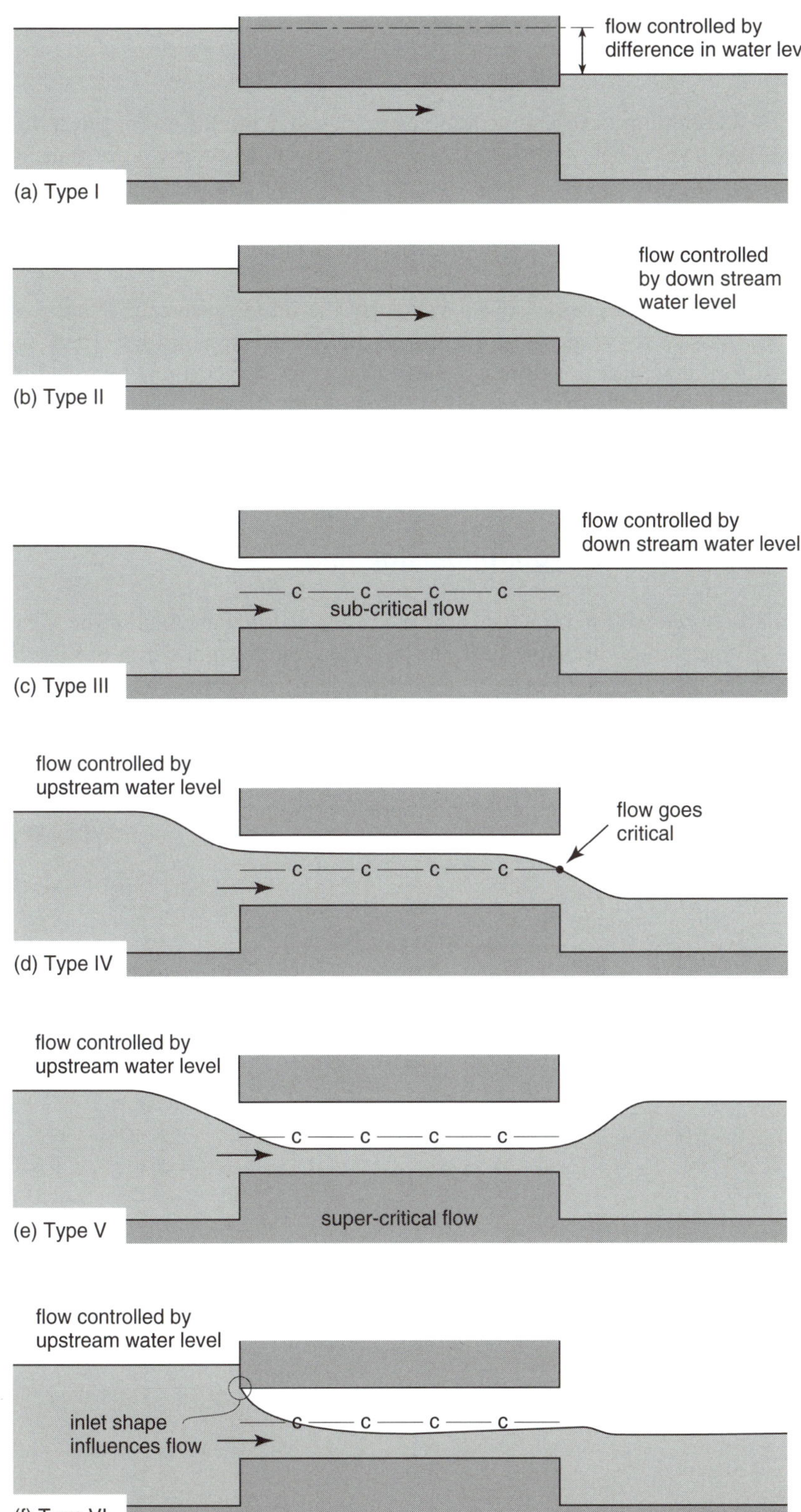


**Figure 7.15** Culvert flow conditions

The final condition occurs when the upstream water level is above the soffit, the downstream level is below and there is a sharp corner at the entrance causing the flow to separate (type VI). Open channel flow occurs in the culvert and is primarily due to the shape of the entrance. But if the entrance is rounded then this could change the flow to pipe flow. Clearly this would improve its discharge capacity.

Because of their complexity and particularly the importance of the shape of the entrance most culvert designs are based on model tests rather than on fundamental formulae. But this does not mean that every culvert must be tested in this way. There has already been extensive testing of culverts over many years and so designers look to the standard handbooks when designing new culverts (see e.g. Portland Cement Association, 1964).

## 7.13 Some examples to test your understanding

1 A broad-crested weir 3.5m wide is to be constructed in a channel of the same width to measure a discharge of 4.3m$^3$/s. When the normal depth of flow is 1.2m, calculate the height of weir needed to measure this flow assuming that the flow must go critical on the weir crest.

2 A broad-crested weir 5.0m wide and 0.5m high is used to measure a discharge of 7.5m$^3$/s. Calculate the water depth upstream of the weir assuming that critical depth occurs on the weir and there are no energy losses.

# Chapter 8

# Pumps and turbines

## 8.1 Introduction

Pumps are a means of adding energy to water. They convert fuel energy such as petrol or diesel into useful water energy using combustion engines or electric motors. In the pipeline problem in Chapter 4 the energy to drive water was obtained from a reservoir located high above the town (Figure 8.1). The energy line drawn from the reservoir to the town showed energy available. Adding a pump to this system increases the available energy and this raises the energy line close to the pump. In this way the discharge from the reservoir to the town can be increased.

Although pumps have been used for thousands of years they were largely small hand- or animal-powered pumps for lifting relatively small quantities of water. It was not until the advent of the steam engine, only two centuries ago, that pumping became an important part of hydraulics.

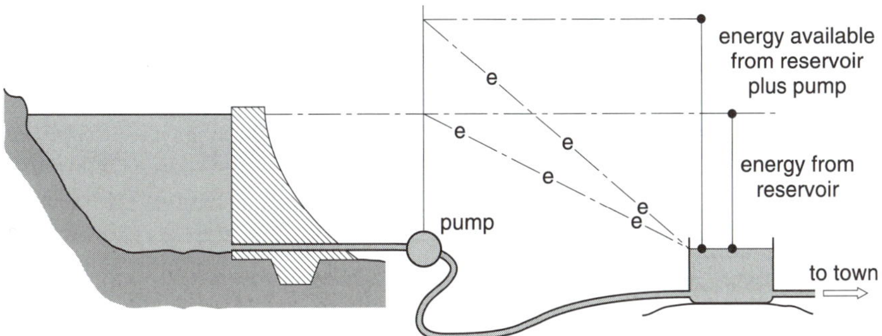


Figure 8.1 Pumps add energy to pipe systems

Turbines are a means of taking energy out of water and were used long before pumps were invented. Modern turbines are used for generating electricity and are popular because they do not pollute the environment and the energy source is renewable.

Because of the importance of pumping much of this chapter is devoted to pumps but a general description of turbines is also provided. Two types of pump are considered:

- Positive displacement pumps
- Roto-dynamic pumps

## 8.2 Positive displacement pumps

Positive displacement pumps usually deliver only small discharges irrespective of head. Typical examples are the piston pump, rotary pump, air-lift pump and the Archimedean screw (Figure 8.2).

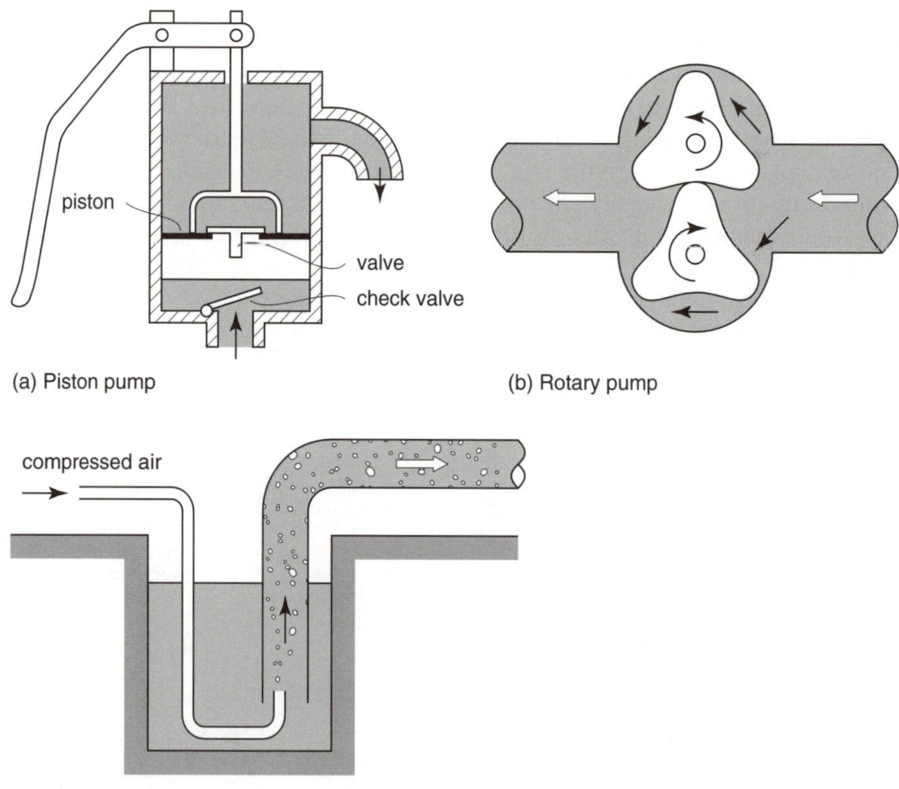


**Figure 8.2 Positive displacement pumps**

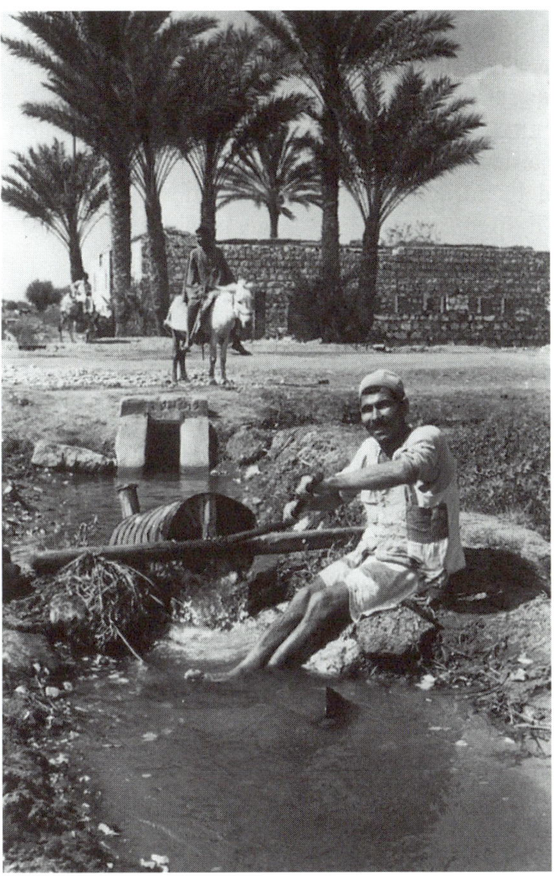

(d) Archimedean screw

**Figure 8.2** *Continued*

The piston pump is often used for domestic water supplies in developing countries for lifting groundwater. A piston moves up and down in a cylinder. When the lever is pushed downwards the piston rises, lifting water above it through the outlet. At the same time it sucks water up the well through the non-return valve and fills the cylinder. When the lever is raised the non-return valve closes and the piston descends allowing water to flow through another valve into the upper part of the cylinder. The process is then repeated. The discharge depends on the energy available from those working the pump handle. The height to which water can be pumped in this way is fixed only by the strength of those pumping and the pump seals, which will begin to leak when the pressure gets too high.

The rotary pump contains two gears which mesh together as they rotate in opposite directions. The liquid becomes trapped between the gears and is forced into the delivery pipe.

The air-lift pump uses an air compressor to force air down a pipe into the inlet of the water pipe. The mixture of air and water, which is less dense than the surrounding water in the well, then rises up above ground level. This pump is not very efficient but it will pump water that has sand and grit in it which would normally damage other pumps.

The Archimedean screw pump has been used for thousands of years and is still used today for pumping irrigation water in Egypt. It comprises a helical screw inside a casing. Water is lifted by turning the screw. Some modern pumping stations also use this idea but the screws are much larger and are driven by a power unit.

## 8.3 Roto-dynamic pumps

All roto-dynamic pumps rely on rotational movement for their pumping action. There are three main types which are described by the way in which water flows through them:

- Centrifugal
- Axial flow
- Mixed flow

### 8.3.1 Centrifugal pumps

Centrifugal pumps are the most widely used of all the roto-dynamic pumps. They are ideally suited to water supply and irrigation schemes, particularly those using pipe systems where there is a requirement for relatively small discharges at high pressures.

To understand how centrifugal pumps work consider first how centrifugal forces occur. Most people will, at some time, have spun a bucket of water around at arm's length (Figure 8.3a) and observed that water stays in the bucket even when it is upside down. Water is held in the bucket by the centrifugal force created by spinning the bucket. The faster the bucket is spun the tighter the water is held. Centrifugal pumps make use of this idea (Figure 8.3b). The bucket is replaced by an **impeller** which spins at high speed inside the pump casing. Water is drawn into the pump from the source of supply through a short length of pipe called the **suction**. As the impeller spins, water is thrown outwards and is collected by the pump casing and guided towards the outlet. This is called the **delivery**.

Some pumps have very simple impellers with straight vanes (Figure 8.3c). These are inefficient because they create a lot of turbulence in the flow and hence energy losses. But they are cheap to make and are used where efficiency is not so important such as in domestic washing machines. Larger pumps need more careful design and have curved vanes so that the water enters and leaves the impeller smoothly. Energy losses are then kept to a minimum and a high level of efficiency of energy use can be achieved. Most impellers have side plates and are called **closed impellers**. When there is debris in the water **open impellers** are used to reduce the risk of blockage.

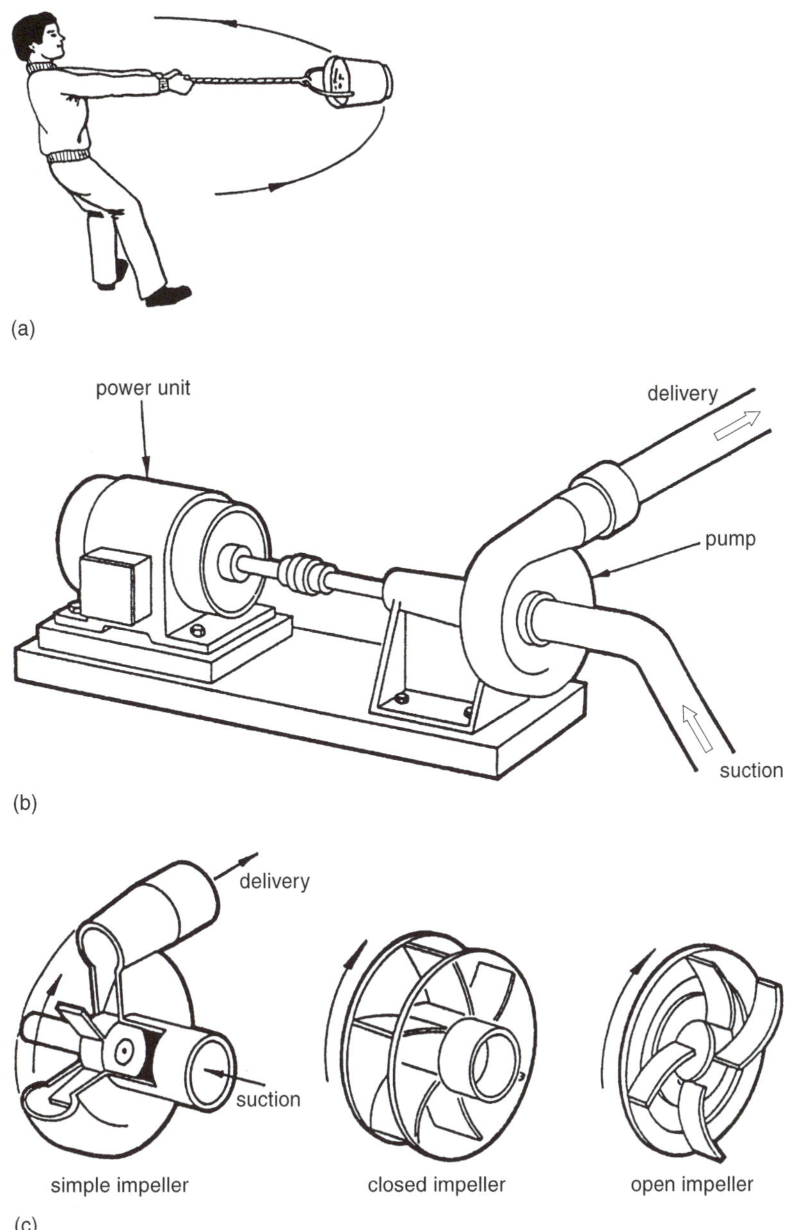


**Figure 8.3 Centrifugal pumps**

Centrifugal pumps are very versatile and can be used for a wide variety of applications. They can deliver water at low heads of just a few metres up to 100m or more. The discharge range is also high, from a few litres per second up to several cubic metres per second. Higher discharges and pressures are achieved by running several pumps together (see section 8.10) or by using a multi-stage pump. This comprises several impellers on a shaft, driven by the same motor, and water is fed from the outlet of one stage into the inlet of the next stage, increasing the pressure at each stage.

### 8.3.2 Axial flow pumps

Axial flow pumps consist of a propeller housed inside a tube which acts as a discharge pipe (Figure 8.4). The power unit turns the propeller by means of a long shaft running down the middle of the pipe and this lifts the water up the pipe. These pumps are very efficient at lifting large volumes of water at low pressure. They are ideally suited for lifting water from rivers or lakes into canals for irrigation and for land drainage where large volumes of water need to be lifted through a few metres. However, they tend to be very expensive because of the high cost of materials, particularly the drive shaft and bearings to support the shafted propeller. For this reason they tend only to be used for large pumping works.

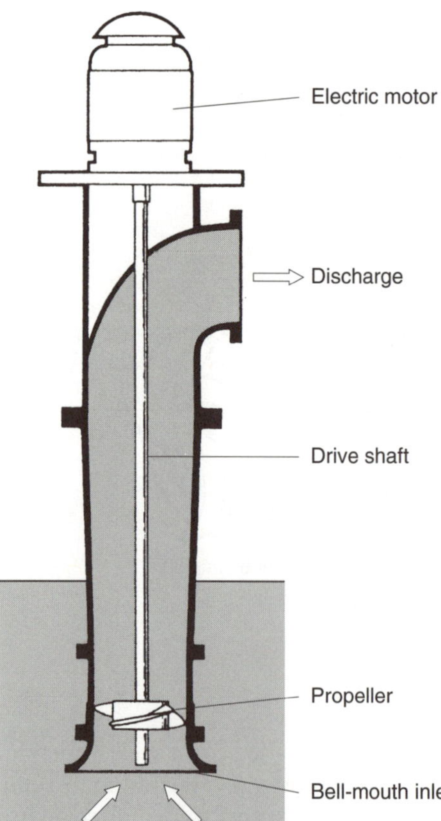


**Figure 8.4** Axial flow pumps

### 8.3.3 Mixed flow pumps

These pumps are a mixture of axial flow and centrifugal pumps and so combine the best features of both pump types. Mixed flow pumps are more efficient at pumping larger quantities of water than centrifugal pumps and are more efficient at pumping to higher pressures than axial flow pumps.

## 8.4 Suction

An aspect of using centrifugal and mixed flow pumps which is not always fully understood and which can seriously impair efficiency is the suction side of the pump. In cases of shallow groundwater or surface water pumping, the pump is often located, for convenience of use, above the water surface and so water is sucked up a short length of pipe into the pump (Figure 8.5). The difference in height between the water surface in the sump and the pump is called the **suction lift**.

When a pump is operating it draws water from the sump in much the same way as you would suck up water through a drinking straw. You do not actually suck up the water, you suck out the air from the straw and create a vacuum. Atmospheric pressure does the rest. It pushes down on the water surface and forces water up the straw to fill the vacuum. So atmospheric pressure provides the driving force but it also puts a limit on how high water can be lifted in this way. It does not depend on the ability of the sucker. At sea level, atmospheric pressure is approximately 10m head of water and so if you were relying on a straw 10.1m long for your water needs there you would surely die of thirst! If you were living up a mountain where atmospheric pressure is less than 10m then the length of your straw would need to be considerably shorter than 10m.

This same principle is applied to pumps. Ideally it should be possible to lift water by suction up to 10m. But because of friction losses in the suction pipe a practical limit for pumps is 7m. Even at this level there will be difficulties in keeping out air and maintaining a vacuum. A more usual limit is 3m. When the depth is more than 3m then a shelf can be excavated below ground level to bring the pump closer to the water. For pumps operating at high altitudes in mountainous regions the suction lift will need to be less than 3m for satisfactory operation.

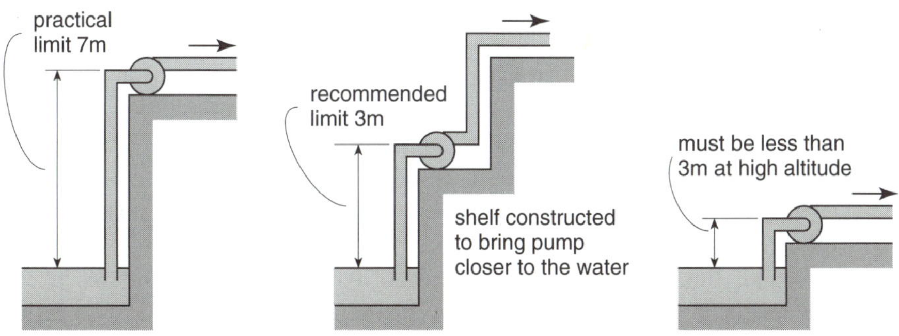


**Figure 8.5** Pump suction

Not all pumps suffer from suction problems. Some pumps are designed to work below the water level in the sump and are called **submersible pumps**. These are often used for deep boreholes and are driven by an electric motor which is also submerged and connected directly to the pump drive shaft. The motor is well sealed from the water but being submerged helps to keep the motor from overheating.

To demonstrate the effects of suction lift on pump discharge a small centrifugal pump was tested for a rural water supply scheme and delivered 6.5 litre/s with a 3m suction lift. When the suction lift was increased to 8m the discharge dropped to 1.2 litre/s – a loss in flow of 5.3 litre/s, i.e. 85% of the original discharge!

Centrifugal pumps will not suck out the air from the suction and will only work when the pump and the suction pipe are full of water. If pumps are located above the sump then it will be necessary to fill the pump and the suction pipe with water before the pump is started up. This process is called **priming**. A small hand pump, located on the pump casing is used to evacuate the air. When pumps are located below the sump then they will naturally fill with water under the influence of gravity and so no priming is required.

A concept sometimes used for limiting suction lift is the **net positive suction head** (NPSH). Manufacturers normally specify a value of NPSH for each discharge to ensure that a pump operates satisfactorily.

The NPSH for an installation can be calculated as follows:

$$\text{NPSH} = P_a - H_s - V_p - h_f$$

where $P_a$ is atmospheric pressure (m), $H_s$ is suction head (m), $V_p$ is the vapour pressure of water (approximately 0.5m) and $h_f$ is the head loss in the suction pipe (approximately 0.75m). The value calculated from the above equation must be greater than that quoted by the pump manufacturer for the pump to operate satisfactorily.

For axial flow pumps, the impeller is best located below the water level in the sump and so no priming is needed.

## 8.5 Delivery

The delivery side of a pump comprises pipes and fittings to connect the pump to the main pipe system. For centrifugal and mixed flow pumps, a sluice valve is connected to the pump outlet to assist in controlling pressure and discharge (Figure 8.6). It is closed before starting so that the pump can be primed. Once the pump is running it is slowly opened to deliver the flow.

A reflux valve is connected downstream of the delivery valve. This allows water to flow one way only – out of the pump and into the pipeline. When a pump stops, water can flow back towards it causing a rapid pressure rise which can seriously damage both the pump and the pipeline (see section 8.13). The reflux valve can help to prevent this by closing and stopping this reverse flow from reaching the pump. Some reflux valves have a small by-pass valve fitted which

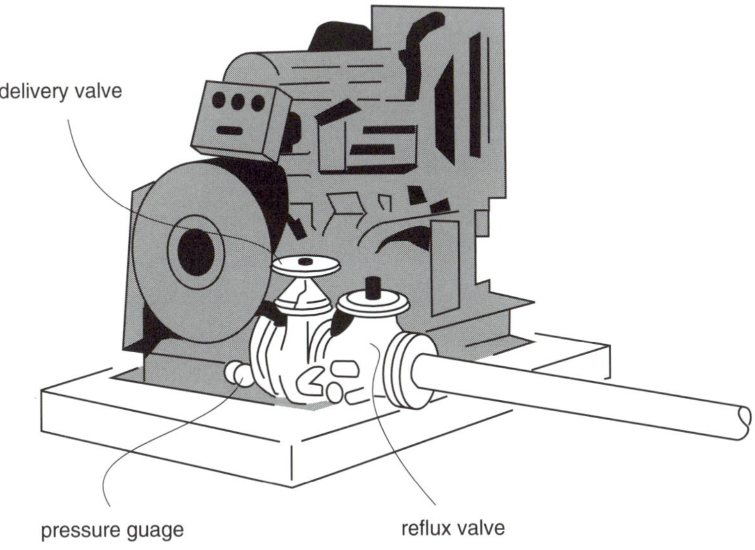


**Figure 8.6** **Delivery side of a centrifugal pump**

allows water stored in the pipe to pass around the valve and be used for priming the pump.

## 8.6 Pumping head

Pumping head is not just the pressure required on the delivery side, it also includes the suction side as well (Figure 8.7). It is the sum of all these components:

$$\text{pumping head (m)} = \text{suction lift (m)} + \text{friction loss in suction (m)} + \text{delivery lift (m)} + \text{friction loss in pipeline (m)}$$

The suction lift refers to the elevation change between the sump water level and the pump, and the delivery lift is the elevation change between the pump and the point of supply, in this case the reservoir water level. Both are fixed values for a given installation. The friction losses in the sump and the delivery will vary depending on the discharge. There are also minor losses at the inlet and outlet to a pipeline but these tend to be very small in comparison with those listed above. To allow for all these minor losses it is common practice to add 10% to the pumping head rather than try to work them out in detail. Strictly speaking velocity energy terms should also be included but these are very small and so they are often ignored.

Pumping head cannot be considered on its own but in relation to the pipeline it will serve. An example of how this is done is explained in section 8.9.

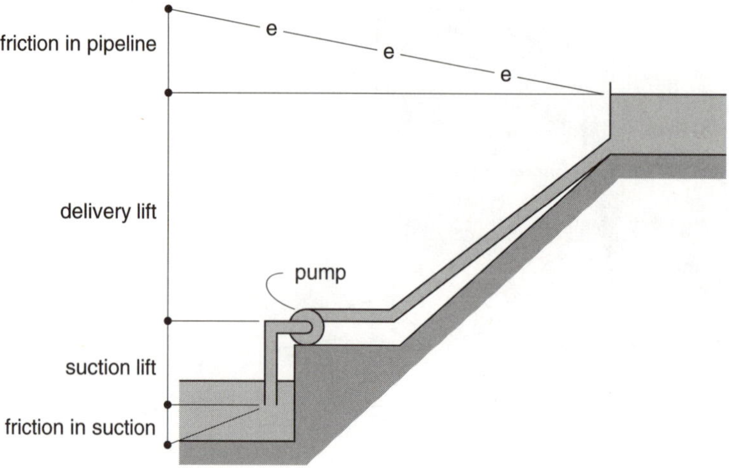


**Figure 8.7 Pumping head**

## 8.7 Pump performance

Small centrifugal pumps are sometimes characterised by the power of their drive motors, e.g. 3HP pump or 5kW pump, or by their delivery diameter, e.g. 50mm pump. Table 8.1 provides some guidance for selection but the full performance characteristics should be used for larger pumps.

All roto-dynamic pumps are factory tested and data are published by the manufacturers on the following characteristics:

- Discharge and head
- Discharge and power
- Discharge and efficiency

These data are usually presented graphically and typical characteristics for all three pump types are shown in Figure 8.8. The curves shown are only for one operating speed. But as pumps can run at many different speeds, several graphs are needed to show their full performance possibilities.

**Table 8.1 Typical discharges from small centrifugal pumps**

| *Pump size (mm)* | *Discharge (litre/s)* |
|---|---|
| 25 | 0–5 |
| 50 | 5–15 |
| 75 | 15–25 |
| 100 | 25–35 |
| 125 | 35–50 |

### 8.7.1 Discharge and head

The behaviour of a pump in terms of its discharge and head is usually of most immediate concern to the user. Will the pump deliver the discharge at the required pressure? A pump can, in fact, deliver a wide range of discharges but there will be changes in pressure as the discharge changes. The speed at which the pump runs can also change. The faster the speed the greater will be the head and discharge.

Figure 8.8a shows typical discharge – head curves for centrifugal, mixed flow and axial flow pumps for a given pump speed. The axes of the graph would normally show discharge in $m^3/s$ and head in m, but in order to show typical changes that occur, the curves have been drawn to show the percentage changes when either the discharge or the head are changed from the normal operating condition represented by the 100% point. So for the centrifugal pump, when the discharge is reduced to 80% of its design flow the head increases to 112% of its design value. Note these values of change are only representative values. They would be different for different pumps and so reference would need to be made to manufacturer's data.

Consider the centrifugal pump first. When it is started up and the delivery valve is closed, there is no discharge and the head is at its maximum. The graph shows that for this pump the head reaches 140% of its design head. As the discharge increases there is a trade-off between discharge and head. When the discharge increases then less head is available.

The discharge–head curves for both the mixed flow and axial flow pumps are similar in shape to that of the centrifugal pump. When the head is high the discharge is low and when the head is low the discharge is high.

The curves for all three pumps are for a given speed of rotation. When the speed is changed the curve will also change. The greater the speed, the greater will be the head and the discharge. So there will be several discharge–head curves for each pump, one for each speed.

### 8.7.2 Discharge and power

All pumps need power to rotate their impellers. The amount of power needed depends on the speed of a pump and the head and discharge required. For centrifugal pumps the power requirement is low when starting up but it rises steadily as the discharge increases (Figure 8.8b). For axial flow pumps the power requirement is quite different. There is a very large power demand when starting up because there is a lot of water and a heavy pump impeller to get moving. Once the pump is running the power demand drops to its normal operating level. Mixed flow pumps operate in between these two contrasting conditions and have a more uniform power demand over the discharge range.

In Chapter 1, power was referred to as the rate of energy use and was calculated by dividing the amount of energy used by the time it takes to use it. This was measured in watts. As this is a very small unit it is more common to use kilowatts (kW). Horse power (HP) is sometimes used to specify power but this is not an SI unit (for conversion 1kW = 1.36HP).

Another way of calculating power ouput is to use pump discharge rather than the volume of water to be pumped. So water power in watts can be calculated using

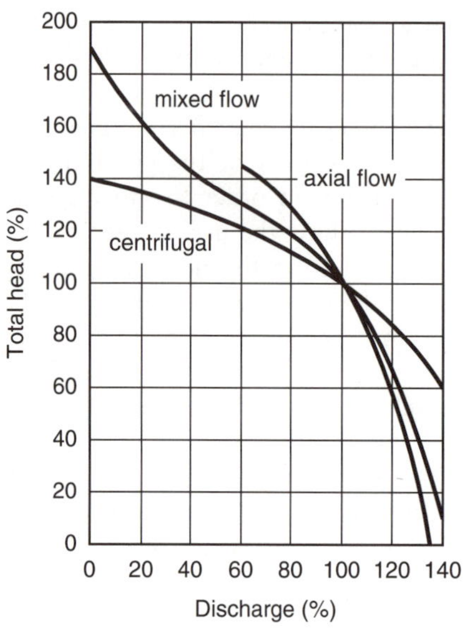


(a) Discharge–head

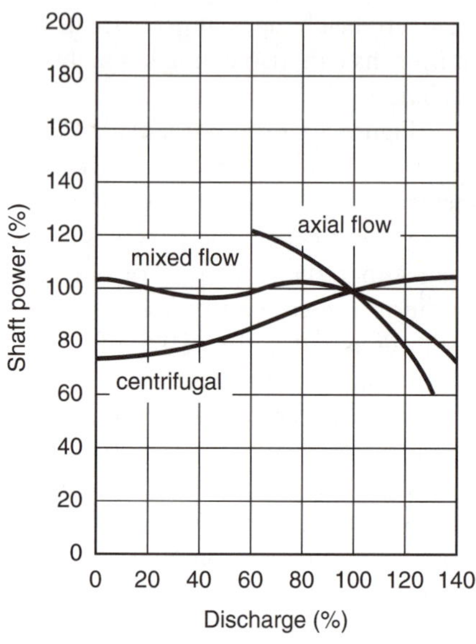


(b) Discharge–power

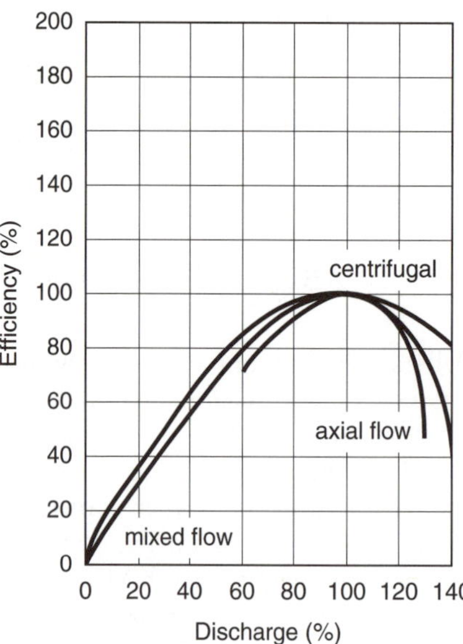


(c) Discharge–efficiency

**Figure 8.8** Pump characteristics

the formula:

$$\text{water power (W)} = \rho g Q H$$

where $g$ is gravity constant (9.81m/s$^2$), $\rho$ is density of water (1000kg/m$^3$), $Q$ is discharge (m$^3$/s) and $H$ is pumping head (m).

By putting in values for $\rho$ and $g$ in the equation and dividing by 1000 to change watts to kilowatts the equation becomes:

$$\text{water power (kW)} = 9.81QH$$

This formula can be conveniently shown as a graph of water power and discharge for a wide range of pumping heads (Figure 8.9). Note that for convenience of units, discharges are given in litres/s.

### 8.7.3 Discharge and efficiency

It is not enough just to meet the head, discharge and power requirements for pumping. Additional power is needed because of losses occurring in transferring fuel energy to water energy via the power unit and pump. The losses in the system

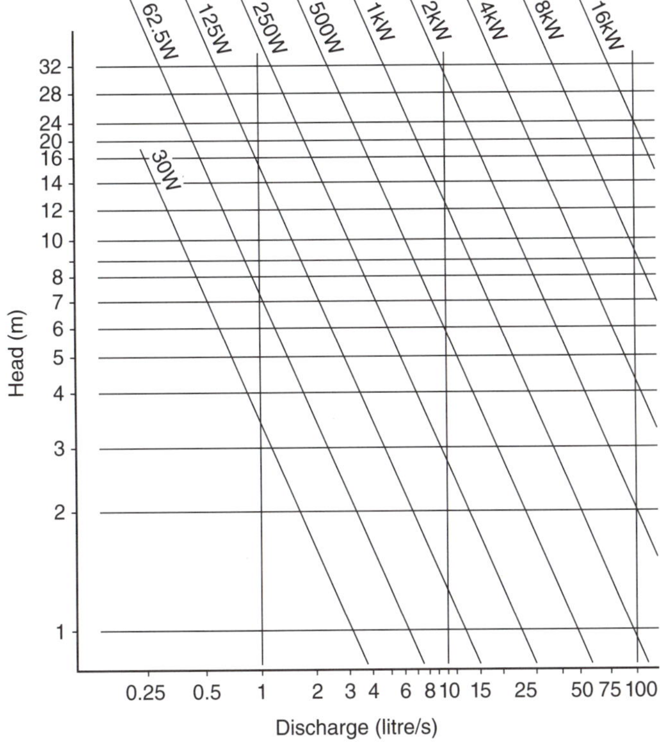


**Figure 8.9** Power requirements for pumps

are caused by friction and water turbulence and are usually expressed as an **efficiency**. There are two ways of looking at efficiency.

#### 8.7.3.1 *Power efficiency*

Power efficiency is a measure of how well the power from the power unit is converted into useful water power in the pump and is calculated as follows:

$$\text{power efficiency (\%)} = \frac{\text{water power output}}{\text{actual power input}} \times 100$$

A system with no friction would have an efficiency of 100% and so all the power input would be transferred to the water. But this is not the case in practice. There is always friction loss in all the components of the power unit and pump. Generally, efficiency increases as the discharge increases. But it rises to some maximum value and then falls again over the remaining discharge range (Figure 8.8c). The maximum efficiency is usually between 30 and 80% and so there is only a limited range of discharges and heads over which pumps operate at maximum efficiency. Outside this range they will still work but they will be less efficient and so more power is needed to operate the same system. Smaller pumps are usually less efficient than larger ones because there is more friction to overcome relative to their size. But inefficiency is less important for small pumps.

#### 8.7.3.2 *Energy efficiency*

Power efficiency provides a good assessment of power use but it is only a snapshot measurement and the efficiency may well vary over time, particularly if there is wear on the power unit and the pump. For this reason energy efficiency is used to see just how well a pump is performing over a period of time:

$$\text{energy efficiency (\%)} = \frac{\text{water energy output}}{\text{actual energy input}} \times 100$$

To calculate energy efficiency the time over which the energy is used must be known, e.g. a day, month or a season.

Water energy output can be calculated by multiplying power by the time over which the pump is used. But this means constant measurement of the power during pump operation. This can be not only time-consuming but also difficult to do. Another easier way is to calculate energy from the volume of water pumped and the head using the following formula:

$$\text{water energy (kWh)} = \frac{\text{volume of water (m}^3\text{)} \times \text{head (m)}}{367}$$

Energy and power efficiencies are often assumed to be the same. In practice this may not be the case. A seasonal assessment of energy efficiency may not always give the same value as power efficiency measured only one or two times during a lengthy period of operation.

An example of calculating energy and power for a pumping system is given in the box.

## Example: Calculating power and energy for pumping water

Each day 600m$^3$ of water is pumped to a tank 10m above the ground (Figure 8.10). Calculate the amount of energy and power required to do this.

To calculate the amount of energy used it is important to specify the time period over which the energy is used, e.g. energy used each day or energy used each month. In this calculation the energy used each day is determined:

$$\text{water energy (kWh)} = \frac{\text{volume of water (m}^3) \times \text{head (m)}}{367}$$

$$\text{water energy} = \frac{600 \times 10}{367} = 16.35\text{kWh}$$

This is the energy required each day.

Now calculate the water power needed. To calculate water power from water energy it is necessary to know the time period over which pumping takes place. If the pump operates for 24 hours each day:

$$\text{water power (kW)} = \frac{\text{energy used per day (kWh)}}{\text{time (h)}} = \frac{16.35}{24} = 0.68\text{kW}$$

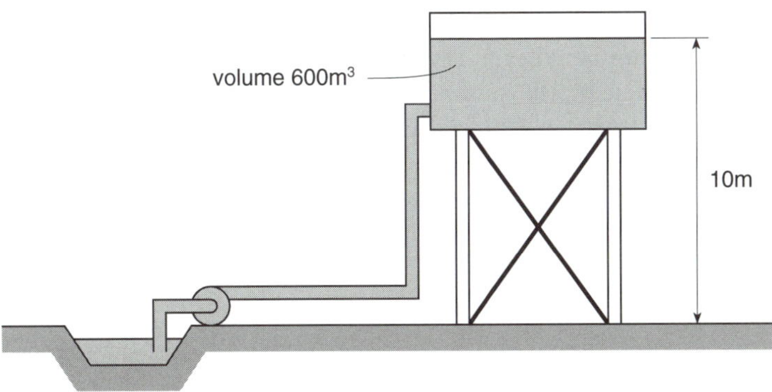


**Figure 8.10** Calculating energy and power

If the pump operates for only 12 hours each day:

$$\text{water power} = \frac{16.35}{12} = 1.36\text{kW}$$

If the pump operates for only 6 hours each day:

$$\text{water power} = \frac{16.35}{6} = 2.73\text{kW}$$

Although the energy used is the same in each case, the rate of using the energy (power) changes with the time period. More power is needed when less time is available for pumping.

An alternative way of calculating water power is to use the discharge and head. Assume that the pump works for only 6 hours a day. First calculate the discharge:

$$\text{discharge } (\text{m}^3/\text{s}) = \frac{\text{volume of water } (\text{m}^3)}{\text{time of pumping (s)}} = \frac{600}{6 \times 3600} = 0.028\text{m}^3/\text{s}$$

and then

$$\text{power (kW)} = 9.81QH = 9.81 \times 0.028 \times 10 = 2.74\text{kW}$$

This is the same power requirement calculated above using the energy approach, showing that both approaches produce the same answer.

## 8.8 Choosing pumps

Manufacturers usually condense all the data for a pump onto one chart for the convenience of the user. But choosing the right pump depends on the **duty point**. This is the point in terms of head and discharge at which a pump normally operates. A general indication of the range of heads and discharges suitable for centrifugal, mixed flow and axial flow pumps has already been given but there is another way of deciding which one to use. The shape of a pump impeller is closely related to its speed of rotation and the pumping head. These factors are combined into a number known as the **specific speed** of the pump, which provides a common base for comparing pumps. It is the speed at which a pump will deliver $1\text{m}^3/\text{s}$ at 1.0m head and is calculated as follows:

$$N_S = \frac{NQ^{1/2}}{H^{3/4}}$$

where $N$ is rotational speed of the pump (rpm), $Q$ is pump discharge ($\text{m}^3/\text{s}$) and $H$ is pumping head (m).

The specific speed is independent of the size of the pump and so it describes the shape of the pump rather than how big it is. But specific speed is not

**Table 8.2 Specific speeds for different pumps**

| *Pump type* | *Specific speed* $N_S$ | *Comments* |
|---|---|---|
| Centrifugal | 10 to 70 | High head – low discharge |
| Mixed flow | 70 to 170 | Medium head – medium discharge |
| Axial flow | above 110 | Low head – large discharge |

dimensionless. It is important to make sure that SI units are used so that the range of specific speeds and pump types is as shown in Table 8.2.

Beware of specific speeds which seem to be quite different to those used here. The main reason is likely to be the use of different units of measurement. The USA still use feet and pounds as their basic units of measurement and so any specific speed they calculate will depend on these units.

## 8.9 Matching a pump with a pipeline

To match a pump to a pipeline the head and discharge required must be known, i.e. the duty point. The discharge–head curves of pumps can then be examined to find one that fits the requirements. There are many pumps on the market and there may be several that can meet the duty point or come close to it. The next step is to examine the efficiency of each pump at the duty point and to select one that will operate at maximum efficiency.

An exact match is not always possible and so, to see just what happens when a pump and pipeline are connected together, a graph of the pumping head required for a range of discharges in the pipeline can be plotted and superimposed on the pump discharge–head curve (Figure 8.11a). The pipeline curve does not start at zero but at some point that represents the delivery lift plus the suction lift (i.e. the elevation change from the water level in the sump to the point of delivery). This is a constant value for a particular installation and is not dependent on the discharge. To this is added the head loss due to friction which does change with discharge. Putting different values of discharge into a head loss formula (e.g. Darcy–Weisbach) will provide the points to plot the graph. Where the two curves cross will be the point at which the pump and the pipeline will operate.

It is usual when selecting a pump to bear in mind that there is not just one pipe diameter that will do the job. Several curves for pipes of different diameters can be drawn to see which gives the best performance. The final choice will depend on matching a pipe with a pump from a hydraulics point of view but equally important will be the cost of the system and its running cost over the life of the system. If, for example, a small-diameter pipe is chosen, the capital cost may be low but the running costs may be high because of the higher friction and energy costs. A true comparison of cost can only be made by working out the running costs, say over a 10-year period, for different systems, and adding this to the capital cost.

A typical example of matching a pump to a pipeline is shown in the box.

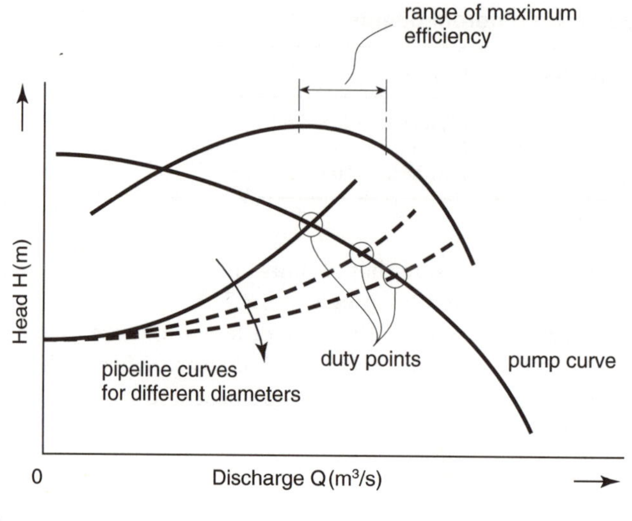


(a)

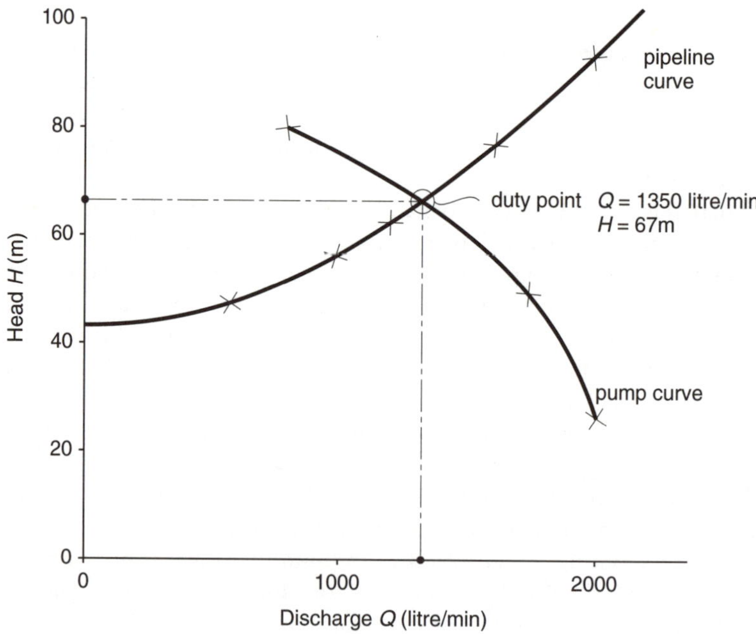


(b)

**Figure 8.11** Matching a pump to a pipeline

## Example: Matching a pump to a pipeline

Water is to be pumped from a river through a 150mm diameter pipeline 950m long to an open storage tank with a water level 45m above the river. A pump is available and has the discharge–head performance characteristics shown below. Calculate the duty point for the pump when the friction factor $\lambda = 0.04$.

| Total head (m) | 30 | 50 | 65 | 80 |
|---|---|---|---|---|
| Discharge (litre/min) | 2000 | 1750 | 1410 | 800 |

The first step is to plot a graph of the pump discharge–head characteristic (Figure 8.11b). Next calculate the head loss in the pipeline for a range of discharge values using the Darcy–Weisbach equation:

$$h_f = \frac{\lambda l v^2}{2gd}$$

When $\lambda = 0.04$, length $l = 950$m and diameter $d = 0.15$m:

$$h_f = \frac{\lambda l v^2}{2gd} = \frac{0.04 \times 950 \times v^2}{2 \times 9.81 \times 0.15} = 12.9v^2$$

But from the discharge equation

$$v = \frac{Q}{a}$$

and so

$$v^2 = \frac{Q^2}{a^2}$$

Calculate area $a$:

$$a = \frac{\pi d^2}{4} = \frac{\pi \times 0.15^2}{4} = 0.017\text{m}^2$$

Using these values calculate

$$h_f = 12.9 \times \frac{Q^2}{0.017^2} = 44\,636Q^2$$

Now calculate values of head loss for different values of $Q$. Remember the values of discharge need to be in SI units of $m^3/s$. These are tabulated in Table 8.3.

**Table 8.3 Values of head loss for different discharges**

| *Discharge (litre/min)* | *Discharge ($m^3/s$)* | *head loss $h_f$ (m)* | *head loss + 45m (m)* |
|---|---|---|---|
| 2000 | 0.033 | 48.6 | 93.6 |
| 1600 | 0.027 | 32.53 | 77.53 |
| 1200 | 0.02 | 17.85 | 62.85 |
| 1000 | 0.017 | 12.30 | 57.30 |
| 500 | 0.008 | 2.85 | 47.8 |

From the graph the duty point is located were the two curves cross. This occurs when

$Q = 1350$ litre/ min

and

$H = 67$m

## 8.10 Pumps in series and in parallel

There are many situations when one centrifugal pump is not enough to deliver the required head or discharge and so two or more pumps are needed to deliver the flow. There may also be circumstances when discharge requirements vary widely, such as in meeting domestic water demand, and it is preferable to have several small pumps available instead of one large one. Centrifugal pumps can be operated together either in **series** or in **parallel** (Figure 8.12).

Pumps are operated in series when extra head is required. Note that the pumps need to be identical. They are connected together with the same suction and delivery pipe but are powered by different motors. The same flow passes through pump 1 and then through pump 2 and so the discharge is the same as it would be for one pump but the head is doubled. The discharge–head curve for two pumps can be obtained by taking the curve for one pump and doubling the head for each value of discharge.

Pumps are operated in parallel when more discharge is required. Again the pumps must be identical. They each have separate suctions but they are connected into a common delivery pipe. With this type of connection the head is the same as for a single pump but the discharge is doubled. The discharge–head curve for the two pumps can be obtained by taking the curve for one pump and doubling the discharge for each value of head.

Pumps in series work well but when one pump breaks down then the whole system is down. Pumps in parallel are useful when there are widely varying demands for water. One pump can operate to provide low flows and the second pump can be brought into operation to provide the larger flows.

## 8.11 Operating pumps

There are some general rules that are used to operate pumps properly.

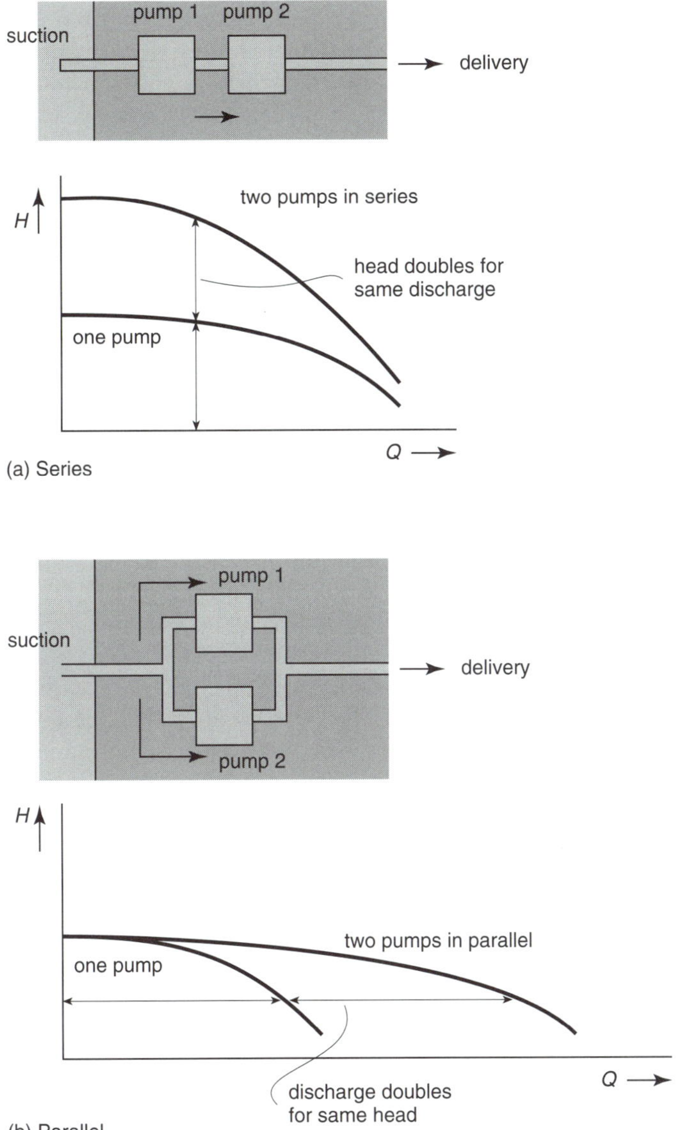


**Figure 8.12 Pumps in series and in parallel**

### 8.11.1 Centrifugal pumps

For centrifugal pumps, control valves are always fitted on the suction and delivery sides of the pump as well as a flap valve on the bottom of the suction pipe. Before starting, the delivery valve must be closed. The pump and the suction pipe are then filled with water for priming. When pumps are located below the sump water level they are primed automatically. Starting pumps with a closed delivery valve does not cause a problem. Contrary to what many people believe, pumps do not blow up when the valve is closed. They reach a steady speed and pressure. Remember the pressure depends only on the speed of rotation of the impeller. The faster it rotates the higher will be the pressure. The delivery valve is then slowly opened, water flows into the pipeline and as the discharge increases the pressure at the pump gradually falls. At the same time the power requirement increases. This gradual change continues until the delivery pipe is full of water and the system is operating at its design head and discharge. These operating procedures are important for several reasons. Suppose for example that the delivery valve was left open as often happens. Not only would it be difficult to prime the pump but also, when it was started, water would surge along the delivery pipe. Such a sudden surge of water might damage valves and fittings along the pipeline. The rapid increase in discharge also causes a rapid increase in power demand, which power units do not like. It is like getting into a car and suddenly trying to put it into top gear and accelerate fast when the engine is cold. The engine will stall and stop. The most sensible way to get moving is to build up the power demand gradually through the use of the gears and clutch. The same idea applies to pumps by opening the delivery valve slowly.

### 8.11.2 Axial flow pumps

Note that axial flow pumps do not have any control valves on either the suction or the delivery. Because of the high power demand when starting up, it is not desirable to start a pump against a closed valve. What is needed, however, on some pumps is a siphon breaker. This allows air into the pump when it stops so that water does not siphon back from the delivery to the sump.

## 8.12 Power units

There are two main types of power unit:

- Internal combustion engines
- Electric motors

### 8.12.1 Internal combustion engines

Many pumping installations do not have easy access to electricity and so rely on petrol (spark ignition) engines or diesel (compression ignition) engines to drive pumps. These engines have a good weight to power output ratio, and are compact in size and relatively cheap due to mass production techniques.

Diesel engines tend to be heavier and more robust than petrol but are more expensive to buy. However, they are also more efficient to run and if operated and maintained properly they have a longer working life and are more reliable than petrol. In some countries petrol-driven pumps have needed replacing after only three years of operation. Diesel pumps operating in similar conditions could be expected to last at least six years. However, it must not be forgotten that engine life is not just measured in years, it is measured in hours of operation and its useful life depends on how well it is operated and serviced. There are cases in developing countries where diesel pumps have been in continual use for 30 years and more. A diesel pump can be up to four times as heavy as an equivalent petrol pump and so if portability is important a petrol engine may be the answer.

### 8.12.2 Electric motors

Electric motors are very efficient in energy use (75–85%) and can be used to drive all sizes and types of pumps. The main drawback is the reliance on a power supply that is outside the control of the pump operator and in some countries is unreliable. Inevitably electrical power supplies usually fail when they are most needed and so back-up generators driven by diesel engines may be needed.

## 8.13 Surge in pumping mains

Water hammer in pipelines has already been discussed in section 4.11 but it can cause particular problems in pumping mains by creating **surges**. This is the slower mass movement of water often resulting from the faster-moving water hammer shock waves.

In pumping mains the process is reversed and it is the surge of water that can set up the water hammer. To see how this happens imagine water being pumped along a pipeline when suddenly the pump stops (Figure 8.13a). The flow in the pipe does not stop immediately but continues to move along the pipe. But as the main driving force has now gone, the flow gradually slows down because of friction. As the flow moves away from the pump and as no water enters the pipe, an empty space forms near the pump. This is called **water column separation** and the pressure in the empty space drops rapidly to the vapour pressure of water.

The flow gradually slows down through friction and stops. But there is now an empty space in the pipe and so water starts to flow back towards the pump gathering speed as it goes. It rapidly refills the void and then comes to a sudden and violent stop as it hits the pump. This is very similar to suddenly closing a valve on a pipeline and results in a high-pressure shock wave which moves up the pipe at high speed (approximately 1000m/s). This can not only burst the pipe but may also seriously damage the pump as well. There are several ways of avoiding this problem:

- *Stop pumps slowly.* When pumps stop slowly water continues to enter the pipe and so the water column does not separate and water hammer is avoided. Electric pumps are a problem because they stop very quickly when the power fails. Diesel pumps take some time to slow down when the fuel is switched off and this is usually enough time to avoid the problem.
- *Use a non-return valve.* Using a non-return valve in the delivery pipeline will allow the flow to pass normally along the pipe but stop water from flowing

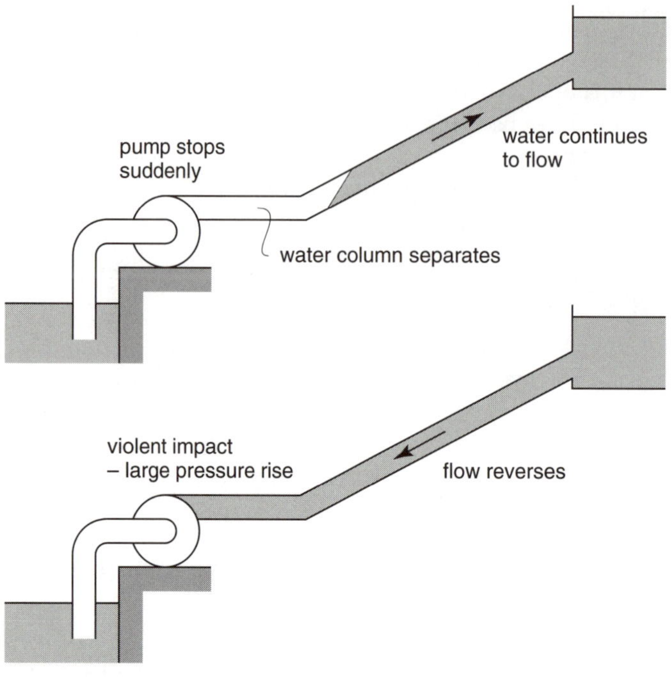


(a) Effects of suddenly stopping a pump

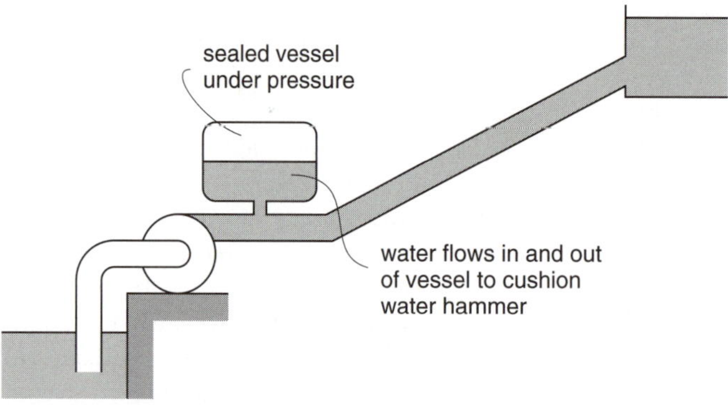


(b) Air vessel used to reduce surge in pumping mains

**Figure 8.13 Surge in pumping mains**

back towards the pump. In this case the valve and the pipe absorb the water hammer pressures and the pump is protected.

- *Use an air vessel*. This is similar in action to a surge tank but in reverse (Figure 8.13b). When a pump stops and the pressure starts to drop, water flows from a pressurised tank into the pipeline to fill the void and stop the water column from separating. When the flow stops and reverses, it flows back into the tank. The water then oscillates back and forth until it eventually stops through friction. Unlike a surge tank, an air vessel is sealed and the air trapped inside acts like a large coiled spring compressing and expanding to dampen the movement of the water in much the same way as a shock absorber on a car dampens the large bumps in the road. This device tends to be expensive and so would only be used on large, important pumping installations where the designers expect serious water hammer problems to occur.

## 8.14 Turbines

Water can also produce energy as well as absorb it. This idea has been exploited for centuries long before rotary pumps were invented. Water wheels were used by the Romans and throughout Europe to grind cereals. Today these wheels have been replaced by turbines which are connected to generators to produce electrical energy. These are used extensively in Scotland for power generation, in mountainous countries such as Switzerland and in many other countries where convenient dam sites can be located to produce the required head. They are not usually the main source of electricity but provide a valuable addition to the main power source which is either coal-, gas- or oil-fired power stations to meet peak demands. Another development has been the pumped storage scheme. In Wales, for example, a small hydro-power plant is used to generate electricity during the day to meet peak demands. During the night when power demand is low, surplus electricity from the main grid is used to pump water back up into the reservoir to generate electricity the next day. This is a way of 'storing' electricity by storing water and is known as **pumped storage**.

There are three main types of turbine (Figure 8.14):

- Impulse turbines
- Reaction turbines
- Axial flow turbines

Impulse turbines are similar in operation to the old water wheel. The most common is the **Pelton wheel**, named after its American inventor, Lester Pelton (1829–1908). This comprises a wheel with specially shaped buckets around its periphery known as the **runner**. Water from a high-level reservoir is directed along a pipe and through a nozzle to produce a high-speed water jet. This is directed at the buckets and causes the runner to rotate. The momentum change of the jet as it hits the moving buckets creates the force for rotation. So by knowing the speed of the jet it is possible to work out this force and the amount of electrical energy that can be generated. Pelton wheels can be very efficient at transferring energy from water to electricity and figures as high as 90% are quoted by manufacturers. They are best suited to high heads above 150m. Some installations have run with heads in excess of 600m.

Reaction turbines are like a centrifugal pump in reverse. The most common design is the **Francis turbine**. Although James Francis (1815–1892) did not invent the turbine he did a great deal to develop the inlet guide vanes and runner blades to

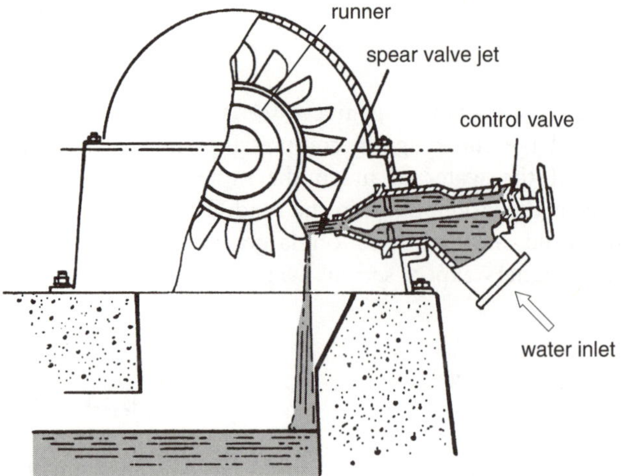


(a) Pelton wheel

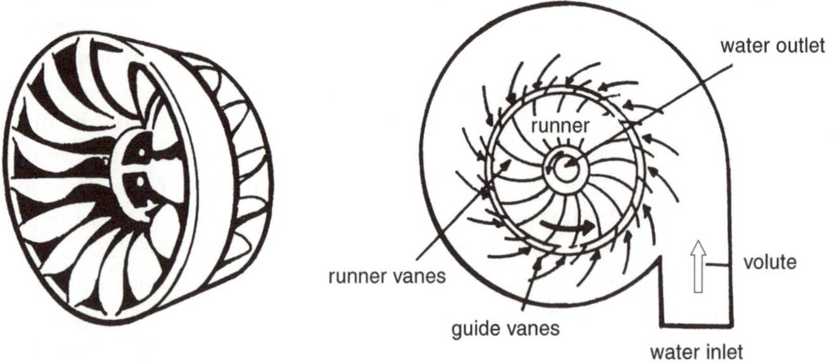


(b) Francis turbine

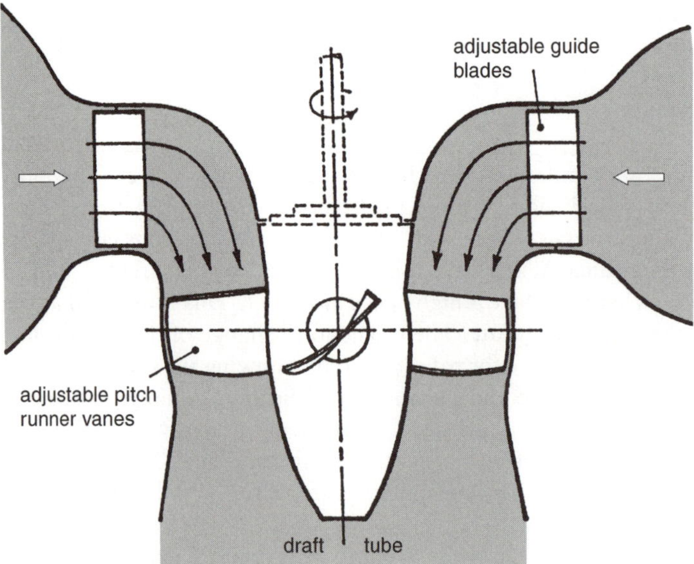


(c) Kaplan turbine

**Figure 8.14** Turbines

improve turbine efficiency and so his name became associated with it. The turbine resembles a centrifugal pump but, instead of the rotating impeller driving the water as in a pump, the runner is driven by the water. Water is fed under pressure and at high velocity around a spiral casing onto the runner and as it rotates the pressure and kinetic energy of the water is transferred to the runner. Francis turbines normally work at heads of 15 to 150m.

Axial flow (or propeller) turbines are known as **Kaplan turbines**. They are named after Victor Kaplan (1876–1934), a German professor who developed this type of turbine with adjustable blades. Axial flow turbines operate like axial flow pumps in reverse. They operate at low heads (less than 30m) and are used in tidal power installations. They have blades on their runners that can be twisted to different angles in order to work at high efficiency over a wide range of operating conditions. This kind of turbine is also used in pumped storage schemes. It is used as a turbine during the day when power demand is high and at night it is connected to an electric motor and used as a pump to lift water back into a high-level reservoir in readiness for the next day.

The power output from a turbine can be calculated using the same formula as was used for pumps:

$$\text{water power output (W)} = \rho g Q H$$

where $g$ is gravity constant (9.81m/s$^2$), $\rho$ is density of water (1000kg/m$^3$), $Q$ is discharge (m$^3$/s) and $H$ is head (m).

As an example, a turbine receiving a discharge of 0.3m$^3$/s from a dam 300m above it would generate a power output of 795kW (1081HP) assuming an efficiency of 90%.

## 8.15 Cavitation

Cavitation occurs in both pumps and turbines (see also section 3.9.2). In pumps it is the result of high water velocities (low pressure) near the centre of an impeller (Figure 8.15). Cavities form in the high-velocity stream and then collapse as they move into the higher-pressure zone near the edge of the impeller blades. The key issue is whether the cavitation causes damage or not. For this reason designers go to great lengths to ensure that the cavities collapse in the main flow, well away from the impeller blades. If this is not possible then stainless steel impellers are used as this is one of the few materials that can resist cavitation damage. But this is a very expensive option and not one to take up lightly.

Cavitation not only erodes the surfaces in contact with water but it can also be very noisy. It also causes vibration and can reduce pumping efficiency. If you have an opportunity to visit a water pumping station then place your ear against the pump casing and you will hear the cavitation. Above all the noise of the pump engines it should be possible to hear a sharp crackling sound. This is the sound of the cavities collapsing as the pressure rises in the pump. The level of the noise produced by the cavitation is a measure of how badly the pump is cavitating.

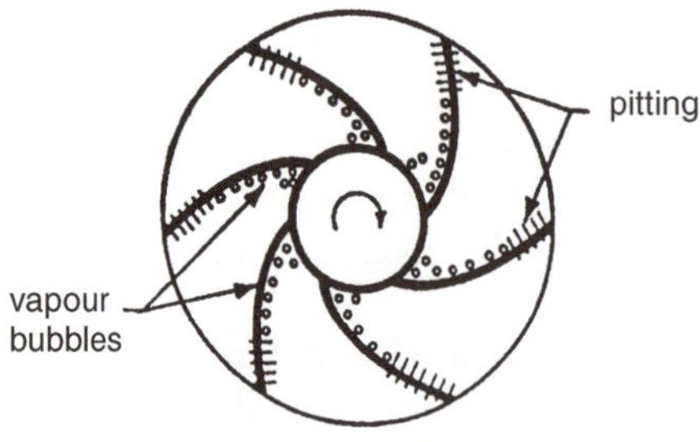


(a)

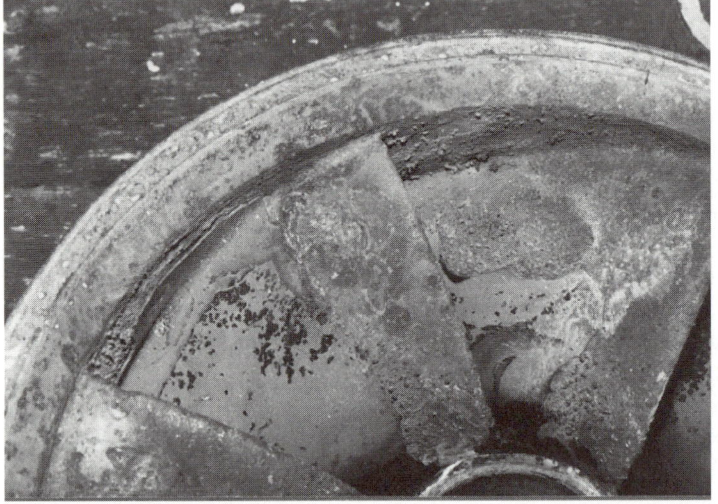

(b) Pitting damage to impeller blades

**Figure 8.15** Cavitation

Cavitation also occurs in turbine runners. High velocities at the turbine inlet produce cavities which then collapse close to the runner blades near the exit.

## 8.16 An example to test your understanding

1 A pump supplies water to a large reservoir through a 2000m long pipeline 400mm in diameter. If the difference in water level between the sump and the reservoir is 20m and the friction factor of the pipeline is $\lambda = 0.03$, calculate the pressure and power output required to deliver a discharge of $0.35\text{m}^3/\text{s}$.

# Answers to questions to test your understanding

Chapter 2

1 137.34kN/m$^2$; 13.09kN/m$^2$.
2 2210kg; 7848N/m$^2$; 3767N; 0.53m from water surface.
3 100.06kN/m$^2$; 10.2m.
4 155kN/m$^2$; 15.82m.
5 13.73kN; 2.83m.
6 11.57kN; 2.69m.

Chapter 3

1 0.0028m$^3$/s; 0.35m/s.
2 2.55m/s; 0.14m$^3$/s; 2.0m/s.
3 3.68m; opening greater than 61mm.
4 7.14m/s; 3.08kN/m$^2$.

Chapter 4

1 19.46m; 5.4m/100m.
2 0.012m$^3$/s.
3 0.02m$^3$/s.
4 0.07m$^3$/s.
5 10.87kN; 288kN/m$^2$.
6 138kN; 137kN.
7 187m.

Chapter 5

1 0.5m; 0.45; 0.29m.
2 0.75m; 0.126m; flow is sub-critical.
3 $d=0.98$m, $b=2.94$m ($b=3d$).
4 For hexagonal channel $d=0.37$m, $b=0.8$m. Note that other answers are possible depending on the choice of channel side slope.
5 2.78; 0.87m; 0.3m.

Chapter 7

1 0.4m.
2 1.45m.

Chapter 8

1 29.38m; 101kW.

# References and further reading

BS3680 *Measurement of Liquid Flow in Open Channels*. British Standards Institution, London (also ISO 748 1979).
(1981) Part 4A *Thin Plate Weirs*
(1981) Part 4C *Flumes*
(1990) Part 4E *Rectangular Broad Crested Weirs*
These are the standards which are the basis for the design, installation and operation of flow measuring structures.

Chadwick, A. and Morfett, J. (1998) *Hydraulics in Civil and Environmental Engineering*, 3rd edition. E & FN Spon, London.
Similar in some ways to Webber, this is another excellent undergraduate text but its coverage of hydraulics is much wider and includes sediment transport, river and canal engineering, coastal engineering and hydrology.

Chow, V.T. (1981) *Open Channel Hydraulics*, International Student Edition. McGraw-Hill, New York.
This is the bible of open channel hydraulics. It is a handbook with lots of information on all aspects of channel flow and design – it is not an elementary text.

Douglas, J.F. (1996) *Solution of Problems in Fluid Mechanics*, Parts I and II. Longman, Harlow, U.K.
This is a good problem-solving oriented text. It approaches the principles of hydraulics by showing how to solve numerical problems.

Hamill, L. (1995) *Understanding Hydraulics*. Macmillan Press, Basingstoke, UK.
This is a book written by a teacher of hydraulics who clearly has a lot of experience of teaching a difficult subject. It is written in a conversational style with the student asking questions and the teacher providing the answers. It is sympathetic to the needs of young engineers but makes no allowances for those with limited mathematical skills.

Hydraulics Research (1983) *Charts for the Hydraulic Design of Channels and Pipes*, 5th edition. Hydraulics Research, Wallingford.
An excellent and widely used book of design charts based on the Colebrook–White equation.

King, H.W. and Brater, E.F. (1996) *Handbook of Hydraulics for the Solution of Hydrostatic and Fluid Flow Problems*, 7th edition. McGraw-Hill, New York.

Very useful for the solution of Manning's equation for channel flow. King's method is used in this text.

Portland Cement Association (1964) *Handbook of Concrete Culvert Pipe Hydraulics*. Chicago, Illinois, USA.

Very comprehensive book on culvert hydraulics and their construction. Although it is primarily supporting concrete culverts they can be made out of other materials as well.

Rouse, H. and Ince, S. (1957) *History of Hydraulics*. Dover Publications, New York.

A comprehensive, well researched and very readable history of hydraulics from the early work of Greek scholars to our modern notions of fluid behaviour. Rouse is a well known authority on hydraulics.

USBR (1974) *Design of Small Dams*. United States Department of the Interior, Bureau of Reclamation.

Lots of useful construction details of hydraulic structures and particularly weirs and spillways.

Vallentine, H.R. (1967) *Water in the Service of Man*. Penguin Books, Harmondsworth, UK.

Sadly this book is now out of print but it may still be available in some libraries. It is an excellent, easy-to-read, introduction to the fundamentals of water flow in pipes, channels and pumps as well as providing a broader appreciation of water and its uses including its history. The text is very descriptive, anecdotal and entertaining in style with lots of good explanations and very little mathematics. Vallentine is clearly an engineer who knows how to communicate his ideas in a practical and interesting way.

Webber, N.B. (1971) *Fluid Mechanics for Civil Engineers*. E & FN Spon, London.

An excellent, comprehensive undergraduate civil engineering textbook covering both basic principles and practical applications. This book is now out of print, but it is widely available in college and university libraries.

# Index